PRAISE FOR GOLF BENEATH THE SURFACE

"After years of traveling the PGA Tour and coaching at the highest level, I've met all the popular golf psychologists. Raymond's rational, practical, and holistic approach to performance psychology is light years ahead of anyone else and now available to everyone in *Golf Beneath the Surface*."

—Nick Clearwater, Golftec VP of Instruction,
***Golf Digest* Top 50, Golf.com Top 100**

"I've spent my whole life playing this great, difficult, and crazy game. I've looked under every rock searching for the next piece of the puzzle that would allow me to play my best golf. I sought out every 'mental expert' I could find looking for that missing piece. All I can say is that Raymond would have helped me find that missing piece. Raymond can explain the what, why, and how golfers can play more freely and confidently game better than anyone I've ever known. I only wish I would have known Raymond when I was still playing on Tour."

—Hal Sutton, PGA Champion, two-time Players
Champion, five-time Ryder Cup team member

"We've all heard that golf is 90 percent mental but rarely know how to practice this area. *Golf Beneath the Surface* offers thought-provoking ideas into what matters most for understanding how your psychology can unlock a path to better golf."

—Melissa Luellen, head women's golf coach, Auburn University

"Raymond is one of the world's leading experts in peak performance and brings that expertise to every golfer in *Golf Beneath the Surface*. *GBTS* is a must-have for anyone looking to take their game to the next level. Rather than giving readers a bunch of tired, outdated golf clichés, he teaches players to understand what the brain is designed to do and why that impacts how we play. After reading this book, you will have a better understanding of your own psychology and be armed with deeper and usable information to play more of your very best golf."

—Chase Cooper, PGA, Axis Golf Academy

"*Golf Beneath the Surface* truly provides helpful, research-backed processes to better players' thoughts, habits, and actions on the course. It replaces overused and outdated golf psychology myths with actionable steps that are proven to work. I can't wait to use the new knowledge myself and will be recommending the book to my students and peers."

—Abby Mann, PGA

"*Golf Beneath the Surface* offers a deep yet approachable understanding of *why* you have the experience that you do with golf. It expertly explains why popular, surface-level notions of the mental game, such as 'just be confident' and 'trust your swing,' have very little to no impact, while at the same time providing guidance for playing with freedom and developing real, sustainable confidence. This book will change the conversation about how to get the most out of your skills and become one of the most influential books on both the mental game and golf ever written."

—Matt Wilson, director of instruction, Baltusrol Golf Club, *Golf Digest* Best Young Teacher in America

Golf Beneath the Surface

Golf
Beneath the
Surface

THE NEW SCIENCE OF
GOLF PSYCHOLOGY

Raymond Prior, PhD

BenBella Books, Inc.
Dallas, TX

BenBella Books, Inc.
10440 N. Central Expressway
Suite 800
Dallas, TX 75231
benbellabooks.com
Send feedback to feedback@benbellabooks.com

BenBella is a federally registered trademark.

Printed in the United States of America
10 9 8 7 6 5 4 3

Library of Congress Control Number: 2022046902
ISBN 9781637743096 (trade paperback)
ISBN 9781637743102 (electronic)

Editing by Camille Cline
Copyediting by Lydia Choi
Proofreading by Jenny Rosen and Marissa Wold Uhrina
Indexing by WordCo Indexing Services, Inc.
Text design and composition by Aaron Edmiston
Cover design by Sarah Avinger
Cover images © iStock / Willard (green), Shutterstock / nexus 7 (flag), and Shutterstock / grebeshkovmaxim (head)
Printed by Lake Book Manufacturing

Special discounts for bulk sales are available.
Please contact bulkorders@benbellabooks.com.

In the last decade, I have been fortunate enough to serve as a consultant to PGA and LPGA Tour players, professional players around the world, countless college golfers, and amateur golfers at all levels, as well as to provide counsel to a variety of PGA teaching professionals and golf academies working to develop the game and those who play it. Being allowed into the minds of so many golfers and coaches has given me uncommon access behind the scenes and to the people who drive the game itself. It is not lost on me how incredible the efforts are by so many just so that others can practice and play. From the groundskeepers and volunteers at tournaments to those giving lessons, washing carts, and picking ranges, golf exists and persists because of people. Thank you for the opportunity to work with you, learn from you, share your experiences, and now write for you.

To any golfer, teaching professional, coach, administrator, or parent who seeks to understand golf on a deeper and more sustainable level, build more consistent performances, understand yourself and others, and enjoy golf more, this book is dedicated to you.

Contents

Introduction

B e a hitter," my Little League Baseball coach yelled to a twelve-year-old me as I stepped up to the plate. *What the hell does it look like I'm doing?* I remember wondering. *I'm literally the only person on the field who can be a hitter right now.*

My coach was doing his best, but his surface-level instruction, although well intentioned, provided no value to me. It offered no usable information for me to apply to my performance; I had no idea what he wanted me to do because I didn't know what he meant and, likely, neither did he.

As a golfer, you've likely been introduced to some surface-level psychology and done your best to apply it to your game. Popular surface-level psychology instructing golfers to "just be positive," "just don't think," and "just be dedicated and prepared" are all well-intentioned sentiments, but they are the golf-psychology equivalent of telling a twelve-year-old baseball player to just "be a hitter."

According to golf historians, performance psychology has been a part of golf in one form or another for about a century. This timeline makes sense, since that was roughly when both golf instruction and the field of sport psychology began. However, approaches to the psychology of golf haven't progressed much since then. While surface-level psychology introduces and describes several important topics, when our psychology is only understood as basic platitudes and pithy catchphrases, the layered questions that lead to growth, sustainable change, and the ability to simplify performance in real time remain either unanswered or answered incorrectly.

There are dozens of books you can read on golf psychology. Some are written by players, some by swing coaches, some by consultants like me. Most are filled with entertaining stories about great players playing great golf. Most are filled with tips, tricks, hacks, personal opinions, and a lot of surface-level psychology. But few of them are, shall we say, overflowing with information backed by actual science about the brain, our psychology, and how to effectively understand and train both. For that reason, throughout this book I will dispel several myths that are outdated, misunderstood, inaccurate, and ultimately detrimental to getting better and playing more freely.

What will also become clear is that many of the surface-level adages and concepts related to building mental toughness that we think of as effective really aren't—and many of the things we once thought weren't important actually are. For example, it turns out that a little bit of anxiety isn't a good thing, and actively thinking about the worst-case scenario actually leads to more stable confidence.

By distilling and organizing the vast ocean of research about the psychology of human performance, we'll see that understanding the levels of our psychology where we can build high performance boils down to only a handful of interrelated areas, with a few key layers in each, and that all of them are supported by rigorously conducted science.

Science has been propelling golf in profound ways, especially in the last decade. These days, club manufacturers hire physicists to research and design clubs that launch higher and farther and are more forgiving than ever; one club designer at a popular manufacturer told me that when he graduated from college, he had a difficult time deciding between designing golf clubs and working for NASA.

Science has also moved golf instruction forward. It's nearly impossible to get a golf lesson or club fitting that doesn't include some combination of motion-capture technology or a launch monitor. Without these things, your lesson becomes just a subjective practice session where maybe you got better, or maybe you didn't.

Similarly, the most effective course-strategy systems are minimizing guesswork in course management by using advanced mathematics to accurately analyze billions of data points about where strokes are gained and lost.

And do you ever wonder why so many professional players are wearing some form of armband or wristwatch that tracks their sleep, workouts, and recovery?

Nearly every area of golf has progressed to an unprecedented degree in the last decade by using science as a guide to go beneath what's on the surface, allowing us to know more about every aspect of the game. Sadly, the exception has been golf psychology, something directly impacting every area of every golfer's game—which is why there's plenty of science in this book.

As a consultant, I'm invested in the knowledge, practices, application, and skills that are most predictive of consistent growth, improved performance, and a fulfilling golf experience. While new clubs, advanced course strategies, and the newest technology can help shave strokes off your game, how effectively we utilize any of those resources depends first and foremost on your psychology.

This book goes beneath the surface using well-designed, meticulously conducted, peer-reviewed, and replicated science as your guide. If the mental tips and tricks we typically hear are the introductory course to golf psychology, *Golf Beneath the Surface* is the expanded and more comprehensive course for those really looking to get more from themselves and their game, not just another series of clichés essentially telling you to "be a hitter."

To organize all of this information, I will start by discussing the brain so that, as a reader, you have some foundational knowledge of how your brain works and how that relates to playing golf. Once we create that foundation in "Your Brain," we will dive into three subsequent sections, ordered to build upon each other in succession: "Awareness," "Habits," and "Framework." When these key areas are understood and consistently trained, they become the strongest psychological predictors of consistent performance and garner a more fulfilling relationship with playing and competing.

The privacy and confidentiality of someone's mind, especially those of my clients, is something that I hold with great reverence and respect. To me, that's sacred space, so I will not be sharing the names of any of my clients. My job as a consultant is to help others understand their minds and train them to pursue the things they want, not to use their names for self-promotion or talk about their successes as if they are in any way my own. Thus, I will use only public information from some players and coaches and provide a few real-life examples from clients who have given me permission to use their experiences anonymously to illustrate a few topics.

Much of the information offered in this book may be different from what you currently understand and might even be a little uncomfortable for you. That's a good thing. There's no sense in wasting pages or your time reading the same surface-level information you already know that isn't challenging you to expand your understanding or empowering you to develop and use your ability. It is my hope that this book will be an informative and pragmatic guide for you to do just that.

Your Brain

O
n a chilly Saturday afternoon in October, I stood between the neighboring ninth and eighteenth greens at Aronimink Golf Club in Newtown Square, Pennsylvania, watching some of the best players in the world compete in the Women's PGA Championship. With its challenging greens and the day's unpredictable winds, Aronimink was proving to be a formidable test.

As I watched players putt out to finish their rounds, I was joined by a highly ranked and respected player; let's call her Emmie. She had made the short walk from the nearby practice putting green to watch and support one of her friends, who had just hit a dazzling iron shot into the difficult eighteenth green and was sizing up a twenty-foot putt for birdie.

Emmie and I talked as we watched the trio of players that made up the group her friend was playing in. Emmie's friend was one of a handful of players who still had a chance to win the tournament and claim the last major of the 2020 season. With a birdie, Emmie's friend could jump up the tightly contested leaderboard, bringing her within striking distance of the tournament leaders going into Sunday's final round. Since all but a few players had finished their rounds, even a two-putt par would ensure a place in one of the final groups the next day. But that's not what happened.

Up until the eighteenth green, Emmie's friend had played composed and committed golf, but her last few strokes were anything but. We watched her leave her twenty-foot birdie putt well short, giving her a slippery four-foot putt for par. She then missed her par putt and had to settle for a three-putt bogey. All three of her putts were taken through defensive, jabby strokes.

As the people around us murmured about what they'd just watched, Emmie turned to me.

"How does that happen?"

Emmie wasn't referring to the results of those final putts, per se. She was asking about what had happened to her friend internally. Emmie's friend, also one of the best players in the world, had clearly been the victim of her own psychology as she closed the round.

"Why do we get nervous like that?" Emmie asked.

For any golfer, regardless of your skill level, you know what this feels like. At some point, we've all had the same experience Emmie's friend did: we struggle to execute because our heart starts pounding faster and harder, our breathing gets shallow and fast, and our muscles become tense. We have a difficult time collecting our thoughts and narrowing our focus. We get nervous.

Nerves are a part of being human and are most certainly a part of playing golf. As common as nerves are, however, they are largely misunderstood, which is what made Emmie's question so poignant.

"Because that's what our brain is designed to do," I replied.

THE HUMAN SUPERCOMPUTER

The human brain is the most complex, high-speed supercomputer on the planet. A few years ago, a team of researchers at the RIKEN research institute in Kobe, Japan, created an artificial neural network of 1.73 billion nerve cells connected by 10.4 trillion synapses to simulate one second of human brain activity. Even with the K Computer, at the time one of the five fastest supercomputers ever built, the researchers couldn't keep up with the human brain's processing speed. They weren't even close. It took the K Computer and 82,944 processors forty minutes to produce just one second of biological brain-processing time. Even in an age of exponential technological growth, the most advanced computing can't even come close to matching the processing power and speed of the human brain.

Having a neuroscientist's depth of knowledge about the brain, its structures, and neural pathways isn't necessary for playing great golf or living a fulfilling life. However, having a foundational understanding of how the brain functions and learns gives us valuable insight and clarity into why and how our brain and body react to specific events, like the one that Emmie's friend was faced with, and thus provides a sound first step to training our mind.

YOUR BRAIN

Let's begin by understanding that your brain is not your mind. Your mind, as we'll address in depth in the coming sections, is what makes you, well, you. The mind is comprised of all those human elements like awareness, beliefs, perceptions, imagination, and creativity. The mind is responsible for creating and interpreting much of the information ultimately processed by the brain. In a sense, our minds are the software from which our supercomputer brains operate. Although they are not the same, the brain and the mind are inextricably linked.

Unlike the mind, the brain is an organ. The brain's functions include a vast array of jobs, including memory, speech, and regulating involuntary movements, just to name a few. While the brain has many functions, its primary and overarching function, above all else, is to keep you alive. Every function that your brain executes falls under the larger umbrella of functions geared to ensure your survival. Prioritizing survival above all else is how our brain evolved to be a supercomputer that can process information at the speed and power of four hundred billion bits per second and leaves modern supercomputers in the dust.

Thousands of years ago, when just about everything was a physical threat to human life, our prehistoric ancestors needed brains that worked and learned as quickly as possible. In a world filled with danger to life and limb, those with the fastest and strongest brains had the highest survival rates. The faster their brains worked, the more likely they were to avoid potentially dangerous consequences. Thus, we can thank our prehistoric ancestors for the way our brains function today.

While the world in which we currently live continues to evolve at a precipitous rate, the human brain has not. Our brain functions and learns just like it did when we were cavepeople. The same high-speed supercomputer designed to find food and avoid getting eaten by a predator is the same brain we use to face modern situations like job interviews, academic tests, and the Sunday back nine of a major. Despite the modern changes to our environment, our brains still work in largely the same way, operating from the same safety-first hardware when we're giving a speech in front of a large crowd or hitting the opening tee shot during the Solheim or Ryder Cup as they did when we were being chased by a saber-toothed tiger.

For a better understanding of how our prehistorically calibrated brain is working and learning under the pressures of our modern world, including golf, let's divide our brain into two parts: old and young. If you were to make a fist with one hand and then cover your fist with your other hand, your fist would represent your old brain, and the hand covering it would represent your young brain. When it comes to understanding how our brain impacts performance, it's particularly important to be familiar with how a trio of brain structures work—two in the old brain and one in the young brain. Together, the trio makes up what's called the "mesocortical limbic pathway," a three-part system responsible for calculating risk and predictability. Put simply, it calculates: *If I do this, what risk is involved, and what might happen?*

The brain structures of import in the old brain are a cluster of regions near the brain stem called the "basal ganglia," which serve as the main hub for basic survival needs, and the limbic system, the headquarters of emotion and memory. The brain structure of import in the young brain is the prefrontal cortex, the brain's executive control center. To answer Emmie's question about why we get nervous, let's break down all three.

WHERE NERVES START

Deep inside our skulls, beneath the cerebral cortex, are the basal ganglia, which make up what is commonly referred to as our "reptilian brain." Evolutionary scientists believe that many of our very distant ancestors who crawled up from the ocean's depths had brains that looked and functioned much like the subcortical areas of our old brain that we still have today.

The basal ganglia are the epicenter for essential survival needs like eating, drinking, reproduction, and social interaction. In response to the things we *need*, the basal ganglia comes online frequently and automatically because it's also the brain's first line of safety-first functioning constantly on patrol, looking for and calculating risk.

Given its prehistoric usefulness, it makes sense that the basal ganglia hold considerable influence over initiating our all-too-familiar "fight, flight, or freeze" response, one of the most universal of all human experiences. When we're in a situation that is important to us and involves some meaningful risk, our basal ganglia kickstart a cascade of physiological reactions to ensure we are ready to take action if needed. More commonly, people refer to our deeply ingrained fight, flight, or freeze response and the corresponding physiological reactions as "nerves."

WHAT NERVES ARE

The cascade of physiological reactions begins with the basal ganglia sending a signal to the body, triggering the release of cortisol. Cortisol is a stress hormone made in the adrenal glands that regulates a wide range of processes throughout the body, including metabolism and digestion.

When we're at rest, more of our blood is in our abdomen than in any other area of our body. The blood in our abdomen serves as the roadway and carrier for our digestion and energy production. In the fight, flight, or freeze response, cortisol is the catalyst that initiates the rapid movement of blood from our abdomen out to our limbs and brain. That visceral feeling of blood moving away from our abdomen and into our extremities is the sensation commonly referred to as having "butterflies in your stomach."

The reason our blood, and any butterflies, migrate to our limbs is because, when immediate action may be required, there's no need to prioritize digestion and energy production—that blood and energy are better served to help us fight, run, or hide. However, for that blood to get to our limbs rapidly enough to take immediate action, it must be pumped there, requiring our heart to beat faster and more heavily. Consequently, our breathing rate must keep up by getting faster, and often shallower, in order for the heart to pump blood quickly. With our cardiorespiratory system firing on all cylinders and our blood closer to the surface of our skin, our body temperature also increases—hence why we feel hot and get those lovely pit stains when we're nervous.

To summarize, we get nervous because the basal ganglia do exactly what they are prehistorically designed to do when faced with risk: quickly, powerfully, and automatically activate and ready our body to take immediate action.

WHERE NERVES CONTINUE

Our basal ganglia are connected to the second member of the mesocortical limbic pathway: the limbic system, the brain's emotional-processing region. It's crucial to understand that our old brain uses the limbic system to tie emotion and memory to decision-making and behavior. Emotion and memory give us the capacity to apply what we've learned from similar past situations to decisions and actions we make in the present and future. So, if you've found teeing off in front of other people to be a nervous experience in the past, your limbic system is what causes you to register that experience as an ongoing trigger for your nerves. This process of tying what we feel directly to events and experiences is a critical component of how our brain learns and reinforces our behaviors. More on that in section three, "Habits."

Our nerves start with the basal ganglia but continue because the limbic system works from the assumption that jump-starting our nerves will make us ready to take immediate action before it's required. Therefore, the limbic system is part of what makes nerves a learned, recurring, and anticipatory response.

THE OLD BRAIN

The basal ganglia and limbic system are two of the major players in our old brain that evolved long before the younger parts of our brain. With its evolutionary head start, our old brain has the capacity to override many of the younger areas of our brain that control functions like rational thinking, largely because it has two salient advantages.

First, our old brain is much faster. According to Evan Gordon, a neuroscientist who specialized in high performance at the University of Texas at Dallas, in any given situation, before any information has the chance to reach the parts of the young brain that can process it consciously and rationally, it goes to the old brain first. This saved the lives of many of our prehistoric ancestors when faced with a pesky saber-toothed tiger, but in a modern-day situation where we want to thrive, the safety-first reflexes of our old brain can be more detrimental than helpful if we respond to nerves in ways that lead to anxiety.

Second, our old brain is not only faster; it's stronger. There are far more neural pathways in our brain devoted to safety and survival than to growing and thriving. In fact, when the safety-first areas of our old brain are activated enough, the areas of our young brain that allow us to think rationally and creatively go offline. Those areas of our young brain weren't strong enough to efficiently keep us alive in a dangerous prehistoric world. Our genetic predisposition as humans heavily favors safety, comfort, certainty, and risk avoidance because that's what kept us alive in a world where thriving wasn't in any way a priority.

Coupled together, the basal ganglia and limbic system, along with a few other structures of our old brain, make quite the survival team. But while they are optimally paired for survival in the prehistoric world, living a life today with only our highly efficient old brain in charge would lead to a never-ending loop of nerves.

As good as it is at keeping us alive, our old brain is also exceptionally inaccurate. Our old brain does not devote any brain matter or neuropathways toward determining if our nerves—or any specific thoughts, emotions, or behaviors, for that matter—are actually necessary.

SAFE . . . BUT NOT SO ACCURATE

We can see how, in a dangerous prehistoric environment, our old brain evolved to err on the side of safety quickly and powerfully. Because everything else took a back seat to survival, our old brain didn't develop the ability to accurately decipher whether any given risk was real or only perceived. Simply put, our old brain is fundamentally flawed in that it doesn't assess risk with any real accuracy. As a result, it detects risk quickly and intensely, often when we aren't actually being threatened.

For the survival of our species, this flaw was a literal lifesaver. Thousands of years ago, it didn't matter whether a rustling in the bushes was a furry little rabbit or a predator looking to make you its next meal. It wasn't worth risking life and limb to find out because, even if most rustlings were indeed rabbits, you only had to be wrong once to meet an untimely demise.

In our modern world, this isn't the case. Situations requiring us to take immediate action to protect life and limb are few and far between compared to those in the prehistoric era. The safety-first areas of our old brain are at times valuable for keeping us safe; however, the old brain's tendency to quickly and intensely overestimate and over-anticipate risk is far less advantageous in situations where we want to take the calculated risks required to pursue the things we want and to execute skills under pressure—for example, when we're playing golf.

THE YOUNG BRAIN

Although we are stuck with the prehistoric survival hardware of our old brain, we do have help from our young brain. Anthropologists and neuroscientists agree that to respond to the ongoing and frequent cycle of inaccurately perceived risk from our old brain, we needed to develop a more deliberate system that could counteract these instinctive safety-first responses. We needed brain structures that would allow us to not only survive but also grow and thrive by thinking consciously and rationally.

Thankfully, as our prehistoric ancestors continued to evolve, they also developed new layers on top of our old brain. Our large neocortex differentiates us from lower-order organisms and makes up our young brain. As humans, our hefty frontal lobes give us the capacity for awareness, reasoning, and the invaluable ability to think about our own thoughts, an ability psychologists call "metacognition."

Metacognition allows us to be aware of, examine, and evaluate our thoughts, feelings, and behaviors. By doing so, we can do more than just react instinctively and habitually to our environment in the same ways over and over. Being able to think and act contrary to how we may instinctively feel is the foundation for developing emotional intelligence, the capacity to be self-aware and to self-regulate.

The foremost portion of the neocortex, and a region of the brain heavily associated with metacognition, is the third member of the mesocortical limbic pathway: the prefrontal cortex. The prefrontal cortex has the capacity for conscious, rational thinking and can significantly influence the information processed by the old brain—specifically, how we learn to respond to our environment and how we think *about* the events and experiences in our lives, both external and internal.

Humans didn't develop the prefrontal cortex until long after the basal ganglia, limbic system, and other areas of our old brain had been cranial residents for thousands of years. As a result, the prefrontal cortex and the other members of our young brain are slower and less powerful. Additionally, our old brain tends to be triggered and come online before our young brain does, which is why it can be easy for us to react habitually and emotionally instead of intentionally and rationally.

Thankfully, we can still use our young brain to influence how accurately our old brain perceives and anticipates threats. In essence, we can influence how our old brain learns and operates by using and training our young brain effectively.

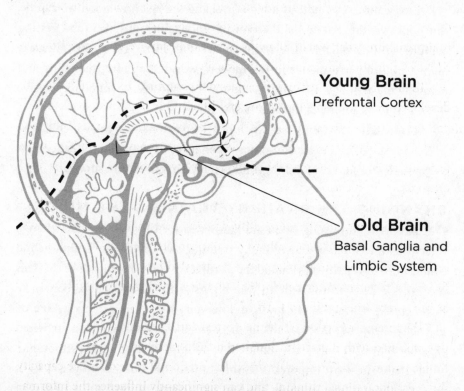

Young Brain
Prefrontal Cortex

Old Brain
Basal Ganglia and
Limbic System

BRAIN SUMMARY

Let's put all the pieces together. Your brain is an organ and the hardware of the human supercomputer. The brain is responsible for a wide range of functions, but, above all else, your brain is designed to ensure your survival. To fulfill this overriding function, it relies heavily on the old brain, which is much faster and stronger than the young brain.

Our old brain is good for surviving, but it's not as good for thriving because it can't distinguish between real and perceived threats. In situations where we're trying to thrive, our old brain easily misconstrues things like emotional discomfort, uncertainty, mistakes, and even its own nerves as real threats to us, despite the fact that the vast majority of the time, these things pose little or no physical threat to us, especially in golf.

If we want to compete at a high level and see just how good we can be, things like failure, emotional discomfort, uncertainty, mistakes, and getting nervous are unavoidable. The more we want to learn, grow, and pursue a higher level of performance in the modern world, the more frequently and intensely these things will occur—and the less valuable it will be to perceive them as threats and react to them habitually.

Fortunately, our young brain includes the prefrontal cortex, which allows us to be aware of and think about our experiences in ways that influence how our brain learns and responds beyond just reacting to ensure survival.

CHANGING THE BRAIN BY TRAINING THE MIND

Our old brain and young brain are hardwired for survival; we can't change their hardware directly. However, by training our minds, our brain's neural connections and pathways can adapt to what we train our minds to do. This process is called "neuroplasticity," the brain's ability to grow and reorganize how neural pathways in our brain and nervous system are arranged. Neuroplasticity allows our brain to change how small clusters of neurons are wired together as well as drastically remap how millions of neurons are structured.

Perhaps the most important reason for understanding neuroplasticity is that it highlights how valuable it is to prioritize our psychology. As a part of our physical body, the brain physically adapts to how we use or don't use our mind, and it's doing so whether we are aware of it or not.

Our supercomputer brains change based on the software we provide to them through our psychology. When we don't take the time to examine and upgrade our psychology, we are effectively leaving our old brain's safety-first hardware to paint our experiences as it sees fit, usually with the same repeated patterns of thought and behaviors. In this way, many golfers continue to play through anxiety, fear of failure, and unstable confidence.

NERVES OR ANXIETY?

Let's clarify a few things about nerves. An accurate understanding of where nerves come from shows us that nerves are not a bad thing in and of themselves. In fact, most of the world's best golfers learn to welcome nerves as a sign that they're in situations they want to be in, like having a chance to win a tournament. After all, very rarely do we get nervous about opportunities that don't include some meaningful risk. But nerves and anxiety are *not* the same.

Too often, we use the words "nervous" and "anxious" interchangeably. Using the two words to mean the same thing contributes to misunderstandings about both. As we've detailed, nerves are an instinctual physiological response triggered by our old brain's most basic hardware. Nerves can feel uncomfortable, but in and of themselves, nerves cannot directly impede us. Nerves create cognitive, neurological, and physical alertness, which is highly beneficial for performance. Think of nerves as a sense of readiness for immediate action in the present moment accompanied by some elevated physiological symptoms.

Anxiety, however, is a fear-based emotion. Specifically, anxiety is a psychological state characterized by extensive worry about the future—typically an imminent event with uncertain outcomes. Since any event that is about to occur is imminent, and the only thing we can be certain about is that things are uncertain, anxiety can be a part of any experience, especially based on how we perceive it. This, of course, includes golf. Each shot we are about to hit is imminent, and there is always some level of uncertainty about where the ball will go.

Let's get specific with how nerves and anxiety are different by understanding how our brain is working as we experience each. To project the future, the prefrontal cortex uses memories of past experiences as precedent. However, to project whether the future is likely to be what we think it *must* or *should* be, and whether that future is perceived as threatening, the prefrontal cortex also requires enough of what we are experiencing in the present moment to match our memories of the past. When enough overlap of past and present information is available suggesting that the future is predictable and non-threatening, the prefrontal cortex is online and in the driver's seat. This is critical to understanding the difference between nerves and anxiety; when our prefrontal cortex is online, we can make conscious, intentional, and rational decisions. When it's offline, we can't.

When there's a wide enough disparity between what we think we *must* or *should* be experiencing based on what we experienced in the past and what we're actually experiencing in the present, or when the future we project is perceived as threatening enough, the prefrontal cortex will then do its best to plan for the future by trying to fill in the disparity so we can avoid any threats, real or perceived. Projecting different versions of what might happen using our core beliefs and perceptions *about* previous experiences in similar situations is our young brain's best attempt to help "do something" to avoid what we don't want to experience. However, when our prefrontal cortex's best efforts to project the future still include levels of constriction and threat that we are unwilling to accept, the result is anxiety.

Our old brain, being older, faster, and stronger, reacts instinctively with nerves so we can live long enough to actually plan for the future, but it's our young brain that creates and fuels anxiety. In other words: nerves from the old brain plus an inability of our young brain to project a future that has acceptable levels of uncertainty and threat creates anxiety.

You might expect the prefrontal cortex to slow down when it lacks information or perceives the future to be threatening and then get back to work when that information is eventually available. But in reality, it's quite the opposite: anxiety is our young brain's way of urging us to "get information" because, if it has information, it can "do something" to feel comfortable, certain, or safe. The less accurate the information gathered by our prefrontal cortex, the more it starts tossing around that lack of information so it can produce all the possible "what if" scenarios for us to consider. And as you might guess, because our old brain is designed for safety and survival but *not* accuracy, it responds to those "what if" scenarios the same as it would respond to real threats.

When this happens, the old brain utilizes its speed and power and takes over, and when it does, the prefrontal cortex, the part of our young brain that can make conscious, intentional, and rational decisions, goes offline, ironically because of its own threatening projections of the future.

Unlike when we're nervous, anxiety is not only emotionally and physically uncomfortable, but it also impairs our cognitive and neurological capacity for making clear decisions because our prefrontal cortex isn't online. Our old brain isn't looking for the best decision about how to respond to a future that does not and may not ever exist; it's only concerned with what seems the safest. So, when you're anxious on the first tee, your old brain doesn't care that the best decision is to focus on your target and make a smooth, free-flowing swing. Instead, its reflexive response is to get you out of that situation as quickly and safely as possible—so it subconsciously chooses to go with the safety-first, guided, tense swing trying not to jerk the ball out of bounds.

Like anxiety, several other psychological and emotional states, such as anger, are not just unpleasant; they are also disruptive to us cognitively and neurologically, which disrupts how we execute physical skills. Information travels in our brain via brain waves, billions of electric impulses that travel along neural pathways. The frequency and intensity of our brain waves changes depending on a variety of factors, most notably our own thoughts and emotions related to events and experiences and whether our prefrontal cortex is online.

Research observing neurological activity shows that when our old brain effectively shuts down our prefrontal cortex, our brain operates on high-frequency and high-intensity brain waves. The amount of activity increases throughout the neurological pathways, making it more difficult for our muscles to receive messages from the brain about how to execute skills effectively.

Several studies, including golf-specific research conducted by neuroscientist Izzy Justice, show that increased traffic in the form of high-frequency and high-intensity brain waves specifically impairs how we execute physical skills in three ways. First, it disrupts the sequencing of physical movements, like that required to strike a golf ball effectively. Second, it makes it more difficult to accurately apply force, such as the amount of force required to swing a golf club at a certain speed, especially for delicate shots like chips and putts. And third, it makes it significantly more difficult to focus on a chosen external target, such as a flagstick in the distance or an aiming point when putting.

When we're nervous, our brain activates our body for action in the present moment with our prefrontal cortex online and operating on low-frequency and low-intensity brain waves. Anxiety, on the other hand, causes our brain to activate our body to avoid a future that is perceived to be too uncertain and too threatening. It takes our prefrontal cortex offline, leaving the rest of our brain operating on high-frequency and high-intensity brain waves that impair us cognitively, neurologically, and physically. Nerves and anxiety are easily confused because they share many of the same physical sensations, but beneath the surface, they are not the same.

Why am I talking about anxiety so much? Well, because golf itself—or any performance venture, for that matter—creates the exact external conditions for triggering anxiety. Alexander Chernev is a professor of marketing at the Kellogg School of Management at Northwestern University who, along with his colleagues, identified the three factors that most significantly diminish our ability to make sound choices: higher levels of task difficulty, greater choice complexity, and—you guessed it—higher levels of uncertainty. Put simply, basic knowledge about how our brain works and an accurate understanding of nerves and anxiety are vital because golf itself creates the exact conditions for our old brain to get nervous and our young brain to create anxiety.

How do we manage anxiety? The first step is to better understand how the brain works. The next step is to understand that the most common methods used to force ourselves to "just relax" or think our way out of nerves and anxiety don't work. Neither do the most common methods for building stable confidence. As we'll see in the coming sections, the majority of ways we try to avoid anxiety and build confidence are ineffective and unreliable because they don't work with how our brain functions and learns. They rely on our prefrontal cortex having accurate information and actually being online, which, in uncertain situations like playing golf under pressure, doesn't happen unless we have trained our awareness accordingly.

MYTH: "A LITTLE BIT OF ANXIETY IS A GOOD THING"

Now that we have a better understanding of the difference between nerves and anxiety, let's address our first myth: a certain amount of anxiety helps us play better golf.

Our brain is an association-making machine. Making connections between events, behaviors, and results is how our brain learns. However, the brain's superb ability to create associations has its limits. Because our old brain is designed to favor certainty and predictability without requiring accuracy, these associations are often riddled with inaccuracy and can lead us to form false associations, relationships between things that aren't actually related.

To see false associations in golf, you only need to watch golf on TV for a few minutes. Invariably, you'll see golfers talking to their golf balls, imploring them to "sit," "get up," or "be right." In truth, most golfers have a habit of talking to their golf balls because they learned to associate this kind of verbal persuasion with actual control over the golf balls. However, in the history of golf, no golf ball has ever been influenced by any amount of verbal persuasion. The fact is, you can talk to your ball and hit a good shot, or you can talk to your golf ball and hit a poor shot—but there's nothing to prove a cause-and-effect relationship between talking to a golf ball and the actual result of the shot. It's harmless, but it's still a false association.

The myth that a little bit of anxiety helps us to perform better, however, is harmful. If you've made this false association, it's not your fault: the idea that we must be at least a little bit anxious to perform at our best has been a consistent and, unfortunately, glamorized notion in surface-level performance psychology. The myth took flight in the early 1900s when Harvard researchers Robert Yerkes and John Dodson concluded that animals needed some level of "arousal," but not too much, in order to learn most effectively.

Their findings gained traction in the 1950s when German researcher Hans Eysenck published a study in which he claimed rats swam faster (improved their performance) when motivated to a certain point but swam slower (decreased their performance) when motivated past a certain point.

However, in his study, Eysenck created the "right amount" of anxiety by holding the rats' heads underwater for differing amounts of time.

The obvious flaw in Eysenck's study is that he failed to consider that perhaps the reason swimming performances decreased for some rats was because, regardless of how "motivated" a rat is, it's really difficult to swim if you can't breathe. His study was also scientifically unsound because he used the terms "motivation," "arousal," and "anxiety" interchangeably when the words do not have the same meaning. And in doing so, the false association between anxiety and performance was born in the form of the Yerkes–Dodson Law, more commonly known as the Inverted-U Theory.

Like Goldilocks trying to find the temperature of porridge that's just right, the Inverted-U Theory suggests that the right amount of anxiety is good for performance—as long as it's not too little or too much. This notion is patently incorrect.

In 2003, a review of psychological literature pertaining to stress and performance revealed that only 4 percent of research using the Inverted-U Theory provided supporting evidence to the theory, while 46 percent of research using the theory found that *any* level of anxiety inhibits performance. Sadly, the myth continues to grow. Before writing this book, I searched for and read every golf psychology book I could find. Of the books I found, the majority of them referenced the Inverted-U Theory in one form or another; many incorrectly described anxiety as "just arousal," and several directly suggested that "a little bit of anxiety is a good thing," effectively encouraging golfers toward anxiety. But, as we've covered, anxiety hinders cognitive capacity and creates the high-frequency and high-intensity brain waves that disrupt one's ability to physically execute their skills.

Let me reiterate that while nerves and anxiety feel physiologically similar at times, they are *not* the same. Being nervous can be helpful because your body activates for immediate action in the present moment and with your prefrontal cortex online. Being anxious isn't helpful, though, because it's rooted in fear of the future to the point that your old brain takes your prefrontal cortex offline, which clouds judgment, takes you out of the present moment, and motivates you to make tense, hesitant strokes and swings. The key difference: nerves feel like a sense of readiness; anxiety is a sense of worry about the future.

Think about some of the best experiences of your life. For example, the best round you've ever played, your wedding day, or the birth of your child. Chances are these events included some nerves, but you were still able to be focused on the present and make clear and conscious decisions about what you wanted to do.

Now compare those nervous experiences with your worst round of golf, the job interview you botched, or fumbling your way through a speech in front of crowd. These experiences were likely marred by anxiety, which caused you to worry about something bad happening and felt like you were losing conscious control of your thoughts and actions, which is exactly what happened.

Let's go back to Emmie's friend who got nervous as she was finishing her round at the Women's PGA Championship. Without knowing exactly what she was thinking or experiencing, my educated guess is that she realized a birdie would put her in the mix to win a major, whereas a bogey would leave more ground for her to try to make up on a difficult final round the next day. She was facing meaningful and uncertain outcomes and got nervous because her old brain was doing exactly what it was designed to do.

In an instant, her old brain quickly and inaccurately overestimated the threat of three-putting, and without accurate information in an uncertain situation, her young brain took those nerves and turned them into a little bit of anxiety, which wasn't helpful to her. Like for anyone else, her nerves were a natural and normal response, but she wasn't able to effectively respond to them and as a result made fearful strokes fueled not by nerves but by anxiety. In this way, her last few putts were executed well below her actual skill level.

If you're someone who has been taught that a little bit of anxiety is a good thing, allow me to make you a better, more accurate offer and explain why this false association between anxiety and playing well isn't real.

Here's a basic false-association check. Consider these questions:

Have you ever played well while feeling anxious?
The answer is probably yes.

Does feeling anxious *always* make you play better?
It doesn't? How interesting.

Here comes the kicker: Does anxiety ever get in the way of playing well?

It does? How interesting.

Does anxiety ever drain your energy, make it harder to execute your skills, or make golf less enjoyable?

It does? How interesting.

When you've played your very best golf and enjoyed golf the most, were you anxious?

No? How interesting—I thought a little bit of anxiety is a good thing.

So let's not proliferate this myth any further by using the terms "nervous" and "anxious" interchangeably. Doing so is like using the terms "tight draw" and "pull hook" to mean the same thing when one is especially useful for playing and enjoying golf and the other . . . well, not so much.

Dispelling this myth is important because it helps us understand that, yes, it is possible to play golf well with some anxiety, and at times that's the internal situation we're faced with. And to be clear, feeling some anxiety is normal. But anxiety is not required, it's not "just arousal," and it's not helping in any way.

Many of the golfers who contact me tell me that worry and anxiety are what keep them from playing more of the golf they really want to play. Their confidence is unstable because it relies on feeling comfort and certainty about the future. They learn to falsely believe that if they are not anxious, it means that they don't care about their golf game or the results they produce. They incorrectly assume that anxiety is required to be highly motivated without a clear understanding of what that anxiety is motivating them to do—which is to play scared and fear failure.

It's harder for us to play the way we want to when we're anxious. We can't avoid anxiety altogether simply based on how our brain is designed. However, accurately understanding how our brain is designed and functions is an invaluable first step toward addressing the habits and beliefs that invite anxiety into our game. What comes next is developing the type of awareness that allows us the space to play and think more freely.

SECTION 2

Awareness

Not long ago, I found myself sitting across from one of the best golfers in the world, although lately not so much. Marco, as we'll call him, was quick-witted, sarcastic, and direct—had he not been a world-class golfer, he would have made an excellent stand-up comic. Despite his relatively young age, Marco had the kind of career most golfers dream about, having already won several tournaments worldwide.

Our conversation was lighthearted, and as Marco talked about how he started golfing and the early years of his career, it was clear that he loved his craft and didn't take himself too seriously. However, the tone of our conversation changed when I asked Marco about what his golf had been like more recently.

Over the last year or so, Marco's play in competition had been steadily getting worse. While he once was near the top of the world rankings, he had dropped well outside of the top 250. He only had a few months left to earn enough money to retain his Tour status.

The more we talked, the clearer it became that Marco's decline in performance was the result of what he was experiencing internally. Despite his best efforts to force himself to feel comfortable and make himself confident, he was wrestling with his thoughts and feelings, and it was only digging him deeper into the hole he was desperately clambering to escape. No matter how hard he tried to get himself to think and feel a certain way and compel himself to play freely, when it came time to play in a tournament, his confidence was unstable, and inside, he was a tumultuous mess.

"I'm just overrun with negative thoughts and feelings," he told me. "My mind just starts going, and I can't control it. The harder I try to fix my thoughts, the worse they get. I don't know what's wrong with me."

"You're finding it difficult to force your thoughts and feelings to fall in line," I empathized.

"Exactly!" Marco replied. "I've never worked so hard to control my mind. I should be more confident, but the more I try to make myself feel confident, the more I just start worrying about having a bad round and hitting bad shots."

"The harder you try to force confident thoughts, the less stable your confidence becomes?" I asked.

Marco's face fell and he nodded.

"Let me ask you this," I said. "What if I told you that from this point forward, no matter what, just don't ever, under any circumstances, have a negative or unproductive thought or feeling ever again. Whether you're on the cut line or in contention to win, you just need to try harder to force yourself to feel confident. In fact, do your best to just not think at all. What would you say to that?"

Marco paused briefly, contemplating. Then with a wry smile, he answered, "I'd say, 'F--k you, Raymond!'"

Mastering only physical golf skills is no longer enough—and likely never has been. Competition will inevitably expose what's going on internally sooner or later. For many golfers, growth and success are hard earned through years of practice and training to hone ball-striking, short-game, and putting skills. But for all the time and energy golfers devote to becoming masters of their craft, many haven't invested much, if any, time learning to master themselves. This was certainly true for Marco.

The inability for Marco to resolve his internal struggles was not for lack of effort; in fact, his internal struggles were because of it. His retort to my sarcastic and clearly ill-advised suggestion was as funny as it was correct. Little did he know, Marco had just introduced himself to a long-neglected part of his performance: his relationship with his inner experience.

Developing physical skills is vitally important; however, you can be as skilled as any golfer in the world, but if you're not addressing your relationship with your inner experience, physical ability will only take you so far.

YOUR INNER EXPERIENCE

Your inner experience is the combination of thoughts, feelings, and sensations you're experiencing internally in any given moment. It's a cornerstone of being human.

Not only do we all have an inner experience, but we also all have a relationship with it: we are always interacting with our thoughts and feelings. As you may recall from the previous section, we are metacognitive creatures—when we think or feel something, we have thoughts and feelings *about* those thoughts and feelings. It's not a matter of *if* we have a relationship with our inner experience—it's a matter of *what type* of relationship it is.

The type of relationship we cultivate with our inner experience plays a vital role in how we respond to the events and experiences in our lives, both external and internal. For this reason, our relationship with our inner experience is perhaps the most important relationship in our lives.

Our inner experience and our relationship with it most heavily revolve around our thoughts. Thoughts reflect what we've learned from previous experiences, our core beliefs, and the direction of our focus. Our thoughts also play a significant role in creating our feelings, and it's our feelings that most heavily reinforce our behaviors. It's important to understand that our feelings are neither right nor wrong; feelings are simply a reaction to our external and internal experiences and our thoughts *about* those experiences.

Thoughts and feelings happen in an instantaneous, rapid-fire sequence, and most experts in psychology and neuroscience agree that thoughts precede feelings. This means that our thoughts serve as one of the primary filters through which any given situation passes, causing our emotional reactions. So, whatever you may feel about any given event or experience in your life, those feelings are not created by the events or experiences themselves. What you feel is created by your thoughts *about* those events and experiences. Your overall inner experience is following what you are thinking *about* anything.

In the coming sections, we'll address the habitual behaviors we form based on how our brain learns; then we will discuss our beliefs, the other primary driving force for the content of our inner experience and our actions. However, examining our habits and reshaping our beliefs are most effective when done through a particular type of relationship with our inner experience. So, before we can effectively do so, we must understand and develop more flexible and durable awareness. Let's start by looking at the type of relationship most people have with their inner experience.

THE DOING MODE OF MIND

Like Marco, many golfers develop an avoidant relationship with their inner experience. When Marco found himself thinking the types of thoughts that led to uncomfortable and undesirable feelings, he responded to those thoughts and feelings by trying to banish them or forcibly replace them with ones he thought he *should* have. In essence, Marco would initiate that internal wrestling match by either trying to push away his thoughts and feelings or by distracting himself and pretending they didn't exist. But fighting his inner experience in this way only opened the door to wrestling with more disruptive thoughts and compounding layers of emotion. The harder he wrestled, the more there was to wrestle against.

The problem-solving and judgmental relationship with our inner experience is what neuroscientist and University of Oxford emeritus professor Mark Williams and his colleagues John Teasdale and Zindel Segal call the "doing mode of mind."

Using golf as an example, here's how they illustrate the doing mode of mind. While playing golf, the doing mode of mind enables us to create an idea of the situation we're currently in and an idea of where we want to be. For example: we are currently on the tee, and we want to get the ball into the hole in as few strokes as possible. The doing mode of mind then focuses on the disparity between where we are and where we want to be to generate behaviors intended to move us in a way that closes the gap between the two—behaviors like picking a target, picking a club, and executing a golf shot.

Naturally, the doing mode of mind works for avoidance as well. If there is something we don't want to happen, the doing mode of mind focuses on widening the gap between our idea of where we are and our idea of what we want to avoid. For example, if what we want to avoid is a rush-hour traffic jam, the doing mode of mind helps to generate behaviors like finding an alternate route or choosing to drive home at a different time in order to move us away from the traffic we seek to avoid.

For external tasks and challenges, the doing mode of mind offers a logical and effective strategy: narrow the gap between where we are and what we desire and widen the gap between where we are and what we want to avoid. It enables us to manage our daily routines and allows us to learn how to swing a golf club and effectively strategize how to play a golf course.

Not surprisingly, in years of research and applied practice, Williams and his colleagues found that, for most people, the doing mode of mind is their default relationship with their own thoughts and feelings because it usually works well for reaching objectives in everyday situations. On the surface, it seems logical, for instance, that a doing mode of mind would work to reduce anxiety and increase confidence. But unfortunately, when it comes to our inner experience, this might be exactly the least effective approach.

As well-equipped as the doing mode of mind is for solving the external challenges around us, it is woefully ill equipped for addressing what we experience internally for two salient reasons. First and foremost, it's of the utmost importance to understand that, above all, the fundamental reason why a doing-mode-of-mind relationship with our inner experience doesn't work is that no matter what we're experiencing internally, our inner experience doesn't need to be "fixed."

Thoughts and feelings happen. Our brains are designed to create, use, organize, explore, expand, interpret, and interact with our thoughts. As Pete Kirchmer, program director of the mPEAK (Mindfulness, Performance Enhancement, Awareness, and Knowledge) program at University of California San Diego's Center for Mindfulness, says, "The mind is designed to pump thoughts like the heart is designed to pump blood."

Telling ourselves or someone else to "quiet your mind" or "just don't think" is surface-level psychology that reflects a fundamental misunderstanding of how our brain and mind work. Thinking and feeling freely is highly beneficial and a significant marker of psychological strength: it signals that one's brain, mind, and body are communicating in high fidelity. Whatever our inner experience is, it's working exactly how it's supposed to by thinking and feeling.

You may be familiar with the phrase "don't fix what isn't broken." This sentiment leads us to the second reason a doing-mode-of-mind relationship with our inner experience doesn't work: the more we try to "fix" it, the worse it'll get. Let's look at a few reasons why.

It Makes Us Feel Worse

In study after study that prompt people to address their thoughts and feelings with a doing mode of mind, psychologists get the same results: trying to fix our thoughts and feelings with an external problem-solving method that highlights the difference between how we feel and how we'd prefer to feel invariably makes us feel worse. Not feeling as confident as we want to isn't especially problematic. Highlighting that we *need to* or *should* feel more confident is what's making us feel worse, trapping us in the unproductive thoughts and behaviors that we hoped it would rescue us from.

It Leads to Overthinking

Overthinking is particularly harmful to our performance because, rather than simplifying and clarifying, it complicates and confuses. Overthinking is the natural consequence of trying to fix our thoughts and feelings by forcefully responding to them with judgment, comparison, and overanalysis. Overthinking often comes in the form of toxic rumination, a self-centered, self-critical, and ongoing self-interrogation fruitlessly preoccupied with trying to uncover all the causes, meanings, and sources of disruptive thoughts, emotional discomfort, poor shots, and uncertainty. It's a losing battle and a surefire method of destabilizing confidence.

But it doesn't end there. Research exploring peoples' habitual patterns of thought repeatedly shows that the more we've previously resorted to overthinking to address our thoughts and feelings—or golf swing, for that matter—the more likely we are to use the familiar but futile strategy again and again, always to the same effect.

It Compounds and Elevates Our Emotions

Our feelings are functional feedback for us to learn and grow—even the uncomfortable ones. But our thoughts and emotions become less functional, and even problematic, when they intensify to the point where they interfere with our ability to think clearly and make conscious and intentional decisions.

Think of feeling nervous on the first tee as a single layer of emotion. A layer or two of emotions won't significantly impede our ability to do anything—this is why feeling nervous isn't a bad thing. However, when we start to think about nerves as a problem that needs to be "fixed," we feel worried about being nervous. Trying not to feel nervous or worried now creates another layer of emotion in the form of doubt. Then, trying to suppress nerves, worry, and doubt so that they won't lead to a bad shot and another bad round of golf creates anxiety. Instead of one layer of emotion, we've now created several additional, intense layers by trying to suppress feeling nervous.

Research on how people respond to their own emotions shows quite clearly that when we suppress our emotions, they get stronger, a process psychologists call "amplification." Amplification is the natural consequence of trying to avoid one's inner experience. We may think that we can control our emotions by ignoring them, bottling them up, or sweeping them under the rug, but the reality is that the more we apply a doing mode of mind to our inner experience, the more our emotions control us by layering and intensifying or by showing up later in more disruptive ways.

It Takes Us off Time

Being "off time" means that we are focused on the past and/or the future instead of the present. If you've ever dwelled on a mistake for an extended period of time or worried about playing a certain hole before you even get there, you know what it's like to be off time.

Although we can think about moments in the past and future, we are, by definition, always physically in the present moment. So, when we're off time, the best-case scenario is that we're somewhat distracted from what we're doing in the present moment. However, the more we try to "fix" our current inner experience, the further off time we become and the more our emotions build upon each other. Frustration, anger, and disappointment are behind time in the past. Fear, worry, and anxiety are ahead of time in the future. On a neurological level, the farther off time we are psychologically, the higher the frequency and intensity of our brain waves and the more disrupted our ability to execute our skills becomes.

Michael Gervais, an author and expert in performance psychology, has an artistic way of describing how our emotions follow our focus when we're off time: he suggests thinking about the present like being inside a raindrop.

As with the present moment passing through time, your raindrop is moving, and you can't physically get out; you're in the raindrop until it hits the ground. As your raindrop moves, you can be at the sides or be centered in it. Going to the sides is like focusing on the past and the future, which makes your raindrop unbalanced because you're not grounded in the present. Space in the present moment is constricted by anger and anxiety.

Learning from our past and planning for the future are valuable at times. But when we're off time in the moments when we want or need to be on time, we become disconnected from our performance.

It Decreases Our Cognitive and Emotional Adaptability

Imagine that you want to get physically stronger, and, to do so, you've decided to do push-ups every day for a month. So, every day you do push-ups, but as soon as you feel even a hint of fatigue or burning in your muscles, you quit for the day. With this avoidant relationship with physical discomfort, how much stronger will you be after a month? Probably not much, if at all.

Because you prioritized alleviating your immediate physical comfort over your long-term strength, your muscle fibers didn't work hard enough to break down and rebuild stronger. You didn't allow yourself to be uncomfortable long enough for your muscles to adapt to an increased level of discomfort. Adaptation plays out in the same way psychologically. The way to increase our ability to adapt to stressful situations and uncomfortable thoughts and emotions isn't to avoid them—it's to accept them.

Moreover, when our adaptability to our own emotional discomfort decreases, we can easily learn to falsely believe that we need to "fix" our emotional state in order to perform well. Doing this creates a situation where trying to fix our inner experience and avoid future emotional discomfort becomes a higher priority than actually performing in the present moment.

It Preoccupies Us with Our Inner Experience

More than one hundred performance-psychology studies, specifically a body of research conducted by author and attentional-focus expert Robert Nideffer, show that when an athlete executes a skill, having a narrow and external focus is most effective. That is, we best execute the skills we painstakingly train when our focus is directed outwardly to where we can see our intended target and then react. In golf, a narrow and external focus is directed toward the target, landing spot, or putting line.

Focusing internally is important at times. For example, focusing on your muscle tension might aid in adjusting your posture and alignment before a shot. However, when it's time to actually play a shot, an internal focus can divide our attention between what we're thinking or feeling and the actual execution of our skills. Despite the common misconception, human beings are *not* efficient multitaskers. We cannot focus internally and externally at the same time without both directions of focus being compromised.

It Creates a Fear of Our Inner Experience

Perhaps the worst part of trying to fix what isn't broken is that we can easily come to fear our own thoughts and feelings.

If every time you have an undesirable thought, you overthink it or suppress it until it amplifies into a full-blown, agonizing inner dialogue, you will naturally learn to fear your own thoughts because they become so much more. You will come to the seemingly logical conclusion that just thinking about making a mistake is a guarantee of a poor round of golf and an unenjoyable experience.

In the same way, we learn to fear our feelings. If every time you feel a twinge of worry, it pushes you more into the past or future and deeper into layers of emotion, it makes sense that you would be anxious about just the idea of feeling anxious.

For many golfers, a doing-mode-of-mind relationship with their inner experience is all they know. The more they learn to fear, suppress, and forcefully "fix" their inner experience, the more it brings them back again and again.

When researchers Costas Papageorgiou and Adrian Wells asked people who are habitual overthinkers why they overthink, their overwhelming answer was that they felt it helped. Habitual overthinkers believe that by not overthinking, things will worsen. Similarly, when researchers asked the same question to people who habitually suppress emotions and fixate on the past and future, the predominant answer was that they felt like they were "doing something" to feel better and improve their situation, and that not doing so would leave them worse off.

But research by Sonja Lyubomirsky and Susan Nolen-Hoeksema shows that when it comes to our inner experience, overthinking, suppression, and being off time causes the opposite. Specifically, they found that the more we bring a doing mode of mind to our inner experience, the more our ability to navigate internal and external experiences significantly deteriorates. And even though a doing mode of mind doesn't help and actually makes things worse, the false belief that it helps by "doing something" keeps the dysfunctional relationship intact.

The other reason we continue to return to the doing mode of mind is because we don't know that there's another option. We're unaware that there's an alternative, not based on controlling our inner experience with force, distraction, and suppression—but rather through awareness.

This awareness is what Williams, Teasdale, and Segal call the "being mode of mind." The being mode of mind is built on our capacities to be intentional, grounded, and accepting of our inner experience. These are capacities we already have, although rarely do we develop them as they relate to our thoughts and feelings. Through such awareness, the being mode of mind is the remedy to the pitfalls of the doing mode of mind.

THE BENEFITS OF THE BEING MODE OF MIND

Through a being mode of mind, we stop trying to ignore, fix, force, and avoid our inner experience. Instead of fixing what isn't broken, we create space to think and act in the present moment through awareness. As you might expect, understanding and training a being mode of mind opens us to several benefits.

We Get Out of Our Heads

A being mode of mind allows us to experience the present moment and our performance directly. Without being subjected to relentless overthinking and toxic rumination, we learn to see our thoughts as just thoughts, memories, projections, perceptions, and ideas—not necessarily as facts or accurate reflections of our current reality. Like passing weather patterns or waves meeting the shore, we learn to experience our thoughts and emotions as passing mental and emotional events that come and go instead of treating them as something to take literally.

The ideas that we "have to be comfortable," "shouldn't feel anxious," or "must never three-putt" can finally be seen as just ideas and not necessarily facts or absolute necessities, which makes it easier to step away from thoughts that lead to overthinking and anxiety.

We Give Our Emotions Space

By seeing thoughts as just thoughts and not necessarily anything more, the being mode of mind gives our emotions license to exist just as they are. We learn to observe unpleasant emotions without the need to "fix" them, force them to be more pleasant, or suppress them. Seeing emotions in this way gives them space to simply be, without having to amplify or layer them.

Emotional discomfort is normal, healthy, and an unavoidable part of life and golf. A willingness to coexist with emotional discomfort without trying to change it keeps the compounding and layering of our emotions to a minimum.

Coexisting with our emotions as they are also allows us to develop what author and researcher Daniel Goleman calls "emotional agility," the capacity to experience a wide range of emotions and more effectively transition between them without losing self-control.

When we develop emotional agility, we can more clearly see that what's best for our future isn't necessarily what's most comfortable for us in the present. Golf, like life, often requires us to experience multiple emotions at once and skillfully navigate them, and research shows that emotional agility is strongly associated with better and more consistent performance, well-being, and general life satisfaction.

We're On Time

You may have heard some players describe the feeling of the game slowing down. Maybe you've experienced the feeling of time slowing down yourself. You may have also experienced feeling as if things are moving too quickly, of time speeding up.

Time doesn't actually slow down or speed up, of course. When we sense that things are slowing down, it's because our mind is synced to the speed of our performance as it's happening. In a being mode of mind, we are able to ground ourselves in the present moment. Without being split between time frames, our focus is on our performance as it's happening, which gives us a sensation that time is playing out more slowly than we are typically accustomed to.

Psychological states that revolve around the present moment and grant access to it, including groundedness, acceptance, and flow state, are characterized by low-frequency and low-intensity brain waves. Specifically, when we are "on time," our brain is operating on alpha and theta brain waves traveling between four to twelve hertz. Alpha waves are an indicator that our prefrontal cortex is online, leading to the capacity for composed, intentional decision-making, and theta waves are an indicator that we are grounded in the present and not off time, lost in wandering thought, or in a triggered habitual response. So, when we are on time psychologically, our brains and bodies execute physical skills better than in psychological states like anxiety, dwelling, and prolonged anger, when our prefrontal cortex is offline and our brain is operating on high-frequency and high-intensity brain waves.

It bears repeating that high-frequency and high-intensity brain waves muddy the communication between the brain and the body and lead to disrupted sequencing of physical movements, a disrupted ability to apply appropriate force, and greater difficulty in focusing on an external target—all vital for playing better and more enjoyable golf.

We Step Away from the Doing Mode of Mind

Through the awareness fostered by the being mode of mind, we can disengage from a doing-mode-of-mind relationship with our inner experience. The being mode of mind helps us become aware of ourselves, our thoughts, and our feelings in ways that direct our focus and efforts where we really want them to go, making us better at executing our skills.

Additionally, without the preoccupation of "fixing" our inner experience, we sidestep the series of thoughts and corresponding feelings and behaviors that make us the primary barrier to our own performance. With the awareness that comes with a being mode of mind, we are better able to recognize at earlier stages the triggers and shifts in our inner experience where we are most likely to engage with the unproductive habits and core beliefs that only cause us to get in our own way.

Through a being mode of mind, an uncomfortable inner experience isn't something to be feared as a precursor to poor and unenjoyable golf. Feeling nervous or having disruptive thoughts isn't the beginning of a downward spiral; these are merely temporary features of our inner experience. Through awareness, our inner experience—even when uncomfortable—promotes and sustains better performances.

But a being mode of mind doesn't happen on its own. We must train a being mode of mind and our awareness through the practice and application of mindfulness. For the remainder of this section, we will discuss mindfulness and how to train it so that we can build a relationship with our inner experience that facilitates growth, delivers more consistent performance, and enriches our golf experience.

MINDFULNESS

Mindfulness as a practice has been around for roughly 2,600 years, with origins rooted in many parts of Asia. Although mindfulness was around long before most performance-enhancement training practices, it is currently backed by a growing and extensive body of modern science. In 1980, only a handful of empirical research studies were published about the effects of mindfulness and its practices. Fast forward to the present day, and more than one thousand scholarly articles are published every year exploring and detailing the effects of mindfulness on medical conditions like chronic pain and obesity, emotional disorders like anxiety and depression, addiction, sleep and recovery, academic performance, business productivity, and sport performance, among many others.

Driven mostly by mobile apps, social media, and business organizations, the mindfulness industry now nets more than a billion dollars annually and continues to grow. The exponential growth and integration of mindfulness into so many different areas of life isn't just because mindfulness is the next fad; it's a reflection of how training to shift into a being mode of mind and being more present improves the quality of our lives and performances.

I admit that I was more than a little skeptical when I was first introduced to mindfulness and its practices. At the time, I didn't see how allowing ourselves to think freely could actually streamline our thoughts. But then I read the mountain of research on mindfulness and its practices used by elite athletes and performers and tried the practices with my clients and myself. The changes were indisputable. In a few short weeks, I observed and experienced a simple but fundamental truth: the quality of our performance and the degree to which we enjoy it are not determined by inevitable fluctuations in our inner experience, like unproductive thoughts and uncomfortable emotions, or by any given external event. Instead, they are determined by whether our relationship with our inner experience gives us the ability to be aware of what we think and feel, accept things as they are, and then reconnect with our performance in the present moment—an ability that can be actively trained through mindfulness.

The benefits of mindfulness extend well beyond the golf course. Modern science continues to highlight incredible neuroplastic changes and the corresponding behaviors of those who make practicing mindfulness a part of their lives.

Neurological research continues to show that practicing mindfulness trains us to be grounded in the present moment more often. As a result of being on time more often, those who practice mindfulness are more likely to be in psychological and neurological states that are associated with faster learning, intrinsic motivation, stable confidence, and flow state.

A massive body of interrelated research featuring studies spearheaded by Ellen Langer, Sara Lazar, Portia Marasigan, Dominique Lippelt, Wendy Phillips, Judson Brewer, and Kristin Neff, among many others, also shows that people who practice mindfulness tend to be happier, more optimistic, more hopeful, and more fulfilled with their chosen crafts. They are more satisfied with their lives and grateful for what they have. They are less anxious, stressed, fearful, and depressed. They are less likely to repeatedly fall into unproductive habit loops or lose self-control in stressful environments. They are more emotionally agile, allowing them to respond to disruptive thoughts and emotions more effectively. They are more likely to engage in behaviors that lead to better health and higher performance related to physical fitness, nutrition, and sleep. They are physically healthier, have stronger immune systems, and even get fewer colds. They are more motivated to pursue passions and interests. They are more conscientious and open-minded, leading to faster and better learning. They are more resilient when faced with challenges and show more grit when pursuing endeavors that are important to them. They are more forgiving and empathic, and they are better able to see others' perspectives. They have closer and more functional relationships with friends, family, and romantic partners.

And a review of sport-performance research condensed by Kristoffer Henriksen, Jakob Hansen, and Carston Hvid Larsen revealed that people who practice mindfulness are also more composed under pressure and have more stable confidence.

The bottom line is that mindfulness, when accurately understood, practiced consistently, and applied purposefully, creates a healthier, more beneficial relationship with all of our experiences, especially our inner experience, opening the door to better and more enjoyable golf and long-term improvement, something that can be learned and trained by anyone.

WHAT IS MINDFULNESS?

Mindfulness is awareness. It is a specific type of awareness cultivated by intentionally paying attention to our experiences, internal and external, as they are in the present moment. Mindfulness comes from paying attention to anything but is often most pronounced when we pay attention to our thoughts, emotions, habits, and core beliefs.

Being mindful is beneficial because it's the exact opposite of the type of attention that stems from a doing mode of mind. The benefits of a being mode of mind are always accessible to us through mindfulness because it is rooted in three internally driven foundational principles: intention, groundedness, and acceptance. Together, these principles make up the vertebrae that give the being mode of mind its durable, yet flexible, backbone.

INTENTION

While Marco and I worked together for a few days, I arranged a round of golf for him at one of the best golf clubs near my home. The club has three courses on the property. While two of the courses are well designed, they both pale in comparison to the championship course, a course that has played host to several PGA Tour events, including several majors. Since Marco had never been to the club before, I informed him that the championship course was consistently ranked as one of the best courses in the country and that playing it was considered a privilege by most professional players.

As you might expect, Marco played his round with great anticipation, savoring every shot in a way he hadn't in quite some time.

"What did you think of the course?" I asked Marco after he had finished.

Marco was enamored with the exquisite design and immaculate condition of the course he had just played. He had purposefully and consciously paid attention to the course, soaking in all it had to offer.

"It was amazing. Everything I thought it would be," he said. "It's without a doubt one of the best courses I've ever played."

Only after Marco's glowing review of his round did I reveal that the course he had played was not the highly touted championship course that Tour players raved about. Instead, I had arranged for him to play one of the other courses, one no more highly rated than courses Marco played all the time.

You may be thinking that I robbed Marco of a chance to play on a truly great golf course, and in part you'd be right. However, what was more valuable to Marco was the lesson learned from the experience, a lesson adapted from an introduction to a series of mindfulness-based programming from mindfulness expert Williams and his colleagues.

In Marco's case, the important lesson learned was not how wonderful a rare round at a magnificent course can be but instead how amazing playing an ordinary course can be if paid attention to in a certain way. Marco paid attention to his round with intention. Through mindfulness, we can learn to pay attention to *any* experience in this way, including our inner experience.

Intention involves paying attention on purpose and with purpose. By purposefully choosing to tune in to our experiences, we become aware of our current reality as it is, what choices we have at our disposal, and the natural consequences of our behaviors. We collect and use information more effectively and can consciously choose with clarity and composure how we respond to any event, internal or external.

By intentionally paying attention in this way, we can change the type of direct experience we have with anything. If intention can transform our direct experience with something as simple as a golf course, imagine how it could change our direct experience with our own thoughts and feelings that impact how we play golf. It is the intentional component to mindfulness training that allows us to interact with our thoughts, feelings, and actions on our own terms rather than being at the whip's end of our default thoughts and feelings.

GROUNDEDNESS

If you've listened to television commentary of golf—or of any sport, really—you've probably heard phrases like "when it matters most," "a big shot," and "a defining moment." These are meant to convey how important a moment or certain shot can *feel*, but the reality is that there is no such thing as a defining moment or when something matters most. What matters most is not the Olympics, the Super Bowl, or any other major championship. Yes, those moments do matter, but *the* moment that matters most to us is always *now*.

Groundedness is an intentional connection to our experiences in the present moment. It's an understanding that there is no moment you've already had, and there's no moment that you're going to have, that is more important than the one you're in right now. Any moment in the past is over and therefore has no direct impact on the present; any moment in the future is unknown and hasn't happened yet and therefore also has no direct impact on the present moment. The only moment available to us with any immediate, and therefore direct, impact on our life and performance is the one we're in right now.

Thinking about the past and future can be important, but when done mindlessly, habitually, or while competing, it interrupts our connection to the present moment. Being off time unnecessarily invites distraction and layers of negative emotions, a common unproductive habit that interferes with our connection to the only moment and the only shot that is currently and directly impacting our game: this one.

ACCEPTANCE

On average, we speak sixteen thousand words each day. Those words all come from thoughts. And if that's how many thoughts we have in order to speak that much, imagine how many unspoken thoughts we must have in a given day. The vast majority of our thoughts are just that: only thoughts and not facts, just subjective evaluations and judgments *about* things, but *not* the things themselves. By definition, beliefs, thoughts, perceptions, interpretations, judgments, and comparisons aren't necessarily facts. They are ideas, memories, notions, projections, and opinions *about* our experiences, but not necessarily relevant, accurate, real, or even worthy of being spoken.

One of the most prominent benefits of mindfulness is that we come to experience our thoughts and feelings as passing internal events. Through acceptance, we are better equipped to deal with disruptive thoughts and emotions because we can accept them without having to believe that they are literally true.

Acceptance is receiving our past, future, and present experiences as they are. Acceptance sees things, like our inner experience, as they currently are and not as we think they *must* or *should* be.

This intentional and grounded shift in our relationship with our thoughts and feelings, while challenging at times, releases us from their control. Instead of a thought *about* failure and feelings of anxiety being taken as precursors to actual failure, we can treat uncomfortable thoughts and feelings as we would other temporary experiences, like passing sights, sounds, tastes, or smells.

Through acceptance, thoughts and feelings are no longer judged for being good or bad, correct or incorrect. Judging in this way falsely assumes that any of the events and experiences of our lives, including our inner experience, *must* or *should* meet our rigid expectations. This then creates cognitive and emotional constriction.

Acceptance doesn't mean giving up on the quality of our performance and the results we authentically want to pursue or that we have to settle for lowered standards. Acceptance is not a resignation that things will always be what they are, whether we like them or not. Acceptance is not passive; it is an active and deliberate interaction with our current reality as it is so that we can create and sustain an urgency for the present moment, the only moment of our life that we can control and have access to.

With acceptance, we can be highly motivated to get better and compete without being attentionally or emotionally beholden to any specific thoughts and feelings or past and future events that no longer and may not ever actually exist.

Acceptance will be an ongoing theme throughout this book because it is a fundamental component to developing self-awareness, self-control, and stable confidence. As opposed to the constriction that comes from trying to avoid or deny our current reality, for those who embrace acceptance, often a deep sense of spaciousness is found.

FROM CONCEPT TO PRACTICE

For those who have experienced anything like Marco's struggles, or even those who sense that they are competing in a doing mode of mind, mindfulness is the road out of a doing-mode-of-mind relationship with our inner experience. Through mindfulness training, we can be more aware of the connections between our golf game, our thoughts, our emotions, and the doing mode of mind.

I do not consider myself to be a mindfulness expert; however, like the experts from whom I've drawn much of my knowledge of mindfulness, I encourage you to engage with the practices described in this section with a combination of patience, self-compassion, persistence, and an open mind. As with any of my clients, whether a tennis player, mixed-martial-arts fighter, linebacker, musician, or golfer, I invite you to let go of the tendency we all have to force our inner experience to be a certain way and instead work to be aware of your thoughts and feelings as they are in each moment.

MINDFULNESS TRAINING

MISCONCEPTIONS AND CLARIFICATION

As popular as mindfulness has become, there are many misconceptions about what it is and what its practices do. The most common misconception about mindfulness is that it is meant to be a state of uninterrupted zen or to get us into "the zone," what psychologists refer to as "flow state." This is *not* true. Flow state is the optimal state of human functioning characterized by a sense of effortlessness of action and skill execution, deep immersion in the task at hand in the present moment, a detachment of ego, elevated levels of acceptance for *all* outcomes, intrinsic motivation without goal striving, and intense enjoyment of whatever is being done. Psychologically, flow state is a state of minimal or no perceived threat. Neurologically, in flow state our brain operates on low-frequency and low-intensity brain waves that make communication between our brain and body as efficient as possible—hence the feeling that skill execution is effortless.

Flow state is a complete fusion between you, your environment, and your performance; however, it relies on many internal and external factors. Thus, it has a range of external moving parts that we cannot always control, like other people, weather conditions, and the difficulty of the task relative to our current skill level. Anyone who's experienced flow state will attest to how wonderful it is—but also to how it can come and go quickly. However, there are several internal components that we *can* control, namely being present, that increase the likelihood of experiencing flow state.

Most research shows that elite-level performers spend about 10 percent of their performance in flow state—but when or for how long that 10 percent comes varies greatly. Sometimes we experience flow state in small doses here and there, while other times we might find ourselves playing large portions of a round of golf in flow state, only to not experience it again for extended periods of time. Additionally, most research shows that athletes are far less likely to find flow state while engaged in unproductive habits, with beliefs that destabilize confidence, and when their primary source of motivation is to gain extrinsic validation. We'll go into more detail about these later. And of particular note, the likeliness of entering flow state significantly decreases when we actively strive to reach or force our way into it.

To be clear, we don't need to be in a flow state to perform well. However, it does provide a valuable frame of reference for how to perform better and more consistently. Specifically, our performance improves when we are grounded in the present moment. So mindfulness and its practices are *not* about creating zen, nor are they intended to force us into flow state. Mindfulness is *not* a special state of mind where nerves, anxiety, or mental time travel never happen. However, one of the benefits for those who make mindfulness practices a regular part of their lives is that flow states become more common simply because they are in the present more often. In fact, you may be noticing that a being mode of mind is strikingly similar to flow state. Although we cannot forcefully step through the flow-state doorway, mindfulness training teaches us to shift to the being mode of mind, which brings us closer to that doorway and increases our chances of passing through it more often.

Another common misconception is that mindfulness and its practices teach us to empty our minds or stop our thoughts and emotions. There's quite a bit of misinformation suggesting that mindfulness is a non-thinking state of mind or a relaxation technique. This is also *not* true. In fact, if you want a surefire method for driving yourself crazy with frustration, try to clear your mind of all thoughts, especially while playing golf. As we've noted at length, our brains and minds are designed to think, and trying to stop them is like trying to stop a train by standing on the tracks. Stopping our inner experience is impossible and ill advised. Without thoughts, we would be miserably unable to function in any environment—and especially while playing golf. Mindfulness training isn't about forcing ourselves to think less; it's about building a relationship with our inner experience and the events of our lives that funnels our awareness and efforts to the present moment more efficiently and nonjudgmentally.

Changing our relationship with our thoughts isn't easy. Because we are so accustomed to the doing mode of mind, mindfulness training can at first feel awkward and clunky. It's important to understand that the awkwardness and clunkiness are just part of the adjustment to becoming more familiar with the being mode of mind, which is foreign to many people. This transition is not unlike the early adjustments of learning a second language and using our first language less frequently. It's a matter of unfamiliarity, established habits, and the appeal for our brain to return to what's familiar to us as we explore a more beneficial language with ourselves.

To that degree, the feeling that they are having "more thoughts" while practicing mindfulness is *not* reflective of an actual increase in thoughts: it's the byproduct of intentionally tuning in to our thoughts. Mindfully tuning into our thoughts reveals the amount and types of thoughts we were unaware of in the doing mode of mind. We've just been tuning out and suppressing what's been there all along.

Harvard psychologists Matthew Killingsworth and Daniel Gilbert conducted a study using a mobile app to ask people three questions: What are you doing at the present moment, what are you thinking about at the present moment, and how happy are you? After collecting more than 250,000 data points, their study revealed that we get caught up in wandering thoughts 47 percent of our waking lives. That's a lot of time spent thinking about things that aren't actually going on. Mindfulness trains us to turn off that autopilot mode of operation, and when we practice it effectively, we can become aware of the other half of our waking life that we've learned to tune out.

Imagine that. You've spent nearly half of your waking life doing something without being mentally engaged; you've been in a doing mode of mind without being aware of it. The doing mode of mind is so common for us that it can be measured in the brain in a network of regions called the "default mode network," discovered by Marcus Raichle, a neurologist at the Washington University School of Medicine.

The default mode network is located in the midline of the brain from front to back. It's called the default mode network because it's the default area of the brain that activates when we aren't focused on a present task. It's the area of the brain activated when our mind is wandering, thinking about the past or the future, ruminating, and when we're in strong emotional states like anxiety. The default mode network has three basic functions: (1) to help create a sense of self, (2) to project that sense of self into the past and future, and (3) to scan for problems. With this trio of functions, we can see why when we're on autopilot we typically default to thoughts and memories about ourselves from the past and the future instead of the present moment. This is partly why we automatically relive mistakes from the past and worry about events coming up in the future—which is how those thought patterns become habits.

Mindfulness training will *not* turn off our thoughts and feelings or prevent wandering thoughts. But not being able to turn off your thoughts is not cause for discouragement; it's an indication that you are learning an awareness of your thoughts and interacting with them differently rather than spending so much time on autopilot.

Finally, it's important to address the misconception that there is such a thing as "being good at mindfulness." There is no hidden agenda or future goal for our thoughts and feelings. Without the need to attain something, mindfulness offers the opportunity to simply be tuned in to the present moment through our body, our breath, our inner experience—whatever each may be in that moment. It's *not* about striving to do something, and, in that way, it opens us to a being mode of mind.

The times when we recognize that we are practicing mindfulness with the intention of "being good at mindfulness," "being relaxed," or trying to "force ourselves to focus on the present" are all signs that we are in a doing mode of mind. A mindful response to these inevitable moments is to acknowledge, without judgment or critique, that these thoughts and feelings of striving are only thoughts and feelings from the doing mode of mind, and then to allow our attention to return to a being mode of mind.

A wandering mind is *not* a sign of failure but instead an opportunity to recognize the doing mode of mind and intentionally practice allowing yourself to shift into a being mode of mind. Mindfulness training is *not* about turning off your thoughts or moving toward a specific thought or feeling. What mindfulness practices train us to do is to tune in to our inner experience and performance with intention, groundedness, and acceptance.

Recently, a team of researchers from the State University of New York at Albany studied the mindfulness practices of one hundred people to examine the reasons why they practiced mindfulness and how that impacted whether they would reap the benefits that mindfulness offers. Almost half of the people in the study practiced mindfulness with the intention of fixing their thoughts and feelings by trying to rid themselves of fear or stress (doing mode of mind). The remaining people in the study practiced mindfulness with the purpose of intentionally being aware of and accepting of whatever thoughts and feelings would arise for them (being mode of mind). The results of the study clearly showed that those who practiced mindfulness with the intent to "be good at mindfulness" and actively manage their inner experience did not report any significant benefits from the practices. However, those who practiced mindfulness with the intention only to be mindful experienced all the benefits of the practices—specifically, less anxiety, less worry, less depression, and richer mindful awareness.

Should you find yourself in any mindfulness practice feeling a growing sense of physical, emotional, or cognitive constriction and frustration, it's likely you have not yet recognized that you've shifted to a doing mode of mind that is striving to "be good at mindfulness." Again, eliminating wandering thoughts is *not* the purpose of any mindfulness practice; the purpose of mindfulness practice is to train our awareness and to allow ourselves to shift into a being mode of mind. There is no such thing as "being bad at mindfulness" because mindfulness is about thinking and feeling freely.

MINDFULNESS PRACTICES

Mindfulness practices come in many forms but typically fall into two general types: single-point and contemplative. There are many versions of mindfulness practices within each form. In this section, I'll explain and provide basic exercises for each type of practice.

BODY-SCAN MINDFULNESS PRACTICE

Truly, an athlete's body is their temple. Golf, like any sport, is a physical challenge that requires us to physically execute our skills in real time, and the body is the vessel for doing so. But how often do we tune in to our bodies through a being mode of mind? It's quite easy to go about our days and our performances, only tuned in to our bodies as they directly relate to how well they are functioning or when they aren't feeling the way we want them to. Rarely do we bring intention, groundedness, and acceptance to the physical portion of our lives and performance.

The body-scan mindfulness practice is done seated or lying down, but it can also be practiced standing as you gain experience with it. A body scan is a practical and foundational mindfulness practice that systematically and sequentially tunes in to the body through a being mode of mind.

For those who are new to mindfulness and its practices, or those returning after some time away, moving your attention intentionally can be challenging at first. For this reason, a body scan follows the breath as a means to guide our attention into each area of the body. As we will learn through our mindfulness practices, our breath is vital because it is always accessible to us and therefore serves as a steadfast anchoring point to the present moment. Following the breath in this way during a body-scan practice grounds our attention in the area of the body we are focusing on as we move through the body from the bottom up.

There are many variations of body-scan practices. The following body-scan practice is adapted from a true pioneer in performance psychology, a mentor to me and a great many others, the late Ken Ravizza. This practice has been sculpted and refined through many years of Dr. Ravizza's work with some of the world's best athletes and performers.

BODY-SCAN MINDFULNESS PRACTICE

Sit in a chair with your feet flat on the ground, your hands on your lap, and an upright posture. Alternatively, you may lie down on your back with your arms resting either on your abdomen or at your sides. Allow your eyes to close gently.

Take a moment to allow your attention to connect with the movement of your breath. There is no need to change your breathing, judge it, or overtly try to control it. Simply allow your attention to wrap around your breath.

Remind yourself that this practice is a time to engage with your body through a being mode of mind—to be aware of your body, however it is.

Your thoughts will inevitably wander away from your breath, body, and practice. This is normal. When at any point you find that your attention has moved away from your breath and the connection to your body, acknowledge this shift in your inner experience and gently allow yourself to bring your attention back to your breath as it is in the present moment. Do this as many times as necessary.

Let's now intentionally follow your breath through your body.

Start by bringing your awareness to your feet. Let your feet rest in your socks, which rest in your shoes, as they rest on the floor. As you inhale, scan for any tension in your feet and allow any tension you find to dissolve as you exhale.

Now move your awareness up your legs to your shins and calves. Breathing into your lower legs, notice any tension in your lower legs as you inhale. Use your breath to release any tension as you exhale.

When you're ready, move your awareness now to the back of your knees and your hamstrings, all the way up to where the back of your legs are in contact with the chair. Following your breath, inhale into your legs, and as you exhale, let the chair take your weight. You carry your weight all day, every day. For just a moment, see how it feels to allow the chair to fully support and hold you.

Now follow your breath to gently move your awareness into your lower back, the middle of your back, and then between the shoulder blades in your upper back. As you inhale, use your breath to scan for any tension in these areas and release any tension you find as you exhale.

Follow your breath and scan your back once more. Should you find any tension as you inhale, release that tension as you exhale.

If need be, at this point, gently reconnect with your breath to guide your awareness of your body.

Follow your breath to shift your awareness now to your hands. Inhale and scan for any tension in your hands. As you exhale, let your hands soften.

Inhale as you follow your breath and awareness up your arms. Take a few breaths to allow your awareness to move away from your wrists, past your elbows, and into your upper arms. With each exhale, you are free to let go of any tension in your arms. Let your arms hang softly.

Gently move your breath and awareness into your shoulders and then into the back of your neck. As you inhale, take note of any tension and release it as you exhale.

Then follow your breath and move your awareness over your scalp, then gently over your forehead, around your eyes, into your cheeks, and through your jaw.

Following your breath into these areas, allow your lips to part slightly and let your tongue lay soft in your mouth as you inhale . . . and exhale. Inhale . . . and exhale. Inhale . . . and exhale.

With your eyes still closed, let the mind drift. Let it go wherever it wants to go without judging or evaluating it; let your thoughts be whatever passing mental events they may be. Then, when you are ready, gently bring your attention back to your breath one last time, noticing that it is always there for you when you need it. When you're ready, bring your attention back into the room around you. Gently blink your eyes open and, at your own pace, invite movement back into your body.

In a body-scan mindfulness practice, we observe our physical sensations and have the option to release muscular tension, but the practice is *not* a relaxation routine. However, while relaxation is not the purpose of any mindfulness practice, because we are interacting with our body as it is through a being mode of mind, it's not uncommon to find a sense of relaxation. By allowing all our thoughts, feelings, and physical sensations the space to exist as they are, they are all free to come and go without being anything more than transient fixtures of our inner experience.

Most mindfulness experts agree that a body-scan mindfulness practice is one of the best starting practices because it incorporates the body, something with which every athlete is already well acquainted, into a simple, sequential exchange through a being mode of mind. Most mindfulness experts also agree that a body-scan practice used daily for about two weeks is one of the best stepping stones to other mindfulness training practices.

The body scan detailed here takes just a few moments and is an effective tool when used before practice, before a round, waiting on a tee box, starting the day, or any time we choose to take a few moments to be mindfully aware of our body. Additionally, keep in mind that all mindfulness practices can be adapted to fit our performance settings and demands.

Once you've completed a week or more of daily body-scan practices as detailed above, you can begin adapting the exercise to your practice and competitive rounds. Shorten your body scan from many breaths and a longer sequence to a handful of breaths and a shorter sequence that you can use in the time from the driving range and practice putting green to the first tee. With practice and repetition, you can even scan your body with a single inhale and exhale between shots. For training mindfulness, a long-form practice like the one detailed earlier is invaluable, but so too is being able to quickly and effectively scan your body to meet your performance demands. Once you have a feel for a body scan, feel free to modify and apply it to fit your performance.

BREATH-CENTERED MINDFULNESS PRACTICE

Single-point mindfulness practices are so named because they focus and refocus us on a singular connection point. The most fundamental of all single-point mindfulness practices is a breath-centered mindfulness practice where our breath serves as the connection point to focus and refocus on the present moment.

Wherever we are, whatever we're doing, whatever we're feeling, whatever we're experiencing, and whatever mode of mind we're in, we're breathing. Our breath is always available to us as an anchor to the present moment. It's not surprising, then, that one of the most basic and effective methods for training composure is through mindful breathing. Any time we want to gain control of ourselves, a connected breath is the beginning of doing just that.

Even in our most pressure-filled moments, we can shift to a being mode of mind by connecting to our breath. However, it's important to distinguish between a connection to our breath and just breathing.

For your next five breaths, bring your focus to your breath with the intention of simply paying attention to it. The purpose here is not to relax or be calm—only to bring focus to the physical sensation of your breathing.

After those five breaths, ask yourself: "Where was the connection point between your focus and your breath?" Or you might ask yourself in a very literal sense, "How do I know I'm breathing?" Both questions bring our focus to some visceral or physical sensation of how we physically and directly experience our breath in the present moment.

The connection point for some golfers is the feeling of the rise and fall of their abdomen. Others connect to their breath through the sensation of air coming in through their nose and out through their mouth. Others connect by feeling the lift and drop of their shoulders. And many golfers connect to their breath through the internal sound of their inhale and exhale.

There is no right or wrong connection point; wherever you connect with your breath is a personal preference. But that connection point underscores the difference between just breathing and being connected to your breath. We breathe all the time, including when we're in a doing mode of mind. So just breathing for the sake of breathing does not serve to ground or compose us. Telling ourselves or someone else to "just breathe" is surface-level psychology, no different than suggesting, "just relax." In contrast, connecting with our breath is the beginning of turning our breath into more than just air moving in and out of our body while our mind is anywhere else because it helps us focus on how we are directly experiencing our breath in this moment.

Once you know where you connect to your breath, you'll know where to ground yourself in the present moment whenever you want. The value of breath-centered mindfulness is our connection to our breath in the moment, keeping us present and giving us a reconnecting point when we find that our thoughts have moved away from the here and now.

As with our body-scan mindfulness practice, it's important to remember that connecting to our breath is not always easy; our brain, mind, and body might pull our attention away with thoughts, sensations, and external distractions. However, connecting and reconnecting to our breath comes with less struggle when we choose to accept the inevitable shifts in our inner experience and external distractions for what they are—temporary shifts in focus and nothing more.

Seeing these shifts and fluctuations as natural and inevitable is a reminder that the purpose of breath-centered mindfulness is *not* to force our connection to our breath and forge an uninterrupted connection for an overly extended period of time. Rather, the times when we recognize that our attention has moved away from our breath are the precise moments that help us become aware of when we have drifted into a doing mode of mind or have drifted to the past or future. Those shifts offer us an invaluable opportunity to use how we directly experience our breath to reconnect with our performance in the present moment, a precious skill for playing golf under pressure.

When practiced consistently, the following breath-centered mindfulness practice is as simple as it is effective.

BREATH-CENTERED MINDFULNESS PRACTICE

Sit in a chair with your feet flat on the ground, your hands on your lap, and an upright posture. Allow your eyes to close gently.

Take a moment to allow your attention to connect with your breath. There is no need to change your breathing, judge it, or overtly try to control it. Simply allow your attention to connect you with your breath.

Remind yourself that this practice is a time to connect with your breath through a being mode of mind; be aware of your breath, however it is.

Your thoughts will inevitably wander away from your connection to your breath. This is normal. When at any point you find your attention moving away from your breath, acknowledge this shift in your inner experience and gently allow yourself to reconnect to your breath. Do this as many times as necessary for the next five to eight minutes.

Breath-centered mindfulness practices are invaluable to athletes because performance happens in the present moment. In any given round, a golfer will face moments where shots have already been taken or there are shots left to be taken that draw attention away from the shot at hand. Mental time travel will happen from time to time, even for the most mindfully trained. Without training ourselves to be aware of when we are psychologically off time, we are often unaware of it until our performance and scorecard have already suffered.

As we train ourselves to connect and reconnect to our breath, we come to understand that the opposite of anxiety is *not* being relaxed. The opposite of being anxious is being *grounded*—because groundedness allows us to be on time and in tune with our life and performance as they are happening. When we're on time, there is little room for past frustrations and fear about a future that doesn't yet, and may never, exist.

Golf challenges our ability to be composed. Thankfully, the most effective training for composure is a breath-centered mindfulness practice. Study after study shows that five to eight minutes a day of breath-centered mindfulness training over a period of at least thirty days builds stronger and more efficient neural pathways in the brain to recognize bodily sensations and cognitive shifts and decreases the amount of cortisol released when we're nervous. These are the building blocks of composure.

To be very clear, while mindful breathing does bring oxygen-rich blood to our brain that can help quiet the old brain's stress response and induce lower-frequency and lower-intensity brain waves, the neurological and physiological changes we experience when connecting with our breath happen as a result of our psychological state shifting from either being off time, judgmental, lost in wandering thoughts, or in a triggered habitual response to being grounded in the present. Our neurology and physiology follow our psychology far more than the other way around. This is why breathing on its own, even deep breathing, isn't enough to build composure under pressure. Composure requires *connected* breathing that psychologically grounds us in the present and a shift to a being mode of mind.

Breath-centered mindfulness practices train us to:

- Intentionally connect to our breath to ground us in the present moment.
- Recognize the doing mode of mind and the natural shifts in our inner experience.
- Observe our inner experience without judgment.
- Intentionally respond to emotional and physical discomfort instead of reacting habitually.
- Intentionally shift to a being mode of mind.
- Compose ourselves.

The breath-centered mindfulness practice detailed above is just five to eight minutes long and can and should be adapted to fit the demands of playing golf.

Once you've built some experience with this breath-centered mindfulness practice, start to adapt it to your practice and competitive rounds. Shorten your breath-centered practice to a minute before your first tee shot. Further, shorten your practice to three to five breaths between shots. And I strongly recommend that you take two or three connected breaths before addressing any shot you're about to play. Where those connected breaths fit into a pre-shot routine can vary, but intentionally grounding ourselves before a shot brings our focus to our performance as it's happening and helps to keep our prefrontal cortex online and operating on lower the frequency and lower intensity of our brain waves, both of which increase the chances of playing a shot as intended.

The extended breath-centered practice is designed to train you in grounding yourself through the connection to your breath at any time and under any circumstances. Having shorter versions will allow you to adapt the practice to your game as you see fit.

CONTEMPLATIVE MINDFULNESS PRACTICE

If a body-scan practice is a friendly wave toward our inner experience and a breath-centered practice is a firm handshake, a contemplative mindfulness practice is a full-on bear hug.

Earlier we discussed the fixated nature of seeing our thoughts as facts and certainties. Treating thoughts and feelings as facts makes the relationship with our inner experience rigid and inflexible. Just as a rigid and inflexible body won't perform well under most conditions, neither will a rigid and inflexible relationship with our own thoughts and feelings.

Contemplative mindfulness practices train a more fluid and flexible relationship with our inner experience. Specifically, the practice offers us the opportunity to interact with our thoughts from a place of acceptance; we observe how our thoughts form and link together without seeking to force, solve, or suppress them and in so doing create space between ourselves and our thoughts, a process called "cognitive defusion."

This space is created simply from seeing our thoughts and feelings for what they are—just thoughts and feelings *about* things, not the things themselves. Cognitive defusion limits the amplification of our thoughts and feelings because it helps us coexist with them. It allows us to make clear and intentional decisions because we are no longer beholden to thoughts and feelings just because, or for whatever reasons, they arise.

In a contemplative mindfulness practice, our thoughts are allowed to be whatever they are and go wherever or whenever they'd like without us trying to suppress them, "fix" them, or distract ourselves from them. As you might expect, when given room to roam, our thoughts will bounce around. But instead of trying to control or avoid our thoughts, observing them with acceptance creates a fluidity and flexibility that makes it easier for us to move past them and focus on our performance in the present moment.

In some ways, contemplative mindfulness is the deep end of the mindfulness and self-discovery pool. At times you will find certain thoughts uncomfortable, while other times you will find insight and clarity. Again, mindfulness practice is *not* about "fixing" the scratchy parts of our inner experience. Of all the mindfulness practices, contemplative mindfulness requires an intentional and devoted sense of acceptance and non-judgment. Thus, contemplative mindfulness is often most effective after some experience with body-scan and breath-centered mindfulness practices to first establish a robust sense of acceptance.

The research on contemplative mindfulness practices clearly shows that eight to ten minutes a day of just observing our inner experience with acceptance is the minimally effective dosage. Most research shows that the optimal dosage is twenty total minutes divided into two ten-minute practices that can be spaced apart according to preference. Below is a basic framework for a contemplative mindfulness practice.

CONTEMPLATIVE MINDFULNESS PRACTICE

Sit in a chair with your feet flat on the ground, your hands on your lap, and an upright posture. Allow your eyes to close gently.

Take a moment to allow your attention to connect with your breath. There is no need to change your breathing, judge it, or overtly try to control it. Simply allow your attention to connect you with your breath.

Remind yourself that this practice is a time to observe your thoughts, fully accepting whatever they may be.

Your thoughts will inevitably wander and stitch together as they see fit. This is normal. When at any point you find yourself judging your thoughts as good or bad, right or wrong, okay or not okay, recognize that you are doing so and gently allow yourself to return to observing your thoughts with full acceptance, whatever they are.

Do this as many times as necessary to allow yourself to observe your thoughts without judgment for the next eight to ten minutes.

Many people find contemplative mindfulness useful in the morning because it establishes a being-mode-of-mind tone for the day and their performance. However, a contemplative mindfulness practice can also be used during a lunch break, in the car or bus ride to the course, or, if you're like me, while walking your dog. With all these practices, however, it's important to start by practicing in a quiet and comfortable place.

Consistent contemplative mindfulness practices train us to:

- Intentionally observe our inner experience through a deep sense of acceptance.
- See thoughts, emotions, and shifts in our inner experience just as they are and nothing more.
- Create space between ourselves and our thoughts.
- Decipher the difference between things and thoughts *about* things.

- Create a being-mode-of-mind relationship with our inner experience.
- Build a fluid and flexible relationship with our thoughts and feelings.
- Allow for self-discovery.

MINDFULNESS AND THE BRAIN

We can think of mindfulness practices like an awareness workout for our brains. We build strength in our mindfulness muscles, and that strength can be seen and measured in our brains. Sara Lazar is a researcher at Harvard University and one of many who have studied how ongoing mindfulness training creates neuroplastic changes in the brain. In her research mapping brain structures, she found that after just eight weeks of daily mindfulness training, areas of the brain associated with memory and learning grew, while at the same time areas of the brain associated with anxiety and stress decreased in size. Her studies provide continued objective evidence that a mindful relationship with our inner experience trains our mind and leads to physical, neuroplastic adaptations in our brain that benefit us and our performance.

The effects of mindfulness were also apparent for Marco. After a few weeks of daily mindfulness training, Marco began to build a different relationship with his inner experience. He recognized that much of his decline in performance and dread of tournament golf was because he was constantly in a doing mode of mind, especially in competition. Once Marco established a feel for mindfulness, he began directing his own practices and trained himself to shift to a being mode of mind even when his inner experience was uncomfortable and uncertain.

To be clear, mindfulness didn't do away with all his disruptive thoughts, mental time travel, or anxiety about competing. What changed is that he stopped trying to "fix" what he thought and felt. He stopped trying to avoid and suppress uncomfortable thoughts and feelings and instead engaged with them mindfully. In the following weeks, he began to feel what it's like for thoughts to be just thoughts, observing them as temporary fixtures of his inner experience that come and go. He began tuning in to his body and mind intentionally, connecting with his breath to ground himself in the present moment, and observing his thoughts with genuine acceptance and non-judgment, which created space for him to play more freely.

MOBILE APPS AND NEUROFEEDBACK

The growth of mindfulness as an industry has led to the development of a multitude of mindfulness resources, including mobile apps that offer guided mindfulness practices and neurofeedback systems that measure brain waves and provide real-time feedback telling us when we are or are not grounded in the present.

These kinds of mobile apps are a good thing. They are evidence of a larger movement that uses technology to better understand and train the mind. As we've discussed, mindfulness has been around for millennia, but it is a new concept and practice for many people, so navigating mindfulness practices can be awkward at first. So using a mobile app or a neurofeedback system as an entryway into mindfulness can be quite valuable to create familiarity with intention, groundedness, and acceptance. Similarly, the neurofeedback industry and its technology are growing to the point where neurofeedback systems are now available to anyone with a mobile device, allowing people to get real-time feedback on their brain activity.

But as valuable as mindfulness mobile apps and neurofeedback systems are as first steps into mindfulness and its practices, they have some note-worthy limitations. First, many of their guided mindfulness practices are scripted with positive affirmations to "build self-esteem." Hearing flowery prose about how "wonderful" and "special" you are certainly feels nice, but it's not rooted in evidence-based mindfulness science because it seeks to change and "fix" your thoughts and feelings rather than observing your thoughts and feelings as they are.

Through acceptance of our inner experience, we can coexist with *all* of our thoughts and feelings. Using guided affirmations designed to make us feel better about ourselves is a hallmark of a doing mode of mind. More-over, unbridled positive affirmations lose credibility quickly and are a sure-fire method for destabilizing confidence. More on this in section four, "Framework."

It's also important to be aware of how much guidance these mindfulness mobile-app practices offer. When you're first introduced to mindfulness and its practices, having guidance is extremely helpful. This section introduces and guides you through three different practices so that you don't have to dive into the deep end of the mindfulness pool without some floaties on.

Using these guided apps to dip our toes into mindfulness practices can be a great way to move into mindful habits. However, optimized mindfulness training and fully developed intention, groundedness, and acceptance require self-guided practices. The more someone else's voice guides our inner experience, tells us how to connect with our breath, or explains how to follow our thoughts, the less we train ourselves to mindfully navigate for ourselves in ways we can use while actually playing golf. Once you feel you understand and are familiar with your mindfulness practices, take ownership of your practice by guiding your own relationship with your body, brain, and mind.

Second, there is some value in using a high-fidelity instrument in the form of a neurofeedback system that can give you accurate and timely feedback about how your brain is experiencing being in the present moment and when it isn't. A wide range of performers use neurofeedback systems because they give direct measurement on brain activity. However, most studies show clear debate as to how much fidelity and utility current neurofeedback technology actually offers.

The reason mindfulness training is supported by so much science is in part because the most attuned instruments we have available to us that give us the most accurate and immediate feedback are our own minds and bodies. The more we use an external instrument like a neurofeedback device, the more we undermine our ability to develop that awareness ourselves. There are no more finely tuned high-fidelity instruments than our mind and body, so to hook ourselves up to a system that does what we can already do—and better—is shortchanging what our minds and bodies have been doing on their own for thousands of years.

Mindfulness apps and neurofeedback systems can be valuable introductory steps into mindfulness practices. And for what it's worth, using them for mindfulness training is better than no mindfulness training at all. If you do use either, keep in mind that most are currently designed as, essentially, mindfulness-practice training aids. They can help direct us to what it feels like to have a grooved swing, but we can't use them on the course. Once we have a sense of mindfulness practices for ourselves, training the practices on our own allows us to bring a bring a being mode of mind to any moment of our golf experience.

EVERYTHING STARTS WITH AWARENESS

Mindfulness isn't a magic potion, nor is it the be-all and end-all. However, when it comes to long-term growth and more stable confidence, mindful awareness offers a range of benefits that cannot be disputed because *everything* starts with awareness. There's not a single viable approach to improving psychological strength or sustainable behavioral change that doesn't begin with awareness.

Everything starts with awareness for the simple but enormously critical reason that becoming aware of something is the first stage of information processing. As a result, awareness is the indispensable keystone for managing ourselves and our performance because everything we do is contingent upon whether we are aware and what type of awareness we bring to it.

In the next sections, we'll discover how we learn habits and how we construct our psychological framework, which generates much of what we think and do and establishes the stability of our confidence. We'll also see that the behaviors and habits that we learn are not always productive and that the beliefs, perceptions, assumptions, and biases within our psychological framework are not always factual, nor are they always beneficial.

As we examine our habits and psychological framework, we'll seek to understand questions and answers about what we do and how we think when we're most consistent in our golf game. However, in doing so, we'll also begin to understand questions and answers for when we get in our own way, fear failure, have unstable confidence, shy away from challenges, and make golf less enjoyable.

I remind my clients that there has never been a golfer in the history of the sport who hasn't been inconvenienced by unwanted thoughts and feelings. Every golfer who has ever played has experienced uncertainty and discomfort and has had their heart broken from time to time. No golfer is immune to the disappointment that comes with failure and struggle. In fact, experiencing and learning to coexist with uncomfortable thoughts and emotional discomfort are unavoidable requirements for long-term growth and being able to perform under pressure. Moreover, a willingness to accept and engage with the sources of our emotional discomfort is the price for a meaningful relationship with any craft, including golf.

One of the most important components to developing mental toughness is to choose to make room for comfortable *and* uncomfortable thoughts and emotions. Research examining the psychological building blocks of resilience show that a radical acceptance of *all* our emotions, even the messy and heavy ones, is the cornerstone of resilience and authentic happiness. Thus, developing mental toughness is *not* built on psychology that ensures experiencing only comfort and certainty but on examining our habits and beliefs as they relate to how much we rely on comfort and certainty. That examination requires honesty, humility, and a willingness to engage with our shortcomings, insecurities, misconceptions, and unproductive thought patterns.

It's greatly important to understand and practice mindfulness before we address our habits and psychological framework because, without interacting with *all* the parts of our inner experience through a being mode of mind, most people will shy away from the vulnerability required to explore, challenge, and even reshape what drives our life and golf experience. Mindfulness training doesn't just train us to pay attention to our inner experience with intention, groundedness, and acceptance—it creates a relationship with our inner experience that allows us to be aware of and mindfully evaluate the core areas that either hold us back or allow us to compete more freely.

Habits

CREATURES OF HABIT

Humans are creatures of habit. More accurately, we are creatures of many habits. Some habits are beneficial; others aren't. This applies to our lives in general and to how we play golf. For some golfers, productive habits allow them to be present, support stable confidence, improve the quality of their practice and performance, and make golf more fun. But for many golfers, unproductive habits keep them from getting better, playing better, and enjoying the game more.

Despite every golfer being a creature of habit, habits are largely misunderstood. There is a wide range of books, videos, and other media on habits that emphasize their importance and tell us to "build good habits." However, most of these resources rely on surface-level psychology and don't have an accurate understanding of what habits are, how they form, why they form, and, perhaps most importantly, how to effectively change them.

Let me take a moment here to note that in the previous section, we learned about mindfulness for a specific reason—and hopefully you're already adopting those practices. We are not practicing mindfulness just for the sake of it. Developing a being-mode-of-mind relationship with our inner experience is also the foundation for making tangible changes to improve our behaviors.

What we do and how we do it matters. What shots you play and how you play them matters. Whether you play a shot with stable confidence or with anxiety matters. The real value that comes from training our minds and using our brains more effectively is that it leads to better and more enjoyable behaviors that impact our lives and golf game. Mindfulness training isn't just about the practices in the previous section; when applied correctly, it's also the key ingredient for stepping away from unproductive habits and forming more productive ones.

Some common unproductive habits many golfers have include dwelling, anxiety, guided swings, and jabby putts. Many clients have told me that they find it increasingly difficult to step away from the habits that keep them from playing freely to the point that they feel they may never play golf freely again.

Sadly, what I'm seeing is that it's becoming more common for golfers of all skill levels to become stuck in the habits of playing scared, getting distracted, and feeling angry or worried, all of which constrict access to their capabilities when they want to use them most. Part of the reason why it's so difficult for us to change the patterns of how we think and act is because the most common methods we take toward changing those habits don't work; they actually work *against* how our brain learns behaviors and forms habits in the first place.

Judson Brewer is the director of research and innovation at Brown University's Mindfulness Center, an author, and one of the world's foremost experts on habits and behavioral change. Dr. Brewer's research is groundbreaking when it comes to how we can step away from harmful habits. In this section, I'll be drawing heavily from his research and applied practices for helping people sustainably change habits that they have learned and reinforced—which, like getting nervous, is exactly what our brain is designed to do.

SLUGGISH LEARNING

Imagine you're a sea slug. Okay, I admit that may be difficult, considering sea slugs don't really have arms or legs; they also live in the ocean, eat algae, and most certainly don't play golf. However, relating to a sea slug isn't as difficult as you may think.

There are literally thousands of scientific studies showing that for all the processing speed and power of the human supercomputer brain, our brains learn behaviors through a remarkably simple process called "reward-based learning." Reward-based learning is rooted in positive and negative reinforcement, and it's as simple as this: we want to do more of the things that feel better and work better (positive reinforcement) and less of the things that feel worse and work poorly (negative reinforcement).

Learning behaviors through reinforcement is so simple that all animals share the same system, down to creatures with the smallest brains and the simplest nervous systems. In 2000, neuroscientist Eric Kandel won a Nobel Prize for his illuminating and humbling discovery that humans learn behaviors in the same way as the sea slug, an organism with only twenty thousand neurons in its entire nervous system—versus our human nervous system that has more than 86 billion neurons.

We still carry this rudimentary learning system today because when it developed, we only had the safety-first portions of our old brains. The areas of our young brain, including the prefrontal cortex, that can learn in more complex ways were still many thousands of years away from developing.

Back in our prehistoric environments when life and limb were at risk, reward-based learning was exceptionally advantageous. Resources like food were scarce and difficult to come by, and our cavepeople ancestors with their yet-to-be-evolved logical, conscious, and creative-thinking young brains needed whatever resources they could get their hands on to survive. When they did, their brains reinforced the behaviors that led to getting those resources. For example, when they ate food, they felt good—and voilà, they survived.

Here again we see how our old brain creates associations between events, behaviors, and what those behaviors do for us. Whenever cavepeople got the resources they needed to survive, their brains would create a positively reinforced association between the resources, the behavior needed to obtain them, and survival, and that association would release dopamine.

Dopamine is a neuromodulator vital for learning behaviors because it helps us remember things by forging a connection to them through making us feel good. Dopamine motivates us to seek rewards, and by seeking rewards we can get the resources we need or perceive that we need. In essence, dopamine is our old brain's way of telling itself to remember where you were and what you did so you can repeat the same behavior in the future. Being

positively reinforced with allowance money for doing your chores or positively reinforcing your dog for sitting by giving it a treat is the same way that
our prehistoric ancestors learned to remember how to behave in ways to get
resources for survival: by being rewarded with dopamine.

As you might guess, we use the same system for avoiding things that
threaten our safety and survival as well. Negative reinforcement is our old
brain helping us learn behaviors that take away or avoid something unpleasant, dangerous, or threatening, real or perceived. For example, if you drove
to work during rush hour every day and found sitting in traffic with people cutting each other off and aimlessly honking their car horns to be a
frustrating, unpleasant experience, you might choose to take a different, less
congested route to work at a different time. Removing the rush-hour traffic
and its accompanying frustration serve as negative reinforcers to make sure
you remember to avoid your previous route. All this is happening in the
exact same way that our ancestors learned not to go to the place where the
saber-toothed tigers hung out.

Reward-based learning is splendidly simple for a good reason—it works.
When it comes to our behaviors, it's of the utmost importance to understand that learning behaviors through positive and negative reinforcement
is our most basic survival tool: remember, seek out, and feel good about the
things that promote survival, and remember, avoid, and feel bad about the
things that may threaten survival. It's so simple and effective that, in most
situations, our brain only requires three basic elements to learn a behavior:
an environmental cue, a behavior, and a reinforcer. Or even more plainly: a
trigger, a behavior, and a reward.

In the case of being positively reinforced to find resources—say, for
example, water—the location of the water is the environmental cue (trigger); drinking the water is the behavior; dopamine and surviving longer are
the positive reinforcers (reward). In the case of being negatively reinforced
to take a different route to work, going to work is the environmental cue
(trigger), taking a different route is the behavior, and decreased emotional
discomfort (in the form of frustration) and saving time are the negative reinforcers (reward).

This positive- and negative-reinforcement system is also the framework
for how our brain learns the behaviors that we consistently repeat, including

the ones that impact how we play golf. As much as we humans like to think that we are thoughtful and deliberate decision makers, we're not. We're creatures of habit, which is why the strongest predictor of future behavior is past behavior. Thus, it's vitally important for us to be mindfully aware of the habits we have. The actions we take now determine the likelihood of continuing in the same old patterns of behavior or making beneficial changes.

HABITS

Being creatures of habit is generally a good thing; without habits, we easily become overwhelmed and exhausted. Habits are behaviors established through reward-based learning that are mostly automatic, that are mostly or completely subconscious, and that come easily to us. They are reinforced behaviors that we engage in without requiring us to consciously think through them.

Habits form when our brain takes behaviors learned through its reward-based learning system and moves those behaviors into an automatic and subconscious memory, often as soon as it can. Not surprisingly, behaviors that are repeated and reinforced often, like checking your cell phone, quickly become habits. Behaviors that are intensely reinforced because they feel really good, like eating tasty food, or that help us avoid what feels really uncomfortable, like choosing a different route to escape rush-hour traffic, also form into habits quickly. Our brains are designed to form habits so that we don't have to consciously learn the same behaviors again and again day after day, freeing up cognitive space in our young brains to learn new things.

Imagine if every time you went to play golf you had to consciously relearn how to tie your shoes or grip a golf club. You and your brain would be exhausted, and you'd run out of cognitive, emotional, and physical energy long before you could learn anything new.

But in habit mode, our brain takes behaviors and puts them into action subconsciously. Neurologically, the faster, stronger parts of our old brain tell the slower, conscious-thinking parts of our young brain, "You're free to think about other things and learn new behaviors while I take care of these behaviors that are familiar and reinforcing."

The division of labor between our old brain and young brain is what allowed the conscious-thinking portions of our brain, like the prefrontal cortex, to develop the ability to think logically and plan for the future. In sum, the faster our old brain took familiar and reinforcing behaviors and turned them into habits, the more our young brain could learn about other things.

Regardless of the behavior, all we need is a trigger, behavior, and reward to form a habit. Once a habit is forged, our old brain subconsciously assumes that, when triggered, the behavior will continue to do what it did before with the same level of reward and puts that habit into what neurologists call "set-it-and-forget-it mode." In set-it-and-forget-it mode, our brain consciously thinks as little as possible to utilize the behavior, which is why many studies show that as much as 90 percent of our decisions are made subconsciously—that is, habitually. For example, set-it-and-forget-it mode is why on average we look at our cell phones one hundred times a day, also often without consciously thinking about it.

Trigger: Boredom.
Behavior: Checking phone.
Reward: Dopamine from scrolling through puppy videos.

It doesn't take very long to create a habit and for a habit to move to set-it-and-forget-it mode. But just because habits form quickly doesn't mean that they are necessarily beneficial for us. Harmful habits—like smoking, overeating, playing fearful golf, and anxiety—form in the same ways that beneficial habits—like exercising, eating healthy, playing freely, and being grounded in the present—do.

Wait. Did I just say that anxiety and groundedness are habits? Yep. Behaviors can be both external, like walking, or internal, like our patterns of thinking. Our patterns of thought in response to triggers are mental behaviors. There are many studies showing that our patterns of thought, like toxic rumination, worry, and even anxiety itself, are learned and strengthened as negatively reinforced habits. Let's look at anxiety as a habit, one common to many golfers.

Anxiety is both something we feel as part of our inner experience and a mental behavior. It's a mental behavior that is negatively reinforced because, in theory, it helps us avoid things that we perceive as threatening, like hitting a bad shot. Avoiding the threat of a bad shot is intensely reinforcing.

Wouldn't it feel better to avoid all your bad shots? Based on how our brain forms habits, anxiety as a behavior only has to happen a few times before our brain forms the habit to respond with anxiety to certain triggers like tight tee shots, playing in front of other people, and even internally experiencing the feeling of anxiety.

Wait. Did I just say that anxiety can be a behavior *and* a trigger? Yep. Just like how behaviors can be both external and internal, so too can triggers. External triggers might be a slippery putt, a comment by someone else, or the hole that seems to ruin your scorecard every time you play it. Internal triggers can be feeling nervous, feeling anxious, certain thoughts and beliefs, or the doing mode of mind.

Remember how in the last section we discussed how we often respond to an uncomfortable inner experience by trying to "fix" it with the doing mode of mind? That dysfunctional relationship with our inner experience is a habit with an internal trigger, behavior, and reward.

Trigger: Uncomfortable inner experience, such as feeling anxious.
Behavior: Trying to "fix" feeling anxious with even more anxiety through the doing mode of mind.
Reward: Feeling like you're solving the problem of your uncomfortable inner experience.

Let's use how our brain forms habits to reiterate why trying to problem-solve our inner experience doesn't work. The doing mode of mind is a relationship with our inner experience that tries to "fix," change, force, avoid, suppress, or distract us from our inner experience. Remember how I said that one of the reasons people go back to the doing mode of mind is because they feel it works? Even though a doing mode of mind makes things worse, we return to it because it *feels* like we're solving a problem—and that offers a sense of reward. Toxic rumination, being off time, worrying, and being anxious are reinforced by the *feeling* that we're "doing something" to fix our inner experience, or the *feeling* that we're avoiding further emotional discomfort.

Our feelings are what reinforce our behaviors the most. Trying to "fix" how we're thinking and feeling seems like "doing something" rather than sitting idly by. For many of our unproductive habits, the feeling that we are "doing something" is particularly reinforcing for us, especially when we aren't aware of better and more productive behaviors available to us.

Even if we can't see it as a physical behavior, the doing mode of mind is happening. Our mental behaviors can become habits just like physical behaviors can. And like physical behaviors, our mental behaviors have tangible outcomes. In golf, those tangible results are shots played out of fear or anger, or trying to hit a good shot to make ourselves feel more confident and alleviate frustration—all habits that are far more likely to produce poor shots than good ones.

CHANGING HABITS

In a recent study, Dr. Brewer and his colleagues used a three-stage approach developed through years of research to help people address the habit of anxiety. After just a few weeks, people in the study showed a 63 percent decrease in anxiety. That's a significant result, and, when compared to the current gold standards for addressing anxiety, Dr. Brewer's approach is unrivaled.

The reason Dr. Brewer's work has been so groundbreaking, and why I will draw heavily upon it throughout the remainder of this section, is because Dr. Brewer's research and approaches do not rely on surface-level psychology. Dr. Brewer's approaches are resoundingly effective because they work with how our brain functions and learns habits through reward-based learning rather than working against our brain or only addressing symptoms.

Currently, the most effective way to change a habit is through Dr. Brewer's aforementioned three-stage process. I hope you've been doing your mindfulness practices and training yourself to shift to a being mode of mind. Dr. Brewer's three-stage process is so effective in large part because it revolves around—you guessed it—mindfulness.

The mindful approach works with how our old brain naturally and instinctively gravitates toward reinforcing behaviors, both internal and external. It doesn't force thoughts, feelings, or actions. It brings mindful awareness to our habits and the natural consequences they produce in the same way that the habits were learned and reinforced in the first place, which allows them to be unlearned and upgraded with better ones.

To start stepping away from unproductive habits, we must become mindfully aware of two things: the habit and its reward-based-learning elements, and the natural consequences that actually come from the habit through our direct experience. Mindful awareness helps our old brain take a habit out of set-it-and-forget-it mode and observe if a behavior is actually helping us or if it's something that's hurting us and our efforts. From there, we can learn a new habit by giving our brain the opportunity to choose something that is better and more productive in a way that matches how it learns behaviors in the first place, which is to choose behaviors that are more reinforcing simply because they feel better and work better.

It's also worth noting that when it comes to forming habits and stepping away from them, repetition is of the utmost importance. It's repetition that psychologically and neurologically grooves our behaviors. Habits are psychologically grooved through repetition because behaviors that are repeated enough become familiar, and both our old brain and young brain associate familiarity with safety and certainty, albeit falsely at times.

Habits are neurologically grooved in our brains through the process of neuroplasticity for both physical and mental behaviors. Specifically, the more we repeat a behavior, the more our brain surrounds the neurons that produce that behavior with a fatty protein called "myelin," which acts like insulation around our neural connections, increasing the speed and efficiency of electrical transmissions in the brain.

The more myelin that surrounds a neural connection, the faster and more effectively the brain sends signals to produce a behavior, whether that's a physical behavior like swinging a golf club or a mental behavior like anxiety. Therefore, the more we repeat a behavior, the more our brain adjusts to make that habit more ingrained. Changing a habit can take time and patience, but research is showing more and more that a mindful approach is the fastest and most effective method for behavioral change because it works with how our brain functions and learns.

IDENTIFYING HABITS

To become mindfully aware of the habits you have, let's compare a few key areas and behaviors from the times when you play how you want and the times when you don't. If it helps, answer the questions in the T-chart on the next page so that you can review your responses and better see the differences between the two.

When you're playing golf the way you want . . .	When you're *not* playing golf the way you want . . .
What are you focused on?	What are you focused on?
What time frame(s) are you playing in most: past, present, or future?	What time frame(s) are you playing in most: past, present, or future?
Who are you focused on?	Who are you focused on?
What mode of mind are you in most often: doing or being?	What mode of mind are you in most often: doing or being?
What does your inner dialogue sound like?	What does your inner dialogue sound like?
How do you respond when things don't go the way you want or expect them to?	How do you respond when things don't go the way you want or expect them to?
Are you trying to force your performance to happen or just allowing it to happen?	Are you trying to force your performance to happen or just allowing it to happen?

This list of questions is by no means comprehensive, so if there are some other areas and behaviors in your game worth examining, feel free to do so. Once you've written your responses to the questions, take a look at them and compare the two sides of the chart. Chances are you're going to see some patterns and important differences between the behaviors that are helping you play the golf you want and those that aren't.

It may also be beneficial for you to answer these questions as part of an ongoing reflection on your golf game. Often when I'm working with collegiate and professional golfers, they will use these questions to review several rounds of golf because they help them take note of their habits more clearly. From there we can get to work, starting with Stage One.

STAGE ONE: BRINGING AWARENESS TO OUR HABITS

Stacy was fed up. When I first met with Stacy (not her real name), she was frustrated, confused, and finding it increasingly difficult to stop doing what she was doing: playing scared. Every time she came to certain shots or situations and experienced certain thoughts and feelings, she would make a guided, steery swing, just trying to keep the ball in play instead of swinging freely and trying to get the ball where she wanted it to go.

As I asked more about her and what she was experiencing, I learned that Stacy had started playing scared while she was in college, and the habit had followed her to the LPGA Tour, where she had been playing for the last few years. As we talked, Stacy told me that when she was in situations where she felt under pressure, like being on the cut line or in contention, and whenever her inner experience became uncomfortable, she would return time and time again to her habit of hitting steery, guided shots.

Stacy told me that she was doing all the things people and the books she had read told her to do—"just trust yourself," "just be disciplined," and "relax and play free." Before I could ask how well those approaches were working for her, Stacy told me what I suspected: trying to apply reason, distraction, and willpower to play freely was only keeping her habits going and making things worse.

Not being able to forcibly change her behavior was also leading to what behaviral psychologists call "echo habits," layered habits that form like ripples from other habits. Her echo habits of anxiety, panic-practicing, over-thinking, and self-criticism were a common but disruptive combination for her golf game.

During a round of golf, Stacy would get anxious and then make a guided swing, trying not to make a mistake. She would then respond to those swings by overthinking her swing mechanics and trying to "do something," which would only make things worse. Then, after a poor round, Stacy would worry, then go to the range and beat balls, searching for confidence or an answer to her troubles. When she would finally leave the course, she would crush herself with self-criticism about how bad of a golfer she was and how she would need to will herself to do better. This pattern would repeat again and again, week after week, and she was perilously close to losing her Tour card. Even more disheartening for Stacy, she was seriously questioning whether she believed in herself and if she wanted to continue playing golf.

After Stacy and I worked together to understand her brain and Stacy had put in a few weeks of mindfulness practice, I asked her to pull out a blank sheet of paper, and together, using the three elements of how our brain learns habits through reward-based learning, we mapped out her habit of playing scared, guided tee shots.

Playing Scared Habit
Trigger: Tight tee shot (usually a dogleg right).
Behavior: Making a defensive, fearful, guided swing.
Reward: Hopefully, "doing something" to keep the ball from going out
    of bounds.

Even though Stacy had been directly experiencing her habits, she hadn't consciously seen them for what they were. But after mapping her habit, she began to see it as a repeating pattern of behavior being triggered by the same or similar events, reinforced by the same or similar rewards.

We also mapped out her unproductive echo habits.

Anxiety Habit

Trigger: Thinking about an upcoming tournament.
Behavior: Anxiety via toxic rumination.
Reward: Feeling like I'm "doing something" to make sure I play well.

Overthinking Habit

Trigger: Poor swing.
Behavior: Overthinking my swing mechanics.
Reward: Feeling like I'm "doing something" to avoid hitting bad shots.

Self-Criticism Habit

Trigger: Not playing well.
Behavior: Berating myself about how terribly I played.
Reward: Motivating myself to "do better."

Stacy isn't the only golfer who's developed some unproductive habits that make it more difficult to play freely and enjoy the game. Here are some other examples of unproductive habits common to many golfers.

Panic-Practice Habit

Trigger: Poor round of golf.
Behavior: Beating balls to feel better (not get better) about playing poorly.
Reward: Conjuring confidence for the next day.

Dwelling Habit

Trigger: Missing a short putt that I always expect to make.
Behavior: Dwelling on the mistake and lamenting that it "shouldn't" have happened.
Reward: Avoiding making the same mistake in the future.

Blaming Habit

Trigger: Failure to make the cut, getting a warning for slow play, getting a bad bounce, etc.

Behavior: Blaming someone/something else, complaining, making excuses.

Reward: Protecting my ego by trying to avoid being the source of my own shortcomings.

Comparing Habit

Trigger: Seeing other players hitting balls on the range or seeing others' scores/rankings.

Behavior: Comparing myself and my game to another player and their game.

Reward: Feeling better and more confident about my own game.

Control Habit

Trigger: Uncertainty of future outcomes in some form or another.

Behavior: Focusing on future outcomes that can't be controlled.

Reward: Feeling like I'm creating a sense of control and certainty about the future.

Worry Habit

Trigger: The potential for other people to judge me and my game negatively.

Behavior: Worrying about other peoples' opinions.

Reward: Protecting my ego and avoiding being judged in unwanted ways.

Protect Your Score Habit

Trigger: Realizing I'm on pace to have a great score.

Behavior: Trying to protect a good score instead of playing for a great score (playing scared).

Reward: Not screwing up a good round.

Entitlement Habit

Trigger: Not getting what I want when and how I feel I "should."

Behavior: Pouting, throwing a pity party, and ruminating about how the world isn't fair and that the things I want "should" happen the way I want them to.

Reward: Protecting my ego by avoiding responsibility for my current shortcomings and the reality that what I want doesn't just happen because I want it to.

As we look at these mapped habits, you may have noticed that some habits don't seem to be that rewarding or work very well. For example, you may have experienced that trying to play scared or dwelling on mistakes doesn't actually work for avoiding mistakes, or that worrying about other people's judgments doesn't actually free you from those judgments.

Reward refers to the result of a behavior that provides some positive or negative reinforcement. The reward, like the feeling we get from dopamine or even just a sense of safety, certainty, or "doing something," is how a behavior is reinforced in the first place. Some habits you map might have behaviors that don't seem that rewarding right now, like being anxious or hitting tense, jerky putts—but at some point, the feelings they produced were rewarding enough for them to become habits. In Stage Two, we'll discuss why our brain continues to choose and even doubles down on behaviors it thinks are rewarding even when they aren't.

After talking through how her brain was learning these unproductive habits, I gave Stacy simple instructions to start mapping the habits that were keeping her from playing golf freely. Stacy's handful of habits is not uncommon, and her experience provides a good example of the importance of Stage One of Dr. Brewer's mindful approach to behavioral change: becoming consciously aware of our habits by mapping them and the elements within them.

Using mindful awareness to map our habits is how we get our old brain to take our habits out of set-it-and-forget-it mode. Please read that again, as it's essential to the work we're talking about here. Without conscious mindful awareness of a habit and its elements, our old brain will keep that habit going and leave it in set-it-and-forget-it mode because it won't see any reason to do otherwise. And when habits remain in set-it-and-forget-it mode, our old brain subconsciously assumes that they are effective, and any effort to change them by using willpower, reasoning, and distraction will be met with significant resistance.

Start with your most obvious habits. Perhaps you get enraged after a few missed putts and that rage follows you for the rest of the round. Perhaps you have a habit of being off time by calculating your final score while you still have holes and shots left to play.

Like Stacy, you may also become aware of a series of interrelated echo habits. Understanding and becoming aware of habits in this way can be exciting and enlightening, but it can also lead to what Dr. Brewer calls an ironic habit trap of immediately trying to fix the habits we are now consciously aware of.

At this point, I'll also reiterate that in Stage One, the awareness we bring to our habits is mindful: intentional, grounded, and accepting. We are paying attention to our habits and their elements on purpose and in the present, and we are accepting what we find without judgment. Not paying attention to our habits in the present keeps them in set-it-and-forget-it mode. And I can guarantee that if you judge your habits through a doing mode of mind as what you *should* or *shouldn't* be doing, you'll feel worse. Changing your habits will be met with even more resistance from your old brain.

One of the most important habits for us to be mindfully aware of as we step away from unproductive habits is the habit of the doing mode of mind. Remember, your inner experience and any mental habits within it are *not* a vending machine that needs to be repaired—only to be met with mindful awareness.

Here's the ironic habit trap to be aware of:

Trigger: Becoming consciously aware of and understanding my habits.
Behavior: Trying to fix them using methods from the doing mode of mind that don't work.
Reward: Feeling like I'm solving my habits (but actually making things worse).

On a neurological level, judging our habits through a doing mode of mind only further activates the neural pathways in the brain that keep habits in set-it-and-forget-it mode.

When discussing the misconceptions about mindfulness in the first section, I touched on the default mode network, the areas of the brain activated when our minds are wandering on autopilot, which tends to happen about half of our waking hours. Many neuroscientists agree that the default mode network contains the areas of the brain where the set-it-and-forget-it mode exists. As it turns out, the default mode network is also activated when we are engaged in repetitive patterns of thoughts and feelings, like toxic rumination, and when we're in strong emotional states like anger or anxiety.

At the center of the default mode network is an area of the brain called the "posterior cingulate cortex," which serves as a connecting hub for several brain regions. It activates in response to reminders and triggers. When the default mode network is activated, our brain also operates on the high-frequency and high-intensity brain waves that disrupt our physical movements and ability to focus on an external target. This is why Stacy, and many other golfers, have real difficulty playing shots the way they intend to when their unproductive mental habits are triggered. Their brain activity won't allow for them to freely execute their skills.

Dr. Brewer and I agree that our mental habits, our repeated patterns of thoughts and feelings and getting caught up in them, are one of the primary obstacles to stepping away from our unproductive physical habits. We also agree that mindfulness is the most effective approach to changing even our most stubborn behaviors. A large body of studies has found that continued mindfulness training quiets the areas of the brain that activate and run our default mode network—the same areas of the brain that activate the high-frequency and high-intensity brain waves that disrupt our ability to execute physical skills.

In a series of recent studies, when comparing fMRI scans, Dr. Brewer found that four brain regions showed different activity between people who practiced mindfulness and those who didn't. Two of those regions were the main hubs of the default mode network. The fMRI scans showed that the default mode network was significantly less active for those with experience practicing mindfulness. In other words, consistent mindfulness training leads to neuroplastic changes that make our brain physically less reactive to triggers and stressors.

Dr. Brewer replicated his study using several real-time neurofeedback experiments to ensure that the reduced activity in the default mode network he had observed was in fact matching changes in physical behavior.

His replication results were confirmed: those who brought a mindful awareness to their mental behaviors were less likely to fall into unproductive physical habits. The program Dr. Brewer used in those studies is the same three-stage program you're reading about right now, and it began with simply bringing mindful awareness to habits without trying to fix the habits themselves.

TWO PATHS OF KNOWING

Think of Stage One as getting to know our habits, or conscious awareness—so that later, when we have the right information and the tools to create change, that awareness will have paved the way for change. When we go too fast by trying to force change too early, we won't have forged both paths of knowing required for sustainable change.

On a fundamental level, as humans we come to know things from two paths. One path is what psychologists call "declarative knowing" or "declarative learning." Declarative knowing is a fancy way of saying "knowing about something and understanding it conceptually." It's the type of knowing you get from reading the latest magazine articles or watching instruction videos online. When we learn about something and understand it conceptually, we can turn that information into applicable knowledge. There's a reason I've devoted so much of this book to helping you learn about your brain and how it works, mindfulness, habits, and later your psychological framework: all of it is valuable declarative knowledge.

But knowing something conceptually and putting that declarative knowledge into action when it counts isn't enough. You can't read a book about how Lorena Ochoa or Arnold Palmer played golf and then walk onto the first tee and instantly play like them. Concepts don't magically lead to improved performance in sustainable ways. We have to directly experience those concepts to learn how to use them.

The second path of knowing is "procedural knowing," or "procedural learning." Procedural knowing is knowing something through our direct experience. There's also a reason why so much of this book is devoted to your individual practice of being aware of your direct experiences through mindfulness. Mindfulness awareness, used to connect with your direct experience, allows you to merge conceptual understanding with your direct experience. And when these two paths of knowing merge, concepts and experiences become wisdom. Wisdom leads to credibility and sustainable change.

When it comes to habit change, both paths of knowing are vital. As you begin to mindfully map your habits, you'll take what you know about the concepts you've learned and tie them to your direct experiences. You may notice, of course, that mindfully mapping doesn't magically lead to change. More is required to bring in procedural knowing through your direct experience.

Like Stacy, most golfers have unproductive habits that have been around longer than they care to admit. Mindfully mapping our habits is a necessary first stage, but it's just that: the first stage to changing our habits. Rushing through Stage One does not provide enough time and repetition for declarative and procedural knowing to merge. So be patient. Mindfully map your habits (triggers, behaviors, and rewards) a few times a day for a week to ten days. The more you map them, the more you will be using mindful awareness to know about your habits conceptually and experience them directly. You'll know you're ready for Stage Two when you can mindfully map your habits quickly and with clarity, almost to the point where you can see them as a trigger, behavior, and reward as they're happening, and possibly even before. Once that point is reached, it's time to show our brain what our habits are really doing by using our awareness of our direct experience with them.

STAGE TWO: BRINGING AWARENESS TO WHAT OUR HABITS ARE DOING

Even as an established professional golfer, Stacy was experiencing two of the most common and damaging habits for any golfer: playing scared and anxiety. The two were echo habits of each other.

But as Stacy began to cruise through Stage One, she could see her habits happening as triggers, behaviors, and rewards, which led Stacy to ask me a logical question.

"Why do these habits persist even when they don't seem to work?"

I cannot emphasize enough how important Stacy's question is and how important it is to understand the *correct* answer. Remember, our behaviors are most reinforced by our feelings. Therefore, paying mindful attention to what a behavior *feels* like and what it does for us is the essence of Stage Two.

The correct answer to Stacy's question is the primary difference between why surface-level psychology doesn't work and why a deeper and more mindful approach does. The correct answer provides us insights into why we act in certain ways and how to move toward more productive habits. Let's start to answer Stacy's question by looking at Stacy's habits, mindfully mapped.

Playing Scared Habit
Trigger: Tight tee shot (usually a dogleg right).
Behavior: Making a defensive, fearful, guided swing.
Reward: Hopefully, "doing something" to keep the ball from going out of bounds.

Anxiety Habit
Trigger: Thinking about an upcoming tournament.
Behavior: Anxiety via toxic rumination.
Reward: Feeling like I'm "doing something" to make sure I play well.

What Stacy didn't see yet is that her habits *were* working, at least according to her old brain. What Stacy was about to understand is that the key to changing a behavior, mental or physical, is *not* the triggers or the behavior itself—it's the reward's value and how that reward works in our brain.

For the sake of clarity, let's quickly recap why and how our brain forms habits. The why: habits create space for our brains to learn new things and not have to think through behaviors every time. Remember, not all behaviors become habits. Our brain has a method for choosing which behaviors to put in set-it-and-forget-it mode to repeat as habits and which behaviors not to. And the all-important how: our brains form a habit based on how rewarding (reinforcing) the behavior is. The more rewarding a behavior is, the stronger the habit.

I'm going to say that again because this is one of the primary reasons why many of the common methods for changing behavior and building mental toughness don't work: the more rewarding a behavior is to our brain, mental or physical, the stronger the habit.

We have an infinite number of behaviors available to us, with infinite variations. To organize our behaviors, our brain creates a hierarchy of those behaviors based on their reward value. A reward value is how reinforcing a behavior is to our brain. In response to a trigger, the behavior with the largest reward value to our old brain is the one it chooses and the one we ultimately act out. Based on how our brain is designed, behaviors that feel the best and behaviors that are most effective for avoiding discomfort, uncertainty, and threats, real or perceived, are the most reinforcing and tend to become our strongest habits.

When Stacy learned her unproductive habits while playing in college, they had large reward values that got reinforced in multiple ways. When she was anxious about playing well enough to be confident, she still played well enough in comparison to the other players who weren't as good as her. She felt some temporary confidence. When she played scared and steered her tee shots, she played well enough compared to the other players, whose best shots weren't any better than Stacy's "don't miss left" swings. She was rewarded in her brain and on the course for both behaviors.

When we're learning a behavior and forming a habit, our brains also learn reward values for the general context around the behavior. Our brains learn reward values for places, people, and things, and they combine all that information associated with the behavior together into a composite reward value. So the reward values for anxiety and playing scared for Stacy not only included the behaviors themselves but also her coach's compliments for "really caring about golf" when she was anxious and still winning tournaments while playing scared. That's how the false association that "a little bit of anxiety is a good thing" began for Stacy.

Of course, the context in which she was playing was changing significantly. Stacy could no longer play scared and play well enough to win. On the LPGA Tour, everyone was as good as or better than she was. But her old brain couldn't register the current details of how rewarding her habits were for her now because her old brain assumed that the behaviors would produce the same reward values they did in the past even though they weren't.

Stacy declaratively knew that anxiety and playing scared were not rewarding. But that conceptual understanding was only half of knowing, which is why no matter how much she told herself to "relax and play freely," she was still anxious and played scared. If declaratively knowing something was enough to think our way to being confident and swinging freely, I would be happily out of a job. But declarative knowing isn't enough for the safety-first portions of our old brain, which, again, are faster and stronger than the rational and conscious-thinking portions of our young brain. Our old brain learns almost exclusively through procedural knowing from our direct experiences. Put simply, it learns based on what we feel.

Reward value registers through our direct experience in the brain within an area called the "orbitofrontal cortex," which is the junction in our brain where emotional, sensory, and physical information from previous experiences and behaviors all mix. You may be noticing that all of these areas of information are ones we *feel* directly.

Until a reward value is updated, it registers to our old brain the same as it did when a habit was established and placed in set-it-and-forget-it mode so that we can quickly retrieve that behavior without our slower, less powerful young brain having to sift through many pieces of information do so. To change a behavior, addressing the behavior itself is *not* enough, whether it's a physical or mental behavior. Instead, we must bring awareness to our direct procedural experience in that behavior so that our old brain can know what the *current* reward value is for the behavior.

But before we address how to update the reward value of a behavior, and while we have some fresh declarative knowledge about how behaviors are learned, become habits, and remain habits despite changing contexts, let's address two common myths that lead to and reinforce unproductive habits for many golfers: willpower and distraction.

MYTH: USING WILLPOWER TO CHANGE OUR BEHAVIORS AND PERFORM BETTER

The number of times you hear television commentators suggesting that a golfer "willed their way to victory" is astonishing. The idea seems simple enough. For example, when we have an important putt, we simply need to "dig down deep" and will the ball into the hole. Or, when we're nervous or anxious, we just need to force ourselves to "relax and trust," "not think," or "be disciplined," and that should work, right? On the surface, willpower seems like it should work, but there are a few significant flaws in relying on willpower.

First, the small number of studies that recognize willpower as a real psychological resource found that people who exerted willpower weren't more successful at accomplishing their goals and, in many cases, performed worse the more they relied on willpower. Those same studies also showed that the more willpower people exerted, the more fatigued and depleted they felt, cognitively, emotionally, and physically. So, even if willpower is real, it's a finite resource that doesn't improve performance and wears us out.

Second, more recent research examining how much power willpower actually offers us has shown that willpower is another false association. The majority of studies show that digging down deep, gritting our teeth, and forcing ourselves to "just swing freely" and "just be disciplined" are counterproductive strategies from the doing mode of mind that we falsely associate with success.

With that in mind, let's do our false-association check:

Have you ever made a putt, made a cut, or hit a good shot by willing it to happen?

The answer is probably yes.

Does willpower *always* make you play better?

It doesn't? How interesting.

Here comes the kicker: Does willpower ever get in the way of you playing well?

Oh, it does? How interesting.

Does willpower ever drain your energy and lead to tension, rushed swings, and jabby forced putts, and does it also make golf less enjoyable, especially when it matters most to you?

It does? How about that.

When you've played your very best golf and enjoyed yourself the most, were you "willpowering" your way through, or did you allow your performance to just happen?

You allowed it to just happen? Interesting, very interesting.

Third, even if willpower did work the way the false association suggests it does in low-pressure situations, when we're in pressure-filled situations that can trigger our unproductive habits, our old brain wants to take over and override our young brain, effectively shutting down our prefrontal cortex. That means that when we're anxious, angry, overexcited, emotionally uncomfortable, or hangry and need willpower the most, the sections of our brain where we can conjure such willpower by telling ourselves to "relax," "be disciplined," or "just trust" are operating at a diminished capacity or not even online. Without the prefrontal cortex online, our old brain subconsciously does whatever it wants based on the amount of constriction and threat it perceives, regardless of whether that perception is accurate or not.

When it comes to willpower as a strategy for tackling the habits that impact our performance, it requires us to rely on the youngest, weakest, and slowest parts of our brain to overpower the oldest, strongest, and fastest parts of our brain. Willpower, whether applied internally or externally, is also a state that is strongly associated with high-frequency brain waves, the opposite of being in flow state.

Willpower as a strategy seems logical on the surface, but if it were as simple as just willing ourselves to relax, be confident, trust our swing, be disciplined, and not be anxious, everyone would always play freely. If you don't believe me, try this for your next round of golf: use willpower to get every putt into the hole, and any time you feel nervous, anxious, or frustrated, just will yourself to "relax and be confident." If willpower works, you should have the calmest and most confident round of golf you've ever had and make every putt.

MYTH: CONTROLLING FOCUS WITH DISTRACTION

Not long ago, I got an email from a professional golfer who was interested in working together but wanted to talk to me about my work before deciding if we would be a good fit. His hesitancy was due to some, let's say, mixed experiences with mental coaches in the past. Most recently, he'd had an experience that was a bit of disaster. Here's what happened.

A few weeks before we met, Terrance wanted some help and had paid a lot of money to meet with a sport psychologist who worked for a professional baseball team. Terrance was getting sick and tired of playing scared, hesitant shots in tournaments; the habit was keeping him from playing the way he wanted to and from posting better scores.

In their meeting, the sport psychologist asked Terrance what his favorite number was. Terrance replied that his favorite number was two. Then the sport psychologist told Terrance that every time he was over a shot and feeling nervous or anxious, he should think of the number two, really make the number clear in his mind, and then play his shot.

Already knowing the answer to the question, I asked Terrance, "How did that work for you?"

Terrance has a great sense of humor. "Thinking of the number two worked about as well as a taking a number two—like crap."

Another client, a Division I golfer, told me that a mental coach told her to count backward from one hundred by threes while she addressed any shot if she was feeling anxious.

"How long did it take before you stopped doing that?" I asked.

"Nine holes."

I can't tell you how many people, especially younger golfers in their teens and early professional careers, have been taught to use some kind of alternate scoring system or mental scorecard, giving themselves points based on how confident they are, how frustrated they get, whether they have the "right level of anxiety," how positive their thoughts are, how confident and in control their body language makes them look, and any number of mental metrics for a round of golf that are simply distractions from playing well.

Like thinking of the number two or counting backward by threes, an alternate scoring system is equally ineffective for getting beneath the surface and addressing the sources of the behaviors and habits that keep golfers from playing more freely. They're distractions, and distractions don't help us play better golf because they take us away from what we're doing and experiencing. Using distractions to avoid our inner experience and habits is the psychological equivalent to rearranging the deck chairs on the Titanic. You're not even delaying the inevitable; if anything, you're only making the situation worse.

Our brain grows tired of being distracted again and again, which is partly why no one sticks with these strategies for very long. Our brain literally rejects them because it takes a lot of conceptual mental energy to try to avoid and distract ourselves from what we are directly experiencing. In essence, it takes a lot of procedural energy to try to fool ourselves into thinking we're not experiencing what we actually are.

Like willpower, distracting ourselves is a version of the doing mode of mind and relies on the younger, slower sections of our brain to overpower the older, faster sections of our brain. Distraction is just another way of saying "avoidance," and, as we established in the last section, trying to avoid our inner experience—especially unpleasant thoughts and feelings—doesn't work and usually makes things worse. As we're establishing in this section, avoiding internal and external triggers doesn't work either and typically makes things worse as well.

More often than not, my clients tell me they want to eliminate distractions. Why? Because they are a barrier to being focused on their performance as it's happening. Being distracted makes it harder to perform well, not easier. Distractions aren't good for us when we want to perform better and more consistently.

Let's use flow state as a frame of reference. Remember, flow state is the optimal state of human functioning largely characterized by complete immersion in the task at hand in the present moment. It's a psychological state void of distraction. If our brain is operating on low-frequency and low-intensity alpha and theta waves, why would we want to invite distractions into our performance and move farther away from that optimal state of functioning?

Recent research shows that these distraction strategies don't work because the things they are meant to distract us from, like triggers and our habits, remain, and distracting ourselves to avoid feeling anxious or playing scared then becomes an echo habit. Now, instead of one unproductive habit of anxiety, we have two unproductive habits: anxiety plus distracting ourselves with a favorite number or doing long division.

Research also shows that people who make distraction a habit are in no uncertain terms training their brain to be chronically distracted to the point of not being able to filter out irrelevancy. Put simply, repeatedly distracting ourselves trains our brain to shift its focus again and again rather than recognizing and focusing on what's relevant.

Here's something that's just as important about being distracted: it doesn't actually feel better. Remember the Harvard study that found that we spend about half of our waking lives on autopilot, distracted in wandering thoughts? To recap, the researchers used an app to ask people three questions: What are you doing at the present moment, what are you thinking about at the present moment, and how happy are you? That same study also revealed that the more distracted we are, the less happy we are, and that our happiness is more heavily impacted by being distracted than by what it is that we're doing.

Distraction is also just another way of saying "multitasking." Contrary to popular belief, research examining attention and task performance shows that when we multitask, we aren't doing multiple things at once. Rather, our brains are constantly toggling back and forth between tasks, allotting only small portions of our cognitive capacity to one task at a time. Although we *feel* like we're getting twice as much done by multitasking, we're actually getting only half as much done—and doing so with lower quality and decreased enjoyment. Some studies even show that persistent distractions in the form of multitasking lead to as much as a ten-point decrease in IQ. Put simply, distraction hurts performance, makes us significantly dumber, and makes what we're doing less enjoyable.

Where we direct and devote our attention is immensely valuable. I mean, seriously, what sounds more enjoyable—keeping an extra scorecard that tracks your body language and doing math homework while you're playing golf, or being present more often when you're playing golf? The things we enjoy the most are made better by being focused on them when they are happening, even when they are difficult, uncertain, and uncomfortable.

By now, hopefully you are starting to understand that using strategies that rely on your young brain to use willpower and distract our old brain don't work. These surface-level strategies do not address the reward value that keeps our habits intact. The reward value and how it registers to our old brain for any of our habits must be updated before sustainable change can happen.

UPDATING REWARD VALUES

If willpower and distractions don't work, then what does? You guessed it—mindful awareness. In order to update the reward value for any behavior, we need to give our brains updated procedural information from our direct experience to show that the reward value it previously established is now outdated. This requires conscious mindful attention to our behaviors in the present moment that so our brain can get a full procedural dose of our direct experience rather than assuming a habit still works like it did when our brain put it into set-it-and-forget-it mode.

Mindful awareness allows our brain to see and feel directly and exactly how rewarding (or unrewarding) a habit is in our current context. When unproductive habits are taken out of set-it-and-forget-it mode, new information gained by paying attention to our direct experiences resets the reward values of those habits and makes room for newer, more productive behaviors.

Think about updating the reward value of a behavior like training your dog not to poop in your house. As Dr. Brewer so deftly says, being mindfully aware of what a behavior directly feels like and what it's directly doing for us right now is like rubbing your brain's orbitofrontal cortex in its own poop so that it can clearly and directly smell how stinky it is. Neurologically, paying attention in this way provides direct procedural knowledge for just how unrewarding a behavior is.

Behaviors won't change if the reward value stays the same, so we must show our old brain through our direct experience that the reward value now is *not* the reward value it previously established and still expects.

Bring mindful awareness to your direct procedural experience of your habits in their current context by asking two purposeful questions. First: What does it feel like to engage in this behavior? This question brings our awareness to the actual emotional, physical, visceral sensations that a behavior produces. Then, ask: What am I getting from this behavior? This brings our awareness to the natural consequences a behavior has for us and for how we play golf.

Mindfully mapping in Stage Two looks the same as in Stage One, with one addition: we add our direct experience in the present moment. Take this example:

Trigger: Feeling nervous about the first shot of a round of golf.
Behavior: Anxiety in the form of worry.
(Outdated) Reward: Feeling like I'm "doing something" to avoid a bad
   shot

Result:
1. What does it feel like to engage in this behavior?
    It feels overwhelming, heavy, tense, rushed, and like a rock in my chest.
2. What am I getting from this behavior?
    Unstable confidence, more uncertainty, rushed swings, and a more difficult and less enjoyable golf experience.

Our old brain updates reward values by using and favoring the most recent and direct information we give it. So when we rub our old brain's orbitofrontal cortex in whatever unpleasant and unproductive direct experience and consequences our habits result in, it starts to rearrange its hierarchy of behaviors by moving less-rewarding behaviors down the priority list. This is what psychologists call "disenchantment." Disenchantment is a long-established awareness technique, which is perhaps why the stereotypical representation of a therapist in movies and television shows often includes someone sitting with their legs crossed, wearing a cardigan, and peering over a pair of glasses perched on the end of their nose, blandly asking, "And how does that make you feel?"

This is really important: when we pay mindful attention to our direct experience with our unproductive habits as they are happening and remove judgment or past experiences to guide us, we can see that a behavior is not rewarding to us right now. We then become less enchanted by those behaviors and are less likely to return to them in the future.

Once our brain knows that something isn't nearly as great as it originally thought it was, it can't unsee that procedural truth in our direct experience. When we pay careful attention to how anxiety only leads to feeling constricted and being less certain, or how playing scared wastes your shots, your old brain can't go back and take a mulligan to pretend you don't feel as bad as you do or end up with the poor results that you keep getting. Every time you pay attention to how demeaning it feels to be too harshly self-critical, or how frustrated and lost you feel when aimlessly beating balls on the range while panic-practicing, you become more aware of what you're getting—not because you willed, distracted, or forced yourself to, but because your brain is now aware of the actual and current natural consequences of those behaviors and will remember how terrible they feel and how poorly they go.

Again, when it comes to habits, repetition is key. The more you rub your old brain's nose in its own unproductive, habitual pile of poop, the more it gains procedural knowledge of just how unrewarding a habit is.

To be clear, Stage Two is *not* an intellectual exercise. We are not appealing to the rational thinking and reasonable decision-making of the slower, less powerful sections of the young brain. Be mindful of the trap of trying to think your way out of unproductive habits.

If, like Stacy, your mind starts trying to problem-solve away worry, playing scared, self-criticism, or comparisons to others, do your best to notice and even mindfully map that doing-mode-of-mind habit as well. Then ask yourself, "What does it *feel* like trying to problem-solve and think my way out of this behavior?" Put your rational and logical thinking mind on hold and observe through a being mode of mind what's happening in your directly felt experience. Let your brain learn how it's already designed to learn. Disenchantment comes through mindful awareness, not willpower, distraction, avoidance, or reasoning, and certainly not through the judgment of the doing mode of mind.

With such procedural knowledge, disenchantment will come not because you have to will yourself to "just not think" or distract yourself with some alternate scoring system but because you are now aware of and remember what happened last time you started overthinking. And the time before that, and the time before that, and the time before that. The same process holds true for anxiety, anger, playing scared, comparing yourself to other golfers, entitlement, or any other unproductive physical or mental habits you've learned.

For the next week or ten days, mindfully map in Stage Two. Start the map in Stage One to bring awareness to the habit to pull it out of set-it-and-forget-it mode. Then add the questions from Stage Two by bringing mindful awareness (intentional, grounded, and accepting) to your direct embodied experience.

Stage Two Mapping Structure

Trigger:

Behavior:

(Outdated) Reward:

Result:
1. What does it feel like to engage in this behavior?
2. What am I getting from this behavior? (Or, what does this behavior do for me?)

Let's look at a few examples from real golfers of the habits we mapped earlier in Stage One.

Overthinking Habit (Division I College Player)
Trigger: Poor swing.
Behavior: Overthinking my swing mechanics.
(Outdated) Reward: Feeling like I'm "doing something" to avoid hitting bad shots.
Result:
1. What does it feel like to engage in this behavior?
   Forced, confused, and angry. Feels like I don't know what to do.
2. What am I getting from this behavior? (Or, what does this behavior do for me?)
   It makes me try to force shots and actively think through something that I've trained for throughout most of my life. It doesn't help me hit better shots. It makes me second-guess myself and makes it much harder to be committed to shots because it complicates everything. I get no confidence from it, and it doesn't fix anything.

Self-Criticism Habit (PGA Tour Player)
Trigger: Not playing well.
Behavior: Berating myself about how terribly I played.
(Outdated) Reward: Motivating myself to "do better."
Result:
1. What does it feel like to engage in this behavior?
   Demeaning, like I'm being scolded. It makes me angry. It feels discouraging.
2. What am I getting from this behavior? (Or, what does this behavior do for me?)

Not confidence, that's for sure. It makes me worry about making mistakes and makes it easy to feel hopeless about playing better. I'm not getting better. If anything, it makes everything worse.

Panic-Practice Habit (LPGA Tour Player)

Trigger: Poor round of golf.

Behavior: Beating balls trying to feel better (not get better) about playing poorly.

(Outdated) Reward: Conjuring confidence for the next day.

Result:

1. What does it feel like to engage in this behavior?
    I feel frustrated, lost, and desperate.

2. What am I getting from this behavior? (Or, what does this behavior do for me?)
    It makes my confidence less stable, makes it easier to second-guess myself, burns through my energy on the first day of a tournament week, and doesn't actually help me find what I'm looking for because I'm not practicing with any real structure.

Dwelling Habit (Division I College Player)

Trigger: Missing a short putt that I always expect to make.

Behavior: Dwelling on the mistake and lamenting that it "shouldn't" have happened.

(Outdated) Reward: Avoiding making the same mistake in the future.

Result:

1. What does it feel like to engage in this behavior?
    I feel angry and cramped, like I'm carrying around extra weight; super crappy.

2. What am I getting from this behavior? (Or, what does this behavior do for me?)
    It keeps me in the past, makes it harder to focus on my next shot, ruins my confidence, and, most of all, doesn't actually keep me from making more mistakes—it leads to them.

Blaming Habit (PGA Tour Player)

Trigger: Failure to make the cut, getting a warning for slow play, getting a bad bounce, etc.

Behavior: Blaming someone/something else, complaining, making excuses.

(Outdated) Reward: Protecting my ego by trying to avoid being the source of my own shortcomings.

Result:

1. What does it feel like to engage in this behavior?

   It feels like I'm so insecure, and I feel small and unprofessional, like I can't handle difficult things. It also makes me feel like I'm a bad person for blaming the people around me who want me to be successful.

2. What am I getting from this behavior? (Or, what does this behavior do for me?)

   Nothing. The more I complain, the worse I am at dealing with what I need to do to play better. The more I make excuses, the less I can rely on myself. The more I blame others, the more they won't like being around me and the less I'll like myself. What I'm getting from this is a shortened career.

Comparing Habit (PGA Tour Player)

Trigger: Seeing other players hitting balls on the range or seeing others' scores/rankings.

Behavior: Comparing myself and my game to another player and their game.

(Outdated) Reward: Feeling better and more confident about my own game.

Result:

1. What does it feel like to engage in this behavior?

   It feels really awful. It makes me feel envious of some players, which doesn't feel good at all. I also feel a lack of confidence when I compare my game to those of players who aren't as good as me because it shows me how little trust I must have in my own game to be looking at players that aren't as good as me to believe in it. That sucks.

2. What am I getting from this behavior? (Or, what does this behavior do for me?)

    The exact opposite of what I want it to do. It gives me less confidence, not more, and it tempts me to start trying to do things that aren't in my bag. It takes me away from the things that I've done to be successful and that lead to success. Basically, it causes me to focus on others more than on myself.

Control Habit (LPGA Tour Player)

Trigger: Uncertainty of future outcomes in some form or another.

Behavior: Focusing on things and future outcomes that can't be controlled.

(Outdated) Reward: Feeling like I'm creating a sense of control and certainty about the future.

Result:

1. What does it feel like to engage in this behavior?

    It feels like things are moving too fast. It feels desperate. It feels like I'm not in control at all.

2. What am I getting from this behavior? (Or, what does this behavior do for me?)

    Not more control, that's for damn sure. It makes me feel less certain about everything. If anything, I feel more anxious the more I focus on and try to control things that I can't control, which makes me try to force shots, and that never ends well.

Worry Habit (PGA Tour Player)

Trigger: The potential for other people to judge me and my game negatively.

Behavior: Worrying about other peoples' opinions.

(Outdated) Reward: Protecting my ego and avoiding being judged in unwanted ways.

Result:

1. What does it feel like to engage in this behavior?

    It makes me feel anxious and constricted. It makes me fearful to do anything that might be seen as not enough by others. It also feels endless—there's never an end to the "what ifs." It just keeps going.

2. What am I getting from this behavior? (Or, what does this behavior do for me?)
   Anxiety. Uncertainty. Fear of failure. Safe, tense, and crappy golf. It's not fun.

Protect Your Score Habit (Division I College Golfer)

Trigger: Realizing that I'm on pace to have a great score.

Behavior: Trying to protect a good score instead of playing for a great score (playing scared).

(Outdated) Reward: Not screwing up a good round.

Result:

1. What does it feel like to engage in this behavior?
   It makes me feel anxious and like I'm wasting a great opportunity to shoot a great score.

2. What am I getting from this behavior? (Or, what does this behavior do for me?)
   It makes me worry about ruining a good round, protect scores on holes that are already over, and leave shots out there on a day when I'm playing great. Wasted chances to go really low because I'm holding back.

Entitlement Habit (Division I College Golfer)

Trigger: Not getting what I want when and how I feel I "should."

Behavior: Pouting, throwing a pity party, and ruminating about how the world isn't fair and that the things I want "should" happen the way I want them to.

(Outdated) Reward: Protecting my ego by avoiding responsibility for my current shortcomings and the reality that what I want doesn't just happen because I want it to.

Result:

1. What does it feel like to engage in this behavior?
   It makes me feel weak, defeated, like the world is against me

and that I'm farther from what I want. Feels like I can't handle difficult things and that I'm a spoiled brat.

2. What am I getting from this behavior? (Or, what does this behavior do for me?)
    Weakened resilience to difficult tasks, an avoidant relationship with failure, a decreased ability to adapt to challenges, becoming less enjoyable to be around.

WON'T THAT SUCK?

As you map your habits in Stage Two, you may be concerned that it will suck to bring awareness to your direct experience with the habits that are unproductive and emotionally uncomfortable. Many times, my clients have expressed concern about bringing awareness to their anxiety, anger, or scared playing and how uncomfortable that will feel. So if you're thinking, "Won't that suck?" . . . the answer is yes, but that's a good thing.

As we can see from most of our unproductive habits, the reward value they offer is some form of temporary relief from discomfort or a false sense of certainty, and that typically feels better to most people than emotional discomfort and uncertainty. In theory, if you can answer enough "what ifs," then you'll have some certainty about the future. But mapping your habits in Stage Two brings awareness to how the "what ifs" actually feel in the moment you engage with them. Mindfully tuning in to our direct experience with our habits just reveals what they're already making us feel and what they're already doing for us.

Tuning in to how our unproductive habits make us feel will make those feelings seem intensified. In reality, that's not what's happening—we're just paying attention to them. The great news is that bringing a mindful awareness to how these habits feel does two wonderful things. First, as we've established, it allows our orbitofrontal cortex to update their reward values, which it does because those behaviors now feel uncomfortable and clearly lead to nothing good for us. We need that discomfort for our old brain to work for us.

Second, mapping our habits in Stage Two will highlight how poorly a habit like self-criticism is already making us feel, but because we're not trying to change, avoid, or "fix" how we feel, that feeling can be experienced directly and pass as a temporary part of our inner experience.

So yes, you're going to feel discomfort, but through a being mode of mind, we won't make ourselves feel worse. By observing our feelings without judgment, we allow them to pass sooner than if we tried to distract ourselves from them.

Here's an email from a client on the PGA Tour who was particularly concerned about being aware of what his anxiety felt like when he started mapping in Stage Two:

> At first, asking myself what my anxiety feels like really sucked. How does worrying about how well I'm going to play make me feel ... awful. It's heavy in my chest and leads to tension. And when I ask what anxiety is doing for me ... all it's doing is leading to more doubt about my game, leading to playing scared, destroying my confidence, and always, always making me focus on the future. BUT ... !!! When I asked these questions without judgment, they went away really quickly. Instead of being anxious all day, I was only anxious for a few minutes.
>
> Raymond, sitting in the discomfort is getting easier each day. Yes, it feels awful, but being able to map my anxiety in Stage Two and not running from the feelings lets them pass along, and that kinda feels awesome.

OUTCOMES ARE NOT BEHAVIORS

As you're mapping in Stage Two, you may be thinking that you'll just map the behaviors you want to eliminate, like bad shots, bad rounds, or losing. However, that won't work and will make things worse for you because those are not behaviors—they're outcomes. Remember, reward-based learning is how we learn behaviors, not outcomes. We don't learn outcomes; we learn behaviors that indirectly influence the outcomes we produce.

Recently, I had a college golf coach tell me that he was having all his players Stage-Two map what it feels like to lose a tournament, which for just about every highly competitive golfer doesn't feel good. However, what this coach was actually doing was creating a fear of losing in his players and reinforcing unproductive behaviors to avoid losing, like anxiety and playing scared. I'll remind you, like I reminded him: no matter how much you try, you *can't* reinforce or incentivize outcomes—*only* behaviors. Outcomes cannot be directly controlled. Trying to reinforce outcomes only reinforces behaviors to avoid negative outcomes and fuels a fear of failure.

You may have heard the phrase that "winning is a habit." It's not. Winning and losing are outcomes, not behaviors. People who get better results more often tend to have more productive habits built on behaviors that increase the odds of successful outcomes. Working hard, practicing effectively, sleeping and eating well, and being present and accepting are habits built on a foundation of productive behaviors. The better outcomes those behaviors tend to produce—such as winning, better scores, improved rankings, making cuts, Tour status, and others—are byproducts, just like how the outcomes we're trying to avoid, like losing, worse scores, missed shots, mistakes, and missed cuts, are predictable byproducts of unproductive habits.

As you're mapping in Stage Two, be sure to map behaviors and not outcomes. Mapping outcomes, especially the ones you don't want, only makes the possibility of not getting them more constricting and threatening and will reinforce the unproductive behaviors you typically use to try to avoid them. Instead, focus on behaviors so that you can be aware of habits that keep you from pursuing the performances and outcomes you do want.

EXPECT A DOUBLE DOWN

Have you ever been to the grocery store or the mall and seen a child have a complete meltdown because their parent wouldn't give in to their demands? It's quite a scene, and it really puts parents in a situation where they are faced with choosing a short-term or a long-term approach. The short-term approach is to end the tantrum by giving in to the child's demands for a toy or candy. For the sake of everyone in the store, this is the option most of us innocent bystanders would prefer because, by making the child more comfortable, we can all be more comfortable.

The long-term option, and the option that wise parents choose, is to weather the storm until the child understands that their behavior will not earn the expected reward. Parents who take this approach are playing the long game. They know that every time they give in to the child's tantrum, they are only reinforcing the behavior, effectively increasing the reward value for throwing a tantrum. They are willing to sit through a tantrum in the short term so that they won't have to deal with tantrums as an ongoing habit in the future.

Where many parents make a mistake is that they'll weather the tantrum storm when it's just some whining and pleading mixed with tears and pouts but will give in to the child's demands when the tantrum escalates into a full-blown meltdown of screams, stomping feet, and—my personal favorite—just falling to the ground and refusing to move.

There's a reason a child will double down on their tantrum at the first sign that they aren't getting the desired toys and candy. It all has to do with how our brain responds when it doesn't get the reward value it expects from our established habits, including the ones that impact how we play golf.

The familiarity and predictability of established habits makes it difficult for our brain to let go of them, much like how a child has a hard time letting go of a familiar tantrum habit when they think the behavior will produce the same rewards it did in the past.

The reason children escalate their tantrums when they don't immediately work, and why even as adults we return to familiar habits, is in part because our brain expects what it used to get. When it doesn't get that established reward value, our brain's response is to do more of a behavior, not less. So when a habit like overthinking doesn't work, many golfers will overthink even more. When Stacy made a tense swing trying to guide the ball and it didn't work out, she continued to do it in the same way that children continue to have a meltdown when they don't get what they want. Basically, if a pouty lip and a few tears don't produce the expected reward value, a full-on tantrum should, right? If a guided, steery, anxious swing doesn't produce the expected shot, an even more guided, steery, and anxious swing should, right?

What Stage Two does for our brain is point out that continuing, and escalating, a behavior doesn't produce the reward value our brain thinks is coming. Becoming aware of how awful a behavior feels and how it's not providing any value to us signals to our brain that there is a discrepancy between what it expects to get from a behavior and what it's actually getting right now. The more we habitually get angry, feel anxious, or play scared without paying attention to and asking how rewarding a behavior is in the present, the more our brain won't signal that something isn't working.

Like children throwing a tantrum, without Stage Two we just continue to double down on habits that don't work for us because our old brain thinks those habits will eventually produce the reward it expects. But with Stage Two, we show our old brain that there are real-life negative consequences to our habits by weathering the behaviors long enough for our brain to realize that they feel like crap and don't work, especially when escalated. It's the same process as when a parent lets their child melt down long enough for the child to realize that falling on the ground and screaming feels terrible and won't lead to the expected toys, despite their best efforts. Stage Two is playing the long game when our brain's tendency—or compulsion—is to double down on the short term.

So, rather than mindlessly continuing a habit, trying to will yourself to stop, or distracting yourself, use your current experience to show your brain that it's not getting what it thinks it is. When your brain doubles down, weather the storm by asking, "What does it feel like to engage in this behavior?" and "What am I getting from this behavior?" Reflect on the answers to those questions so that your brain will see the discrepancy between an established expectation and your current reality in your direct experience. That's what updates the reward value of habits and stops the tantrums—but it requires acceptance and patience to allow yourself to weather the storm long enough for your brain to catch up.

BUT I LIKE PIZZA

As you're mapping in Stage Two, you may notice that some of your habits are productive up to a certain point, and then they aren't. Put another way, some habits are beneficial in moderation but not when overindulged. For me, that habit is eating pizza. I love pizza and have a habit of eating it just about as often as I can. The habit itself isn't unproductive, but as much as I hate to admit it, there is such a thing as too much pizza. There is a tipping point when eating pizza is no longer beneficial, just as there are tipping points for many of the habits that affect how we play golf.

Dana Small is a neuroscientist and professor of psychiatry and psychology at the Yale School of Medicine. In a series of studies, Dr. Small scanned people's brains to measure their brain activity when they ate their favorite candies. People would choose their favorite candy bar, and then Dr. Small would feed them bites of it while their brain activity was measured using a

PET scanner or an fMRI machine. As people took each bite, they were asked to rate how much they would like another bite using a scale from -10 to +10. -10 was scored as "Awful—eating more would make me sick," and +10 was scored as "I really want another piece."

As you might expect, people started the study the same way I start eating a pizza—at a +10. Knowing what we now know about the brain and reward values for behaviors, you'd also be right to expect that, as people ate more of their favorite candy bars and were asked to rate how much they wanted another piece, the ratings started dropping from "I really want another piece," to something pleasant like "Another piece would be nice," to something neutral or indifferent, and finally into displeasure and disgust. It didn't take long before partaking in their favorite indulgence created unpleasant feelings and became an unproductive experience.

The measurements of people's brain activity through the experiment showed some interesting and important results. The posterior cingulate cortex, the region of our brain that activates when we get stuck in habitual behaviors and serves as the hub for the default mode network, was the only brain region that was activated during both craving and disgust. That is, wanting more and wanting less of something activate the same brain region.

But this is the same region that quiets when we're mindful. This finding is really important for changing our habits because it highlights that many of our habits aren't just completely productive or unproductive; there's a gradient to them. Many are productive up until a point of diminishing returns, but unless we're paying mindful attention to the behaviors, how they make us feel, and what they do for us, we'll miss the point at which a behavior goes from being helpful to harmful.

Back to the pizza. When I see pizza, I want to eat it. After a slice, my brain feels good, thanks to some pepperoni- and green chili–flavored dopamine, and my brain urges me to eat more. But if I continue to eat, it won't take long before I'll have devoured an entire pizza, which won't make me feel good and isn't healthy in any way.

Whether we go past the tipping point with our habits and into the land of diminishing returns depends on whether we're paying attention to the behavior itself and what it's doing for us. The participants in Dr. Small's studies paid attention because they were prompted to pay attention to how they felt and what they were getting after each bite. Likewise, being mindful will help you and your brain recognize when enough turns into too much. But on the golf course or at practice, we aren't prompted to pay attention to when habits like anger and panic-practice go past the tipping point and become destructive to our game and confidence.

Consider a habit like anger, one common to golfers at all skill levels. Research conducted by Raymond Novaco, a professor of psychology at the University of California, Irvine, and an expert on anger, shows that short stints of low-intensity frustration can be constructive. For example, his research found that frustration can help us to energize ourselves, provide clarity, summon courage, encourage us to be assertive without being overly aggressive, and promote personal control and empowerment when we are faced with important choices.

However, his research also shows that when frustration intensifies to anger for prolonged periods of time, or when anger becomes too elevated, it quickly goes from being constructive to being destructive. Past a point of diminishing returns, intense anger significantly clouds judgment and decision-making, causes us to engage in ego-protective echo habits, tends to make us self-righteous, leads to dwelling on past events, corrodes relationships with ourselves and others, and significantly inhibits our ability to decipher what's true and what only seems true and what's relevant and what's not.

For every golfer, practicing is required to develop physical skills and play better—it's an invaluable habit to develop. However, practicing goes from being helpful to harmful when we're practicing for the purpose of building confidence rather than building competence. Practicing with the purpose to make ourselves *feel* better instead of practicing to *get* better is panic-practice that goes past a point of diminishing returns. Doing so usually involves high-frequency and high-intensity brain waves that disrupt our physical movements. Practicing in this way tends to make getting better much more difficult because it requires you to multitask between getting better and feeling better, which compromises both objectives.

As amazing as pizza is, after a certain amount it doesn't taste or feel very good. Mapping in Stage Two allows us to identify which habits are not beneficial in any way, like anxiety, and which habits can be beneficial for us if we're mindful of the points of diminishing returns. When you're mapping in Stage Two and asking yourself, "What does it feel like to engage in this behavior?" and "What does this behavior do for me?" pay attention to where the behavior passes the tipping point of being helpful to being harmful.

STAGE THREE: UPGRADING TO A BETTER OPTION

Now that you have some clarity regarding the tipping points for your habits as you've mapped in Stage Two, you might be feeling a bit disenchanted and ready to change those habits into ones that are more productive.

To recap, we need three conditions to change a behavior. First, we have to be mindfully aware of an unproductive habit and its elements—that's Stage One. In Stage Two, we mindfully and directly experience the habit to see how it feels and what it does for us, which updates the habit's reward value. And finally, we need to offer our brain an upgrade by giving it what Dr. Brewer calls a "better option." That's Stage Three.

Stacy made her way through Stage One and Stage Two in just a few weeks; she became keenly aware of her habits of playing scared and of anxiety and understood that both made her feel like crap and only led to poor and less enjoyable golf. Let's look at each of her habits, mapped through Stage Two.

Playing Scared Habit
Trigger: Tight tee shot (usually a dogleg right).
Behavior: Making a defensive, fearful, guided swing.
(Outdated) Reward: Hopefully, "doing something" to keep the ball
    from going out of bounds.
Result:
1. What does it feel like to engage in this behavior?
   It makes me feel worried, tense, rushed, embarrassed, and heavy.
2. What am I getting from this behavior? (Or, what does this
   behavior do for me?)
   Unstable confidence, anxiety, rushed swings, feeling hopeless
   about golf going forward, making golf more difficult, making
   golf less enjoyable.

Anxiety Habit

Trigger: Thinking about an upcoming tournament.

Behavior: Anxiety via toxic rumination.

Reward: Feeling like I'm "doing something" to make sure I play well.

Result:

1. What does it feel like to engage in this behavior?
   It feels overwhelming, tense, and like I don't have enough room to breathe.

2. What am I getting from this behavior? (Or, what does this behavior do for me?)
   Unstable confidence, more uncertainty, rushed swings, making golf more difficult, making golf less enjoyable.

Here's the good news for Stacy and for us. When it comes to choosing between behaviors, our orbitofrontal cortex is like that golfer who is always swapping out one driver for another, constantly searching for something better. As we know, for a new habit to form and replace an old habit in a sustained way, the reward value must be greater than the reward value of the old habit. Given the choice between two behaviors, our brain will choose the one that has a larger reward value.

We're not looking for just any option. A better option is a specific habit that allows us to step out of an unproductive one because it feels better, works better, and doesn't continue to feed the previous habit. Distracting yourself with an alternate scoring method or by doing long division on the course won't work—because being distracted doesn't actually feel that good and doesn't address the anxiety itself. The anxiety will remain intact, and distracting ourselves taxes our brain rather quickly.

When it comes to finding a better option, it is important that we're not just looking to substitute one unproductive habit for another. Replacing cigarettes with cupcakes only creates another unproductive habit; replacing anxiety about hitting poor shots with distraction in the form of advanced math creates the same situation.

The essence of Stage Three is to offer ourselves and our brain a better option, an upgraded behavior that replaces an unproductive habit when faced with the same triggers. What could that better option be? You guessed it:

mindfulness. Specifically, we're looking for mindful behaviors from the being mode of mind that ground us in the present and/or grant us access to the present moment. They do so effectively and consistently because mindful behaviors fit two important criteria.

First, mindful behaviors are internally driven. As opposed to relying on something external that cannot be controlled, the more we respond to the same triggers with internally driven mindful behaviors, the more consistent and effective our responses can be. Because mindful behaviors are internally driven, they are always immediately accessible and never run out; thus, we can use them as often as needed and in a wide range of situations.

Second, the reward value for mindful behaviors is greater and therefore feels better than that of unproductive habits. Simply put, our brain prefers behaviors that feel better. Once the reward value for a previous habit has been lowered, our brain is designed to choose an upgrade so long as that better option feels materially better than the previous option did.

Mindful behaviors are not magic; they just need to be better than the alternatives. We can effectively substitute a mindful behavior for habits like anger, anxiety, overthinking, and self-criticism because it will feel better than all these unproductive behaviors. Specifically, behaviors from the being mode of mind feel better than those from the doing mode of mind because they allow us access to the present moment and ground us in it.

Being grounded in the present moment is a dopamine-rich state for our brain, which is why the flow state is so enjoyable and why, in the Harvard study mentioned previously, people who live more of their lives being present are happier and enjoy even mundane experiences more than those who don't.

It's worth noting that when we talk about what "feels better," we're not necessarily talking about behaviors that magically and suddenly make us feel comfortable or grant absolute certainty. We're not looking for behaviors that make us go from feeling anxious to feeling relaxed. What we're really looking for, and what mindful behaviors provide, is a sense of space.

CONSTRICTION AND SPACE

Stable confidence is *not* built on comfort or certainty. Stable confidence is built on a sense of space in the present moment and an acceptance of the uncertain future. In fact, building confidence by trying to manufacture comfort and certainty is what makes confidence unstable. Mindful behaviors create space for us to coexist with our thoughts and feelings without them dictating how we ultimately choose to act just because they exist.

On a neurological level, a sense of space feels really good to our brain, especially compared to behaviors like anxiety, overly harsh self-criticism, distraction, and anger, which all create a sense of constriction. Space is our brain being reinforced by dopamine and operating at low-frequency and low-intensity brain waves, the ones associated with flow state.

Constriction is one of our brain's evolutionary defense mechanisms that protects us from threat. Physical constriction, like tucking in our arms and legs and curling into a ball, protects us from physical harm by shielding our vital organs. Psychological and emotional constriction, like overthinking, dwelling, toxic rumination, and anxiety, are meant to avoid potential future harm.

Constriction is also an indicator that our old brain is effectively shutting down our prefrontal cortex, that it's in survival mode, and that we're at a diminished cognitive capacity. In a prehistoric world, constriction was immensely valuable, but on the golf course in the modern world, it causes us to get in our own way because that constriction, and the high-frequency and high-intensity brain waves that come with it, disrupt our brain's ability to send messages to our body for any other reason than survival.

Conversely, the sense of space that mindful behaviors create quiets the faster and stronger safety-first portions of our old brain and allows the prefrontal cortex to stay online so it can think clearly and rationally. Let's look at the difference between constriction and space in our direct experience.

Try this. Bring to mind a recent time that you were playing golf when you were overthinking, playing scared, anxious, or angry. It could be on the first tee, after a mistake, before a specific tee shot, or as a result of a missed putt. Do your best to recall enough of the experience so that you can feel it directly.

When you have that experience clear in your mind, notice what you feel in your body. Does it feel like a sense of constriction and tightness, or does it feel spacious and free?

Now bring to mind a recent time when you were playing confidently and really enjoying the game. Do your best to recall enough about that experience so that you can feel it in your body.

When you have that experience clear in your mind, notice where you feel that experience in your body. Does it feel like a sense of constriction and tightness, or does it feel spacious and free?

Once you compare your direct experiences, it's obvious why numerous research studies have concluded that we prefer space to constriction—physically, psychologically, and emotionally. And of course, every golfer in the world would prefer to play with a sense of space instead of feeling constricted. It just feels better, and that matters because our brain prefers space to constriction. Space is one of the key elements that stable confidence is built upon.

Because mindful behaviors are always accessible and have a larger reward value compared to the harmful habits we've discussed, they provide us with better options that help us step away from unproductive habits—and, over time, those mindful behaviors can eventually develop into productive habits. In the remainder of this section, I'll detail what mindful behaviors do, offer a few specific mindful behaviors, and provide structure for how we can use them.

MINDFUL BEHAVIORS

Mindful behaviors are not a quick fix, life hack, or trick for our brain. They feel and work better than unproductive habits namely because they allow us to sit in some emotional discomfort long enough for the safety-first portions of our old brain to realize that we're not in actual or unmanageable danger. Sitting outside of our comfort zone long enough creates space for our brain to realize that it doesn't need to retreat to stay safe, which is ultimately what leads to growth.

Our prehistoric brain is designed to warn us when we're moving somewhere uncertain or potentially threatening—that is, when we're moving out of our comfort zone. Remember, the survival portions of our old brain only see the world as safe or unsafe but without any real accuracy. In response to triggers and our own unproductive mental habits that it perceives as unsafe, our old brain shuts down the prefrontal cortex, which is the area of the brain that can see a middle ground between comfort and danger. That middle ground is where we find space to play freely and where we can learn and grow.

Obviously, the world and our inner experience isn't always dangerous. Hitting a golf ball out of bounds is only a threat to a scorecard and almost

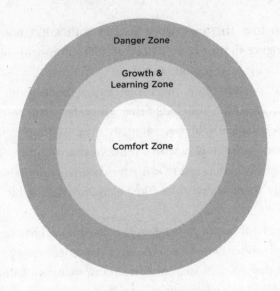

never directly threatens a golfer's physical safety. Mindful behaviors allow us to sit in discomfort long enough for our old brain to pump the brakes before resorting to shutting down the prefrontal cortex and retreating to the familiarity of anxiety, anger, and safe-but-steery swings.

Whether we're facing a difficult tee shot or our best score ever, or feeling anxious, mindful behaviors allow us to approach uncertain and unfamiliar experiences without retreating to the perceived safety of unproductive habits. As I mentioned in the previous section, the more we allow ourselves to coexist with discomfort and uncertainty, the more our comfort zone will grow, and the more we will adapt and build a tolerance for discomfort and uncertainty. On a fundamental level, this is how we learn and grow. Mindful behaviors are also the behaviors most strongly associated with those lovely low-frequency and low-intensity alpha and theta brain waves of flow state.

Let's look at two specific mindful behaviors that are internally driven, feel better than unproductive habits, create space for us to play freely, and move us into our growth zone.

BETTER OPTION: GROUNDEDNESS

Let's start with a mental behavior you're already training through your mindfulness practices: groundedness using connected breathing. In Stage Three, we are offering our brain an internally driven better option that doesn't feed our previous habits. Anything from the doing mode of mind won't work because that's already the source of many of our unproductive habits. One of the most streamlined routes to a being mode of mind is grounding ourselves through connected breathing.

When Stacy found herself feeling the first signs of anxiety—that familiar tightness in her chest and the sense that she had to answer all the "what ifs"—she offered her brain a better option by connecting with her breath in the same way that she did during her breath-centered mindfulness practice. Again, it's important to note the key difference between just breathing and taking a few connected breaths, which grounds us in the present moment by focusing on the breath itself. Breathing is something we do all the time, but connecting with our breath brings our awareness to our directly felt experience of the breath itself and serves as an anchor to our experience in the present moment, not just moving air.

Instead of falling back on her old, unproductive habits when faced with the same triggers, Stacy would connect with her breath by asking herself, "How do I know I'm breathing?" Rather than trying to force her feelings or thoughts away or trying to distract herself, Stacy would bring a mindful awareness to where and how she experienced her breath and simply observe. Because connecting with her breath to ground herself is always available, feels markedly better than being anxious, and doesn't feed her previous habits, Stacy was able to sit in some discomfort just long enough for her old brain to realize that the discomfort and uncertainty she was experiencing was not an unmanageable threat to her. She created space for her prefrontal cortex to stay online. And therein lies the space for us to be able to play a shot freely rather than play one dictated by fear and anxiety. Connecting with our breath is an anchor we can use any time we find ourselves gravitating toward unproductive habits.

You may be wondering: Why isn't groundedness through connecting with our breath just another form of distraction? I'm so glad you asked. Unlike a distraction that is trying to take us *out* of discomfort and uncertainty with avoidance and multitasking, connecting to our breath allows us to stay *in* our current experience with what we're doing, when we're doing it. Groundedness is about being in our experience, not trying to "fix," escape, or suppress it. Trying to "fix," escape, or avoid discomfort and uncertainty signals to our safety-first old brain that it's time to retreat into the familiar habits of our comfort zone.

On a basic but vital level, groundedness created by connecting with our breath brings us *into* our present experience, not out of it. Groundedness isn't about avoidance of what we're experiencing; it's about an urgency to be present but composed within it. Groundedness has a higher reward value than dwelling on the past or worrying about the future and provides the space for us to step away from unproductive behaviors instead of keeping them going. It always offers us the opportunity to shift to a being mode of mind.

Additionally, to effectively and consciously process information, our prefrontal cortex needs to be online. The psychological state where our prefrontal cortex is always online is when we are grounded in the present. When we are grounded and our prefrontal cortex is online, our subconscious decision-making—which typically accounts for 70 to 90 percent of all decision-making—decreases, while our conscious decision-making—typically accounting for less than 30 percent of all decision-making—increases. Put simply, when are grounded, we give ourselves and our brain more conscious control to make decisions intentionally rather than simply reacting habitually.

Trigger: Any external or internal trigger.

Better Option: Groundedness through connected breathing ("How do I know I'm breathing?").

Reward:
1. What does it feel like to engage in this behavior?
   More spacious than from previous habits.
2. What do I get from this behavior?
   Being present, more space to play freely, clarity of thought, conscious decision-making, and more enjoyable golf.

BETTER OPTION: CURIOSITY

Watching pro golfers play practice rounds never gets old to me. They have so much fun just trying to figure out how to best play a course. Those rounds often consist of players comparing notes, hitting shots just to see how a ball will react, and experimenting with what lines they can take off the tee. There's an exploration and a playfulness to their curiosity that allows them to learn a course in a way that is enjoyable and productive. Everything is interesting to them: good shots, bad shots, misreads, tight lies, even the grain on the greens. If you've ever been to a practice round, you've seen this. Players are laughing and usually playing great golf. There's a tournament around the corner, and yet they are fully immersed in the present moment.

My observations of such a childlike curiosity by the best golfers in the world spurred me to explore a large body of research on curiosity. As it turns out, the right kind of curiosity is one of our most rewarding and productive mindful behaviors—and a fantastically better option for us and our brain when we're looking to step out of unproductive habits like anxiety, worry, anger, or anything else keeping us from playing better golf and really enjoying the game.

When triggered by discomfort or uncertainty in any of their forms, our brain's default response is to retreat and find something it thinks is safer and more familiar. This default setting is why we develop and reinforce so many of our unproductive habits in the first place. But curiosity is different. Rather than retreating and repeating unproductive habits, mindful curiosity explores unpleasant thoughts, feelings, and external experiences in a way that disarms the safety-first portions of our old brain. In a non-judgmental way, it allows us to explore our current experiences to see them for what they are and how well they are working for us. Like composure cultivated through a connection to our breath, mindful curiosity creates enough space to quiet our default survival settings and help us step away from unproductive habits.

Curiosity is not applied through willpower. Curiosity is something we allow that brings us into our present experience as it's happening rather than distract us from it. When it comes to our unproductive habits and interacting with our inner experience, mindful curiosity has become a favorite mindful behavior of almost all of my clients, especially golfers. What they love about curiosity is that it doesn't tire them out trying to force thoughts, feelings, or habits to change. Curiosity naturally moves them forward, building their ability to be aware of their habits and navigate the challenges of competing so that they can learn both declaratively and procedurally.

But when it comes to stepping away from unproductive habits, not just any form of curiosity will do. Jordan Litman is a professor of psychology at the University of Maine at Machias, and Paul Silvia is a professor of psychology at the University of North Carolina at Greensboro. Both research curiosity and how it relates to learning and motivation. In a series of studies, Dr. Litman and Dr. Silva have identified two primary types of curiosity: deprivation curiosity and interest curiosity.

Deprivation curiosity is the type of curiosity we apply when there is a gap in information that creates a restless, unpleasant, "need to know" psychological and emotional state. In other words, deprivation curiosity creates constriction. On the other hand, interest curiosity creates an enjoyable, almost playful, and spacious investigation and thirst for knowledge. Essentially, curiosity is how we search for information and knowledge, and the type of curiosity we use will create either constriction or space.

Deprivation Curiosity

Deprivation curiosity is from the doing mode of mind and driven by uncertainty. Often, we're looking for a specific reason why something is or isn't happening as we expect or prefer it to. When we're faced with a gap in information, we have an urge to get that information so that we can feel better. For example, deprivation curiosity is the type of restless urge to fill the uncertainty you experience when you're playing trivia and you don't quite know the name of that one actress who was in that one movie; it's the restless urge we get when our phone buzzes with an alert and we find it hard to focus on what we're doing because we really want to know who the text is from. It's the same restless sense we get when we don't know why we're feeling nervous or lacking confidence—our brain starts itching to find information that will figure things out or solve the feeling of uncertainty.

Once we find the information needed to fill the gap, either by googling that actress's name or by picking up your phone to see that your friend texted you a cute puppy meme, we feel better. Deprivation curiosity urges us to find missing and uncertain information, after which we feel good because we're more certain, even if that certainty is bad news.

Have you noticed that airlines show how many minutes, or hours, a flight is delayed on the monitors in airports? That's because, to scratch the itch created by deprivation curiosity, people would rather have bad news that is certain than no news, which is uncertain. Not knowing that a flight is delayed by a half hour makes people more restless than knowing their flight is delayed by two hours. It's a bit of a "better the devil you know than the devil you don't" situation for our brain because our old brain equates the familiar predictability of bad news with safety—even though we can't ever really be certain of any potential future.

As humans, the vast majority of us have a habit of constantly trying to project the future to create a sense of predictability and certainty. Often our projection habit comes in the form of deprivation curiosity. But what if the information we seek isn't a Google search away? What if the gap in our information can't be filled? When the information we feel we *need* isn't readily available or can't be answered, deprivation curiosity keeps us restlessly searching where answers that lead to predictability and certainty can't be found. Here again we see why trying to "fix" our inner experience with a doing mode of mind doesn't work and typically makes things worse.

Interest Curiosity

As humans, our curiosity can also be piqued broadly without necessarily having to fill in some specific piece of information we're missing. Interest curiosity is a beginner's mindset driven by a desire to simply learn without a specific endpoint in mind.

In his postdoctoral research, Cardiff University senior research fellow and psychologist Matthias Gruber showed that at peak interest curiosity, dopamine centers in our brains fire with increasing intensity, leading to stronger associations with memory. Put another way, Gruber demonstrated that interest curiosity has a large reward value and helps us learn quickly and effectively.

Acquiring information through interest curiosity is a mindful behavior that works with reward-based learning. When compared to deprivation curiosity, interest curiosity feels better because it doesn't require any specific answer, comfort, or certainty for us to learn from our direct experiences. It's the difference between searching the internet for an exact answer that doesn't exist and searching the internet just to learn more about a topic in general. The latter option feels better, keeps us grounded in the present, and is a nonjudgmental means of addressing our habits by helping us learn.

Specifically, interest curiosity directed toward our unproductive habits creates a nonjudgmental space highlighting the mapping we've done in

Stage One and Stage Two. In a way, it shows our brain in a neutral tone, "Hmm, how interesting that you want to use that habit when you now know how crappy it feels and that it doesn't work anymore."

As I mentioned before, for many of the professional athletes I work with, interest curiosity has become their favorite mindful behavior and a much better option; it feels almost playful but still allows them to hold themselves accountable for their performance. When these athletes recognize that they are being triggered or are acting on an unproductive habit, they respond with, "Hmm, how interesting that I think being anxious and playing scared are actually going to make me play better when they make me feel tense and play hesitant, steery shots." Interest curiosity brings their focus to the present in a way that allows them to connect with their performance as it's happening and creates enough space for them to execute more freely. It takes some time and repetition, but most are surprised at how quickly their established, unproductive habits begin to seem almost silly when they bring a mindful interest curiosity to them.

PLAYING IN THE RAIN

Now let's put interest curiosity into a tangible, practical structure. If you've mindfully mapped your habits in Stages One and Two, your brain is ready for an upgrade to a better option. Here's a simple and structured approach to applying interest curiosity. The RAIN method was developed by meditation teacher and mindfulness expert Michele McDonald and provides a simple and practical structure for addressing our habits with interest curiosity; the following is an adaptation of the method to match what we have discussed.

Recognize

Everything starts with awareness because awareness is the first line of information processing for us and our brains. RAIN begins by being aware of triggers, behaviors, or our unproductive habits. Think of this like Stage One mapping; we're seeing our habits and their elements before or as they are happening.

Accept

Rather than trying to ignore, fix, force, suppress, will, or distract ourselves from our thoughts, feelings, or habits, we accept them nonjudgmentally—but without treating them as facts or something we *must* engage with. Acceptance is what gives our old brain enough time to understand that we're not in danger so it can calm down and let our prefrontal cortex stay online. Acceptance is also a mindful behavior that we will discuss more in the next section.

Interest (Curiosity)

Rather than letting a habit simply keep going or trying to wrestle with it, we inject interest curiosity. We nonjudgmentally point out to ourselves that we're applying a behavior that feels crappy and doesn't work. Specifically, we use the phrase "Hmm, how interesting that I think_____ will_____ when what it really does is_____." For example: "Hmm, how interesting that I think complaining about having a terrible lie is helpful when all complaining does is make it harder for me to play the shot I'm faced with."

Interest curiosity simply and effectively observes our triggers and behaviors and reminds us of what we've mapped in Stage Two. It nonjudgmentally recalls what a behavior feels like and what we're getting from it. In short, it reminds our brain of the updated reward value for a habit while also offering it a better option.

For Stacy's anxiety habit, her phrase looked like: "Hmm, how interesting that I think toxic rumination while playing tournament golf will create confidence when what it really does is make me feel anxious and lead to more uncertainty."

For Stacy's playing-scared habit, her phrase looked like: "Hmm, how interesting that I think playing a scared, steery, guided tee shot will help me play this hole better when what it really does is make me feel like I'm wasting my ability and result in worse tee shots."

Now

Notice how recognition, acceptance, and interest curiosity allow our prefrontal cortex to stay online or come back online sooner, creating a sense of space for us to make clear decisions and committed swings. Rather than trying to force ourselves to "not think" or "just trust," we have space to step away from unproductive habits by shifting our focus to the present moment and our performance as it's happening now.

Taking yourself through the RAIN method when you notice the triggers and behaviors you want to step away from is quick and simple, but it does require you to have effectively mapped your habits in Stage One and Stage Two. And like a connected breath, the more you practice and use it, the shorter the process will become. Eventually, RAIN can become a habit itself that you can use anytime: before a round, on the course, in response to the ups and downs of golf, or whenever you notice you're in a habit that isn't productive for you. Here are a few responses from some of my clients who have used RAIN.

Sitting in discomfort by being curious is getting easier than before. That in and of itself feels awesome. I haven't gone into anxiety or feeling bad for myself when I get uncomfortable like I did when I played scared. It's a totally different experience. There's so much space compared to before, I don't know what to do with it all.

—PGA Tour Player

I'm so proud of how I played today and how I managed myself on the golf course. I started with a rough patch with the putter, but instead of letting my inner dialogue get harsh and critical, I got curious instead, and it was almost like it was so easy to see how that wouldn't work, and I could focus on hitting good shots. For the rest of the round, I putted freely and holed a few crucial putts. HUGE PROGRESS!!

R—Missed a three-footer in the final pairing.

A—Accept it and the frustration I feel.

I—"Hmm, how curious that I think telling myself how awful I am at putting will make me feel more confident and help me make more putts when really it feels terrible and leads to hesitant strokes."

N—Connect with my breath and focus on playing the next putt how I want to.

—LPGA Tour Player

Recognize—That I'm practicing to make myself feel better (rather than practicing to get better) by just searching aimlessly for a feeling with my driver.

Accept—Yep, that's what I was doing, but it's not something that I must do.

Interest—"Hmm, how interesting that right before a tournament I start searching for the perfect feeling to make me confident with my driver when that only makes me less confident and less comfortable with my driver, especially since I've been hitting it well."

Now—Ground myself and focus on the fundamentals that I've built my swing on.

—Division I College Golfer

RAIN

Recognize—Identify the triggers or behaviors of an unproductive habit.
Accept—Sit in your current experience without trying to fight it or ignore it.
Interest (Curiosity)—Nonjudgmentally get curious about your habit and what it does for you.
Now—Refocus on your performance as it's happening.

Let's look at what interest curiosity sounds like for the earlier example habits of some other players.

Overthinking Habit (Division I College Player)
Recognize—My habitual reaction to making one or two bad swings.
Accept—Okay, I'm starting to overthink. That's been my habit.
Interest—"Hmm, how interesting that I feel like thinking more and more will make me more confident and help me fix my swing when what it really does is make me feel less confident and make my

swing instantly worse because I'm overthinking something I can do in my sleep."

Now—That swing is over. This swing is now. See the target and react, then see what happens.

Self-Criticism Habit (PGA Tour Player)

Recognize—When I don't play well and when I start crushing myself for it.

Accept—Be willing to experience my thoughts as just thoughts, even harsh ones.

Interest—"Hmm, how interesting that I continue to scold myself like I'm a child when all that does is make me more angry, hopeless, and worried, which isn't in any way making things better for me."

Now—How about I focus on what I can do right now instead of crushing myself for something that has already happened?

Panic-Practice Habit (LPGA Tour Player)

Recognize—Being triggered by a poor round of golf or practicing to alleviate frustration.

Accept—Sit with the discomfort of having a poor round.

Interest—"Hmm, how interesting that I think hitting balls through frustration and without any structure will fix a poor round and help me get better and play better tomorrow when it just makes me second-guess myself more."

Now—Connect with my breath and get back to a fundamental drill my coach and I know works.

Dwelling Habit (Division I College Player)

Recognize—Making a mistake and continuing to dwell on it.

Accept—Allow myself to see dwelling on a mistake as just thoughts *about* a past event.

Interest—"Hmm, how interesting that I think dwelling on a mistake will fix something that's already happened and help me avoid making mistakes in the future when it can't do either and just makes it harder for me to focus on my next shot, which usually leads to more mistakes."

Now—Choose to let go of the mistake and focus on playing a committed shot now.

Blaming Habit (PGA Tour Player)

Recognize—Blaming, complaining, and making excuses for not playing well or getting the outcomes I want.

Accept—Okay, I'm doing the same thing again, but it's not something I have to do.

Interest—"Hmm, how interesting that I think blaming others, complaining about the course, and making excuses is going to help make a crappy situation better when really it only makes me feel worse about my abilities, causes me to play worse, and makes me less enjoyable to be around."

Now—Be present and consider what I can do right now to get better, play better, and move my career forward.

Comparing Habit (PGA Tour Player)

Recognize—When I'm at the tipping point where I'm paying more attention to other players' games than to my own.

Accept—Okay, you're comparing yourself to others to try to build confidence.

Interest—"Hmm, how interesting that I think comparing my game to other players' and focusing on what they do will help me play better and build stable confidence in my game when what that really does is make me question my own strengths, feel jealous of others, and start trying to do what other players are doing."

Now—Focus on what I can do right now to improve what I do to play my game.

A quick note about the habit of comparing ourselves to other people. Karen Pine is an author and a professor at the University of Hertfordshire. In a study where she surveyed five thousand people, including athletes, she found that of all the productive habits identified as being keys to a more fulfilling and high-performing life, self-acceptance was the most predictive habit of satisfaction and more stable confidence. The same study revealed that despite self-acceptance being perhaps the most valuable habit we can learn and reinforce, the vast majority of people reported habitually comparing themselves to others.

Control Habit (LPGA Tour Player)

Recognize—Feeling out of control and focusing on things that I can't actually control—scores, mostly.

Accept—Be willing to sit with the frustration and feeling that I'm not in control.

Interest—"Hmm, how interesting that I think trying to control scores that have either already happened or haven't happened yet and that I can't control will give me a sense of control and help me play better right now when what it really does is make me feel like I don't have any control.

Now—Ask myself, "What can I control right now that will actually give me some control?"

Worry Habit (PGA Tour Player)

Recognize—The feeling of not wanting others to judge me negatively.

Accept—Acknowledge this worrying habit and what it feels like without trying to do anything to fix it.

Interest—"Hmm, how interesting that I think asking myself 'What if' a million times will actually lead to an answer that makes me stop worrying when it's literally never, ever done that and has only made me worry more."

Now—Be present with what I'm doing now.

Protect Your Score Habit (Division I College Golfer)

Recognize—Being on pace for a great score and feeling like I need to protect it.

Accept—Understand that the feeling that ruining a great round would be a failure is just a thought about the future; it hasn't actually happened.

Interest—"Hmm, how interesting that I think playing to not ruin a
   great score will keep me from ruining a great round when that's
   exactly what it does. It feels like a total waste to hold back my best
   golf in favor of playing some average golf."

Now—Focus on playing the next shot how I want to play it and not
   how my habit dictates that I should play it.

Entitlement Habit (Division I College Golfer)

Recognize—Feeling that I should get selected by a team and play as
   well as I want just because I want to.

Accept—That I want what I want and that I'm not going to get
   selected and play better just because I feel like I should.

Interest—"Hmm, how interesting that I think things that are earned and
   sometimes unfair should happen just because I want them to when
   doing so makes me a less likeable person to my team and coaches."

Now—What can I apply effort to right now to get better and that will
   actually move me toward getting selected instead of pouting about
   my circumstances?

Some players I work with also find it beneficial to map out a habit in all
three stages with a mindful behavior as a better option to help expand their
RAIN process. Full mapping allows them to think through how they want to
apply this process and simplify it on the course. Here's an example of a fully
mapped impatience habit from an LPGA Tour player.

Impatience with the Speed of Change Habit

Trigger: Change happening slower than I feel it "should" happen.

Behavior: Impatience, worry, tension, frustration, anger, jumping from
   drill to drill looking for a quick fix.

(Outdated) Reward: Hopefully, the familiar feeling that I'm "doing
   something" to make a change.

Result:

1. What does it feel like to engage in this behavior?
    It makes me feel like I'm totally lost, have no bearing of where
    I am, and am more confused.

Better Option: Coexist with the discomfort and be patient in it. Stick with the change because it is a better way of doing something. Accept the pain and frustration that comes along with making changes; otherwise, nothing will change. My thoughts about the outcomes are just thoughts about the outcomes. They are not themselves the mechanisms for change, just thoughts about how fast and easy I think change "should" be.

OLD HABITS TO NEW HABITS

As we've seen throughout this section, our habits have a profound impact on how we play golf and how much we enjoy the game. You may also be noticing that our unproductive habits have some obvious commonalities in that they tend to stem from the doing mode of mind, take us out of the present moment, create high-frequency and high-intensity brain waves that disrupt our physical skills, and create constriction and perceived threat.

Conversely, you may also be starting to notice that mindful behaviors are better options because they stem from the being mode of mind, allow us access to the present moment, and ground us in it. Being grounded in the present feels better to our brain, as evidenced by the low-frequency and low-intensity brain waves and the sense of space that mindful behaviors create.

Regardless of what mental or physical habits you have right now, if they don't work for you now, they can be upgraded. Taking a mindful approach works with how your brain learned your habits in the first place and uses the same reward-based learning to learn new habits that feel better and work better. You might be surprised at how quickly a mindful approach makes old habits outdated and urges us toward new habits that are more aligned with the golf experience we want to have.

Unproductive Behaviors/Habits	Better Option: Mindful Behaviors
Anything from the doing mode of mind	Anything from the being mode of mind
Avoidance	Groundedness
Anxiety	Interest curiosity
Dwelling	Acceptance
Distraction	Personal values
Willpower	
Overthinking	(More on acceptance and personal values in the next section, "Framework")
Rumination	
Panic-practicing	
Impatience	
Overly harsh self-criticism	
Attempting to create certainty	
Deprivation curiosity	
Prolonged and intense anger	
Attempting to control outcomes	
Comparing to others	
Complaining/blaming/making excuses	
Entitlement	
Steery, guided, forced strokes and swings	
What do we feel when we engage in these behaviors/habits?	**What do we feel when we engage in these behaviors/habits?**
All the downsides of the doing mode of mind	All the benefits of the being mode of mind
Constricted	Spacious
Threatened	Accepting
Fearful	Composed
Frustrated	Strong, like persisting
Without control	Undeterred
Trapped	Motivated
Confused	
Weak, like giving up	
Overwhelmed	

What do we get from these behaviors/habits?	What do we get from these behaviors/habits?
Fear of failure	More stable confidence
Tension	Composure
Second-guessing	Clarity
Being off time	Groundedness
More mistakes	Fewer mistakes
Habitual/subconscious decision-making	Intentional/conscious decision-making
A less fun golf experience	A more enjoyable golf experience
Hindered learning and progress; a retreat to our comfort zone	Accelerated learning and progress; entering our growth zone
High-frequency and high-intensity brain waves (farther from flow state)	Low-frequency and low-intensity brain waves (closer to flow state)
More unproductive echo habits	More mindful behaviors as echo habits
Further reinforcement of unproductive habits	Further reinforcement of mindful behaviors

SECTION 4

Framework

So far, we've introduced groundedness through connected breathing and interest curiosity as mindful behaviors and better options. In this section, we'll discuss a few other mindful behaviors in the context of our psychological framework. Our habits are born from reward-based learning, but they are raised by our beliefs. Stepping away from unproductive habits like anxiety or playing scared is more difficult when our psychological framework is constructed in a way that reinforces them. On the other hand, beliefs that reinforce productive habits build stable confidence and allow us to play freely more often.

STABLE CONFIDENCE

Stable confidence is one of the most sought-after elements of golf. Look at any driving range, golf lesson, magazine, or clinic, and you'll see golfers trying to find confidence in any number of ways. Some golfers seek confidence in rituals or superstitions. Some get pep talks and positive affirmations from a coach, a teammate, or themselves. Some meticulously tinker with their equipment. Some take the "fake it till you make it" approach. Some resort to toxic rumination and overthinking, while others conjure up images of past successes to stoke their confidence. Some seek confidence by comparing themselves to others, and some try to simply convince themselves just how good they are.

There are few stones left unturned by golfers of all levels in search of confidence. But the cruel irony is that the more stones we turn over, the less stable our confidence becomes. Constantly searching for stable confidence in these unstable sources creates a never-ending search to find something where it can't be found.

And yet, there are some golfers who aren't searching for confidence by grasping at straws. To those still turning over stones, players with stable confidence are deemed the "lucky ones," making them the envy of those who want what they have. But these few golfers with stable confidence aren't privy to a secret or some special genetic code. Rather, in one way or another, they have come to an accurate understanding of what stable confidence is, where it comes from, and what it does—and thus, they know how to create and sustain it.

WHAT STABLE CONFIDENCE IS . . . AND ISN'T

So why do most people go to, and continuously return to, unstable methods of building confidence? It's simple: the most common notions about confidence are mistaken.

When researchers asked people to briefly define confidence, these were the most common ideas that were shared: being certain and assured of outcomes, being comfortable, how easy something is, unwavering positivity, unwavering positive beliefs, acting confident, the result of past positive outcomes, lofty goals, arrogance, and being outspoken. But none of these provide an accurate definition of stable confidence.

Stable confidence is *not* built upon comfort, certainty, assuredness, absolute predictability, ease, blanket positivity, or arrogance. Stable confidence does *not* come from past results, unyielding beliefs, lofty goals, or outspokenness. And most certainly, stable confidence *cannot* be made by being faked. Stable confidence is a credible sense of space in the present moment and a willing acceptance of an uncertain future.

Consider how confident you are when you get into your car and drive to another location, assuming you're of driving age. You've driven countless times before, so you have a certain level of established driving skill. Although the average road leaves less than two feet of space on either side of your vehicle, I'll venture a guess that that's enough space for you to effectively execute your driving ability to get where you want to go, even though driving inherently involves some risk. Making mistakes while driving can come with some undesired consequences, but I'll surmise you're willing to accept the risk that you may drift from your lane every now and then.

In short, you understand that there's limited space on the road and that there's some calculated risk getting behind the wheel. Still, you believe there is enough space for you to drive freely, and you willingly accept the potential consequences. With this combination of space to drive and acceptance of uncertainty, you have all the stable confidence you need to drive.

Now consider how confident you'd be if, instead of the standard space on either side of your car, the lanes were only as wide as your car and not an inch wider. Additionally, if you were to veer outside your lane even in the slightest, a river of molten lava would await you on either side. You'd still have the same level of driving experience and skill, but, with no space to maneuver within your lane, you'd probably feel significant constriction. Instead of a willingness to accept the consequences of going outside your razor-thin margin for error, you'd be doing all you can to avoid a future that includes boiling in lava. Instead of being confident, you'd understandably be hesitant and anxious, and you'd drive in an overly protective way.

The difference between these two imaginary driving scenarios demonstrates what stable confidence is, where it comes from, and what it does. Our thoughts are not unlike the width of a hypothetical road or the consequences of drifting from that road. Thoughts like *I have to be perfect* constrict the space we give ourselves to maneuver and compete within. At the same time, when our thoughts create a future filled with overly threatening consequences, we become unwilling to accept that potential future and will behave in ways to protect ourselves from it. Thoughts like *I have to make every putt inside five feet, and if I don't, that proves I'm a terrible player* provide almost no margin for error to avoid a future that no golfer wants to accept. With constricting and threatening thoughts, confidence is rendered unstable, even for skilled, experienced, and accomplished golfers.

WHERE STABLE CONFIDENCE COMES FROM

Just like our hypothetical overly narrow road and consequence of certain death, our thoughts—specifically our beliefs—can constrict us in the present moment and create a future threatening enough that our priority becomes protecting ourselves from what we don't want to happen. This makes it almost impossible to play freely. On the other hand, our thoughts can create space in the present and project a future we are willing to accept, even if it's uncertain and includes discomfort: that's stable confidence. Stable confidence comes from thinking in ways that create credible space for us to execute our skills in the present moment, even if we're uncomfortable, and project a future that we are willing to accept, even if that future isn't quite what we want.

One of the reasons why all the stone-turning methods don't work in any sustainable ways is because none of them are sources of *stable* confidence. Several research studies have examined the most common approaches to building confidence, finding again and again just how unstable confidence is when built from unstable sources. The confidence built through the most common approaches may initially produce a sense of comfort and certainty, but that fragile confidence won't hold up when tested under pressure and replicated across different settings and more challenging conditions. Riddled with inherent instability, the most commonly utilized methods for building confidence are the fool's-gold versions of confidence, looking and feeling like confidence at first glance but lacking any substance and lasting value.

Contrary to popular belief, the most stable source of confidence is a credible inner dialogue. As humans, we are always having a conversation with ourselves. The ongoing personal conversation with yourself, the running commentary about you, is your inner dialogue. Our inner dialogue is how we hear and talk to ourselves through our thoughts.

Having a credible inner dialogue means that when you say something to yourself, it's meaningful and makes sense to you, and you can believe it. As we discussed in the second section, events and experiences don't directly make us feel anything—it's what we tell ourselves *about* events that make us feel what we feel. Confidence is a feeling and therefore is created and sustained (or not sustained) by our thoughts. Thus, the most stable source of confidence is a credible conversation with ourselves.

WHAT STABLE CONFIDENCE DOES

Another reason many people struggle to build stable confidence is because they don't know what stable confidence does. Stable confidence doesn't necessarily make us more comfortable or certain, and it doesn't guarantee that we won't make mistakes or fail. Stable confidence doesn't entirely protect us from emotional discomfort, nor does it protect us from being unsatisfied with our performance or being judged by others. What stable confidence does is give us credible permission to play freely, knowing there are no guarantees.

Growth, progress, and our best performances happen at metaphorical forks in the road, what psychologists call "choice points." Choice points test how you've trained your mind, body, and golf game. At these choice points, we either go for what we want or protect ourselves from what we don't. We invest time, energy, effort, and part of ourselves into pursuing what's meaningful to us, but there are no guarantees that our investments will pay off. We all face choice points where there are many actions we can take, but the simple truth is that we can either intentionally choose actions to pursue or default to actions that avoid unfavorable consequences. What stable confidence does is give us permission to step forward and pursue what we want, knowing that our best efforts may still not be enough to assure success.

The difference between how most golfers perform on the range versus in competition highlights the difference between unstable and stable confidence and what it does. On the range, it's easy to give ourselves permission to swing freely. Using our road analogy from before, the range is just about as wide of a road as we can find, with essentially no consequences for mistakes. On the range, we don't have to perform on command, so a less credible inner dialogue and unstable confidence will suffice.

But the road narrows as soon as we arrive on the first tee and there are tangible consequences of success and failure. In competition, scores count. There are people who win and people who lose. Playing a round of golf has choice points built into it that the driving range and practice rounds don't. Moments like the first shot of a round, a missed short putt, realizing you just made three birdies in a row, realizing you're on your way to a personal-best score with a few holes left, or having to make a putt to stay in a match are all moments that require far more stable confidence than on the driving range.

At these choice points, we can try to avoid failure or try to pursue success, knowing there is no guarantee that things will go how we want. It's as simple as that. Standing at meaningful choice points, when results matter, we can either stay where we are and protect ourselves from mistakes, failures, uncertainty, and emotional discomfort, or we can step forward to have a chance to experience the thrill of competing authentically in pursuit of the results we want.

To be clear, I'm not talking about cutting every corner off the tee or firing at every tucked pin or using any specific course strategy, per se. The shots you choose and the way you manage the course are up to you. This book is not about course management and when to take conservative or aggressive targets. I'm talking about the difference between playing scared and playing freely. Playing freely means playing shots with the intention of playing the best shot you can rather than trying to protect yourself from mistakes. Unstable confidence is why even the best players in the world make swings that try not to hit the ball somewhere instead of trying to play the ball where they want it to go.

As you might expect, stable confidence also impacts how our brain responds to choice points where results matter but are uncertain. For those with unstable confidence, brain activity in competitive conditions looks quite different from that in low-stakes environments. Although the same physical skills are required to be successful in both environments, our brain knows the difference between playing a practice round or hitting balls on the driving range and playing when the score counts. There's no amount of willpower, distraction, or positive affirmation telling us a first tee shot is the same as the shot we just hit on the driving range that can credibly convince our brain that the two shots are the same. Stable confidence is required for our brain to honestly acknowledge that they are indeed different—and it allows us to play freely regardless.

There's a certain level of vulnerability at choice points because there is always a risk that we may fall short. At these moments, our safety net often tells us to avoid failure, play it safe, hold back, soften the blow of potential disappointment or embarrassment, and guard our ego and self-esteem. As we've seen reviewing our unproductive habits, the cruel irony is that the more we try to protect ourselves from falling short, the more we ensure that our efforts will come up short. We typically default to thoughts and behaviors that seek comfort and certainty. That's the deprivation of the doing mode of mind. Even worse, the more we try to avoid failure when we come to choice points, the more avoiding failure will become a familiar and ingrained habit we'll return to whenever we face similar situations.

As you've seen so far, the most common methods for building confidence don't do what stable confidence does: give us credible permission to execute our skills how we want to when it counts but when there are also no guarantees. At some point, every golfer is faced with the question: What if my best isn't good enough? Stable confidence allows us to accept the risk of failure so that we can freely pursue success. That permission is not granted unless we've built a psychological framework that generates an inner dialogue credible enough to answer such a fundamental and existential question.

To illustrate how a credible inner dialogue is the primary source of stable confidence, let's look at one of the most common and most famous methods of seeking confidence: faking it until you make it.

MYTH: JUST FAKE IT TILL YOU MAKE IT

In 2012, Harvard researcher Amy Cuddy gave a TED Talk titled "Your Body Language May Shape Who You Are." In her talk, Dr. Cuddy detailed her research asking people to pose with open body language and an upright posture for a period of time. The pose would be a stance similar to what a superhero might have when showing up to save the day, standing upright with their hands on their hips. Her assertion was that body language in the form of a "power pose" communicates to our brain that we are powerful and therefore builds confidence in the now-famous "fake it till you make it" approach.

What she found in her initial research was that people did indeed act more confidently this way. This "act confident to be confident" approach became wildly popular because it appealed to many people looking for a quick and easy way to create confidence. Imagine how great it would be if all you had to do was stand like a superhero for a few minutes to have the confidence to play freely anywhere, under any conditions, and against anyone. The idea was so captivating, Dr. Cuddy's TED Talk went viral across multiple platforms and news outlets and has more than 65 million views to date.

If you're thinking that the "fake it till you make it" approach seems too good to be true, you're right. When researchers replicated Dr. Cuddy's studies eleven different times under a range of conditions and with larger sample sizes, every study found that acting confident doesn't work as Dr. Cuddy's initial research suggested. Michigan State University psychology professor Joseph Cesario reviewed the studies replicating the "fake it till you make it" approach popular with so many people, and after his review, he concluded that faking confidence leads to a brief sense of comfort before leaving people feeling even less confident than before.

The rise and fall of the "fake it till you make it" approach exemplifies why so many people, especially golfers, are constantly searching for confidence. There are so many things we repeatedly do that fool us into thinking that they build stable confidence. They look and feel like the real thing initially, but they don't cultivate the confidence we can use when we really need it.

Faking confidence leaves people with less stable confidence than before because simply changing your body language is surface-level psychology that does not address the source of where stable confidence comes from: a credible inner dialogue. Faking body language lacks credibility. No matter how much confidence you fake or what superhero you emulate, you'll know you're lying to yourself.

Positive affirmations, tinkering, toxic rumination, comparisons to others, and recalling past successes are equally unstable sources of confidence. They tend to make us feel a sense of confidence, but only temporarily. Studies observing brain activity and brain chemistry show that positive affirmations activate pleasure centers in the brain and produce a quick flood of neurotransmitters and hormones—dopamine and serotonin, to be exact. The same reactions happen when setting goals, reliving past successes, faking confidence, and comparing ourselves favorably to others. Unlike mindful behaviors, each of these methods produces brain activity and a chemical rush that fades away quickly once our skills are tested under meaningful or difficult conditions.

Being assured of outcomes and being comfortable don't build stable confidence because they cannot be credibly guaranteed. Let's face it: sometimes even good shots don't go well, sometimes we're confused about what to do, and sometimes golf makes us intensely uncomfortable. These methods quickly and easily stop being credible once they reach a point where we know we're not being honest with ourselves about our current reality, our current ability, or what we can truthfully be certain about.

If previous accomplishments built stable confidence, all anyone would have to do is be successful once to be confident enough to continue to produce successful results forever. Clearly, this isn't the case. Being successful in the past is in no way a guarantee of success in the future. The same limitation holds true for future goals. Lofty goals are just ideas of desired future outcomes and are in no way a guarantee that those ideas will come to fruition. They feel good to create, but they ultimately lack credibility when the rubber hits the road because they can't be assured.

Comparing ourselves to other golfers is perhaps the least stable source of confidence. The more competitive the level of golf becomes, the less likely it is that we can credibly and favorably compare ourselves to others. The differences between the best golfers in the world are razor-thin. In any given tournament, there are many golfers who are good enough to win. Even the top-ranked golfers in the world can't look down the range or at the leaderboard, compare themselves to all other golfers, and always credibly tell themselves, "I'm the best player here; therefore, I can be confident." The smaller the differences in skill between players, the less credible the comparison to others becomes, making the confidence built on that comparison unstable.

We can see why building stable confidence comes with great difficulty for many players. They're trying to build stable confidence using unstable sources, namely different versions of comfort and certainty, because they don't have an accurate understanding of what they're building or where to build from. Only an inner dialogue that credibly creates space in the present and a willingly accepted future builds stable confidence.

Our inner dialogue is the spokesperson for our beliefs, perceptions, and explanatory styles. Now that we have an accurate definition of stable confidence, where it comes from, and what it does, we'll explore our beliefs and the thoughts they produce. We'll look at what that work entails, how to evaluate our beliefs, and how to build an inner dialogue that creates more credible space in the present moment and a willingness to accept an uncertain future.

PSYCHOLOGICAL FRAMEWORK

Our psychological framework is our collection of thoughts, assumptions, mental images, ideas, perceptions, and beliefs, both conscious and implicit. It is a subjective rendering of the events and experiences of our lives, dictating what they mean to us. Your psychological framework is how you understand yourself, your life, and the world around you, including your golf game. While many components make up our psychological framework, chief among them is our beliefs.

Beliefs are a person's most central ideas. More specifically, our beliefs are our most central ideas *about* the events and experiences of our lives. Along with our direct experiences, our beliefs are perhaps the strongest force behind why and how we do what we do because they determine what events and experiences mean to us. Beliefs act as a lens through which we interpret the world around us: they strongly influence our priorities and values; direct our focus; and generate our inner dialogue, all of which ultimately guide our behaviors. Some beliefs empower us and promote things like stable confidence and resilience. However, we can also develop beliefs that create self-imposed limitations, like fear of failure and entitlement.

On a basic level, the purpose of a belief is to produce and reinforce behaviors, both mental and physical. Therefore, different beliefs produce and reinforce different behaviors. Differing beliefs is why people can interpret and respond to the same event with a variety of different reactions. For example, people will have different responses to a breakup with a romantic partner or to the results of an election, just as they may have differing responses to things like a missed putt or teeing off in front of a crowd.

For any situation or event, our beliefs help us make sense of the world by answering two questions: What does this mean, and, more specifically, what does this mean about me? That meaning heavily impacts how stable our confidence will be and how we will act in situations where stable confidence is required. Thus, our beliefs are one of the primary sources of our actions, thoughts, and feelings—including confidence.

BELIEFS

Beliefs and perceptions work in tandem to drive our thoughts, emotions, and behaviors. For example, if we believe that being embarrassed in front of other people is the worst thing that could ever happen to us, a significant level of anxiety and perceived threat will be triggered if we do anything in front of other people. That anxiety will make it much more likely that we'll behave in ways to avoid embarrassment instead of performing freely. You've likely seen this play out in your golf game at some point—if you believe that missing short putts means you're a terrible putter, you'll perceive missed short putts, or even just the idea of missing a short putt, as threatening and constricting. These thoughts will gear you toward trying not to make mistakes instead of putting as best as you can, especially in front of other people. Here we can see how our beliefs determine which events will be triggering to us and which behaviors will get reinforced into habits.

This interplay between our beliefs and behaviors is why our psychological framework runs the show behind the scenes for everything we do, including playing golf, and why we don't have a choice in the matter. Nature and nurture pale in comparison to the immeasurable influence of our beliefs.

You could be the most talented golfer in the world with all the physical attributes that greatness requires and have been flawlessly nurtured by the best coaches and trainers your whole career—but if your core belief is "I absolutely cannot fail because, if I do, it will mean that I have wasted my life," there's no amount of nature or nurture that will counterbalance the fear of failure and the self-sabotaging behaviors that your belief will generate. Make no mistake, you will be extremely motivated. But over time and under pressure, the constriction and perceived threat that this belief creates will motivate you to avoid failure and almost never give yourself permission to play freely when results matter to you. Just as importantly, even if a belief like this is flat-out untrue, it will still shape how we see ourselves, the world, and our golf game if we treat it as truth. Our beliefs are powerful enough that they don't even have to be correct to take effect.

MYTH: PERCEPTION IS REALITY

You may have heard that "perception is reality." It isn't. Perception is perception and reality is reality. As fast and strong as our supercomputer human brain is, the amount of information, specifically sensory information, available to us is overwhelming. This is especially true in stressful and pressure-filled environments, when our young brain can't consciously process all the information coming at us without being overloaded and overworked. Our young brain must filter out information that it perceives isn't relevant or valuable enough to take up precious processing time. As a result, what registers to our conscious mind isn't ever the whole picture or what makes up actual reality around us or even within us. Instead, what we experience is a subjectively curated portrait of what we've trained our mind to perceive as meaningful, most notably through our beliefs.

So perception is not reality; it's a subjective rendering of reality based on what we *believe* to be true, not necessarily what is actually true. You may be asking: How do we come to believe things that aren't true? I'm so glad you asked. There are two primary reasons. First, we are not born with beliefs. Beliefs are learned mostly while we're children trying to make sense of the world. The majority of our beliefs are adopted through the most consistent and intense words and actions of the adults in our lives, as well as from our own early and ongoing responses to our direct experiences.

For example, at one point in your life you may have believed that a jolly, fat man shimmied his way down your chimney every Christmas to deliver presents based on whether you were a good boy or girl. Or you might have believed that every time you lost a tooth, a magical fairy in a tutu replaced your teeth with money while you slept—that is, assuming she could get past the monster you believed was living under your bed. We learned those beliefs because someone else told us they were true. Those messages then gained credibility with consistent actions, traditions, and our own thought patterns about them. And for a period of our lives, we had beliefs *about* a jolly, fat man or a nocturnal fairy or a scary monster that we perceived were absolutely true, even though they weren't.

We learn other inaccurate, although less magical, beliefs in the same way. Just as we came to believe that Santa, the Tooth Fairy, and the monster under the bed were real, we can also learn to believe that anything less than perfect isn't good enough, that other people's opinions of us are worth more than our own, or that our golf game reflects our self-worth. Therefore, it's important to understand that just because a belief exists doesn't mean it's true. Moreover, beliefs aren't true just because a belief persists.

The second reason we learn to believe things that aren't true is that the more we buy into our own beliefs, the stronger they become. Strengthening our established beliefs is part of a process called "confirmation bias," our strong tendency to subjectively search for, interpret, prioritize, favor, and recall information in ways that confirm and support what we already believe while at the same time subjectively devaluing, dismissing, ignoring, and overlooking information that disputes our current beliefs and lends evidence to different ones.

Through confirmation bias, we favor and interpret things like presents under a tree on Christmas morning or a silver dollar under our pillow as evidence that Santa and the Tooth Fairy exist and are doing exactly what we were told they would. However, at the same time, we overlook information like how we never directly see Santa or the Tooth Fairy because, conveniently, they only come around while we're sleeping. We look for and favor indirect and subjective evidence to confirm what we already believe instead of the objective and direct evidence to the contrary.

Confirmation biases play out in our beliefs about anything, including ourselves and our golf game. Just as we might fortify our beliefs that Santa and the Tooth Fairy are real, we might also strengthen our resolve with beliefs like "I must never hit bad shots because that would mean I'm a bad golfer." Through the lens of this belief, nerves aren't just a feeling, a wayward drive isn't just one shot in a round of many shots, and a misjudged wedge shot isn't just a shot that went longer or shorter than intended. They are interpreted as mounting evidence to confirm what we already believe *about* what mistakes mean for us personally. Regardless of our belief or how accurate it is, we are far more likely to strengthen our established beliefs than to develop newer, beneficial beliefs unless we intentionally stop to mindfully examine and evaluate them.

Perception is not reality because much of what we perceive is rooted in our beliefs, making them subject to the same learned inaccuracies and confirmation biases. Regardless of how real they may directly *feel* to us, our perceptions are not necessarily reality. Studies that test how accurately we assess risk, perceive changes in our environment, and predict future events repeatedly show that as humans, we are not nearly as astute with our perceptions as we think we are. In fact, we tend to grossly overestimate how likely negative events are to happen and how bad the consequences will be when they do.

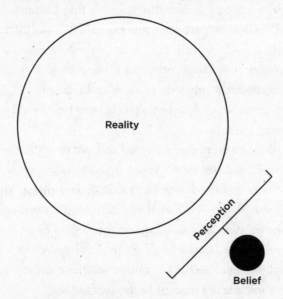

As inaccurate as our perceptions can be, they still matter. As humans, when we perceive a threat to be minimal or manageable, we are inclined to give ourselves permission to take the calculated risks required to pursue what we want. With a low or manageable level of perceived threat, we are motivated to thrive. Conversely, like every other animal, we act defensively when we perceive a significant or unmanageable level of threat. When the perceived threat level is too high, we prioritize surviving over thriving, and when we come to choice points, we opt for the safety net.

Like our habits, nothing in our psychological framework is random. Everything within it has been learned and reinforced. Thus, hoping our beliefs will randomly fall in line and build stable confidence without our intentionally examining them is a hit-and-hope strategy. It leads to unstable confidence far more often than not. Chances are we'll learn and reinforce beliefs that are inaccurate and overly biased, making it more likely for us to learn to perceive something as threatening when it isn't. For example, when people are surveyed about what they fear most, people generally fear public speaking more than anything else. And sure, public speaking comes with some risk of embarrassing yourself in front of others, but it most certainly poses far less threat than death itself, which usually ranks around fifth on the list of what people fear most. While even the deepest sense of embarrassment is not as threatening as death is, the *belief* that it is creates a *perception* that it is. This perception leads to patterns of thought that create anxiety about public speaking.

Our brains respond directly to what we believe, and our psychological framework is the engine that drives much of our life and golf game, more so than nature or nurture because our beliefs don't have to be rooted in reality to impact our direct experiences with anything. You can see why there's no pre-shot routine, positive affirmation, or "fake it till you make it" approach to confidence that can overpower a belief that constricts space in the present moment and projects a future that is perceived as a threat. This is another reason why so many golfers who tell themselves, "Just trust your swing"— no matter how much they've practiced or what previous success they've had—still have real difficulty "just trusting" their swing. The deepest levels of credibility come from our beliefs, which is why no matter how hard you train, how good you get, or how successful you've been, you cannot consistently outperform your psychological framework.

Needless to say, it's more effective for us to frontload our psychology consciously and intentionally before stable confidence is required than it is to passively hope for our beliefs and habits to fall in line. The upside is that our psychological framework can be credibly relearned and reinforced in ways that move us in the directions we want to go when it's most important to us—if we're willing to do the inner work required.

THE INNER WORK

There are only three things we can train: our body, our craft, and our mind. Training all three areas for optimization is difficult and requires us to consistently commit significant time, energy, and resources. Training to get the most from our bodies requires building and maintaining muscular strength and flexibility, managing nutrition, and committing to effective rest and recovery. Seeing how good we can be at a craft, like golf, requires us to learn and practice skill sets, understand strategies and equipment, and ultimately decide how to best utilize them all.

Training to get the most out of our psychological framework is the inner work, and it's difficult for a few noteworthy reasons. First, no one can do the inner work for you. No one becomes successful alone—parents, coaches, teachers, friends, and teammates all contribute to our growth—but those people can't do the work that only you can do.

We may learn how to train our bodies from the instruction of a trainer, but no one can work out for you. We may learn how to build a golf swing, chip, or putt from a coach or how to understand the strategies of course management and its skill set from teammates and coaches, but no one can practice those skills and gain that knowledge for you. Nobody can make you want to do the work to train your body or craft for extended periods of time.

The same is true for doing the inner work. Many people and resources can help us learn how to use our minds more effectively. That's my job in a nutshell. This book is one of those resources and will provide you with guidance for training your mind, but you will have to train and apply that information on your own.

Second, change in general is hard for us humans, largely because real behavioral change requires us to change not only our habits but also our underlying beliefs. There's a reason why more than 80 percent of New Year's resolutions fail; people start and stop diets and start and stop physical-activity routines several times before finally sticking with them long enough to lose weight and improve their physical health. Changing what we do and how we do it stems from our habits and psychological framework because the reward value for any behavior is heavily influenced by our beliefs. We have to address the beliefs and thought patterns that lead to our behaviors and reinforce them for change to be sustainable.

Even when we are motivated to make changes, it's difficult to step away from some beliefs that we've adopted and strengthened for years. As we work through the remainder of this section, we will be examining our beliefs and evaluating them for their accuracy and utility. I encourage you to keep the following in mind: just because we believe something doesn't make it true. Just because we've believed something for a long time doesn't make it true. Just because we believe something strongly doesn't make it true. Just because other people believe something doesn't make it true. Just because a belief is popular doesn't make it true. Just because we feel a belief directly doesn't make it true.

Similarly, as we systematically examine and evaluate our beliefs, you may find it difficult to let go of your current beliefs and develop new ones. We have a strong tendency to cling to the things that are predictable, that are familiar, and that come easily to us. Our established and repeatedly confirmed beliefs and perceptions are deeply familiar, easily accessed, and give us some sense of predictability, even when what they predict is us playing hesitant golf and trying to steer the ball. Many of our beliefs are tightly woven to our emotions; letting go of these beliefs tends to come with some emotional discomfort because we must explore unfamiliar, and at times uncomfortable, ways of thinking about familiar events and experiences.

Letting go of familiar things that make our lives easier and more predictable so that we can commit to things that are less familiar and require more effort to establish is difficult, and that's okay. The inner work doesn't happen overnight. The process and approaches are simple, but they are not easily done. Like training our bodies and learning the skills within the game of golf, the inner work requires patience, persistence, and an open mind.

It's worth noting that letting go of certain beliefs may be difficult because, like our habits, they may have been beneficial in the past. Consider the example of my client Li. Between the ages of ten and twenty-two, Li was exceedingly confident as a golfer. Her confidence came from an inner dialogue stemming from her belief: "I am confident that I can play well and win as long as I can tell myself I'm the best player in the field."

We can see here that her confidence was built upon comparing herself to other players. Li's approach to confidence is familiar to many golfers, especially young ones. Through the junior- and high-school levels of her amateur career, Li's belief worked wonderfully.

After an early growth spurt in elementary school that continued through high school, Li could hit the ball farther than just about every player she knew. And since she had twenty-four-hour access to one of the best practice facilities in the country with some of the best coaches in the game, Li was good enough that she could credibly tell herself that she was the best player in almost every event she played. She could credibly tell herself this because she was almost a foot taller, far more athletic, and indeed a better player than almost everyone she played against. Training her body and practicing her skills, along with her belief about how she stacked up against other players, led to more than twenty scholarship offers to some of the most prestigious collegiate golf programs in the United States.

When I started working with Li, she had just finished her first season at one of the NCAA's top golf programs, and it had not gone well. She was a better player than she had ever been, thanks to having excellent coaches, spending hours in the weight room each week, having her meals planned to the calorie, and having access to top-of-the-line equipment. However, all that confidence Li had ridden high on for most of her life was now gone because she could no longer credibly tell herself that she was the best player around. In fact, she wasn't even the best player in her recruiting class. The belief that she had built her confidence on and the habits it had produced didn't work in her new, more competitive conditions, and that confidence was now unstable because she had reached a level of competition that required a more stable source.

Like Li, many of us get by for a while in conditions where our psychological framework's unexamined areas can be covered up by physical ability and advanced skills. For many golfers, these conditions include practice, familiar courses, favorable weather, or playing against lesser competition. Doing the inner work is difficult because, like Li, we typically resist letting go of beliefs that are familiar, predictable, and beneficial right up until they aren't. It's easier to try to convince yourself that you're the best, like Li tried to do for her first collegiate season, than it is to reconcile with the fact that what we believe won't serve us in the same way because the level of competition or conditions require something more credible.

Finally, the inner work is difficult because it doesn't take much for our old brain to perceive threat, even from thoughts that seem mostly innocuous. Thanks to the dangerous prehistoric conditions from which our old brain evolved, our old brain quickly and powerfully overestimates the likelihood and amount of threat around us. So, as we're working to build a psychological framework that promotes space and acceptance, our brains aren't exactly helping us with that work. Since the old brain is designed to err on the side of safety, it's not very good at assessing what's really dangerous in our modern world. Again, more evidence that perception is not reality.

Safety and survival have a deep-rooted level of credibility for every human because of how our brain evolved. At times, training your mind will feel like swimming upstream against your old brain's safety-first current. However, when we do the inner work, the credibility that comes from learning to step away from outdated beliefs and choosing to live and play freely is profound.

Doing the inner work means looking at our beliefs and logically assessing them, so in this section we will be tapping into the power of our prefrontal cortex more than in the last section, though there will be some significant overlap. In fact, if you'd like to think of your beliefs as mental behaviors to assess them, that's okay. Once we have a structure for being aware of and evaluating our beliefs, we can begin to discredit our outdated beliefs and shape new ones that generate a more credible inner dialogue, one that gives us permission to pursue the types of performances we want.

At times, this work will need to be done and applied to your performance against feedback from your old brain giving you warning signs and telling you to play it safe and retreat to your comfort zone. So, much like when we examined our habits, be prepared to weather a double-down tantrum from your beliefs from time to time.

Here's the good news: a massive overhaul is rarely required. Building a higher-performing psychological framework is about favoring evolution over revolution. Research from many different fields shows that making small shifts in how we think drastically changes and enhances our ability to thrive over time. As you do the inner work, each tweak you make may not seem like much on its own or in that moment, but it will be the beginning of a more credible inner dialogue and more stable confidence.

Our thoughts are the words in the story of our lives and golf game. Every alteration and evolution, even the smallest ones, reshape our story from that point forward. If you've ever had a golf lesson or been fit for clubs, you know that even a few degrees of change in shot dispersion have a significant impact over a round of golf, even more impact over the course of a tournament, and even more impact over the course of an entire season.

The first step toward evolving how we think is to understand how thoughts constrict or create space and how thoughts project a threatening or acceptable future.

SHAPES OF THOUGHTS

Unlike the old brain, the young brain is keenly affected by images and words. The prefrontal cortex's propensity for images and words allows us to learn things like confidence and groundedness and to adapt that knowledge through more than just having to experience them firsthand. Therefore, it stands to reason that doing the inner work with clarity of images and words improves our ability to declaratively learn new beliefs so that we can experience those new beliefs procedurally.

A'S AND V'S

To create an image of what our thoughts look like, we'll assign them to one of two shapes, each shape with a top and a bottom portion. A-shaped thoughts lack credibility for building stable confidence and lead to a range of negative emotions that make it more difficult to compete freely. Conversely, V-shaped thoughts are credible and build stable confidence, even in difficult conditions.

The open space at the top portion of each shape represents the amount of perceived space a thought or belief creates for us in the present moment. A-shaped thoughts have a narrow top portion because they constrict the space within which we live and compete. Similar to the overly narrow road in our earlier lava-road scenario, constricted space in the present moment means that we perceive a smaller margin for error. As you can guess, just the perception of a constricted space is enough to warrant the activation of our old brain, making it easy for nerves to become anxiety or for any number of unproductive habits to be triggered and reinforced.

On the other hand, V-shaped thoughts have a wider top portion because they provide us enough space in the present moment for us to live and play more freely. Like driving in a regular-size lane, the perceived space, or margin for error, at the top portion of a V-shaped thought isn't infinite but is perceived as enough to execute shots as intended. The space created by V-shaped thoughts doesn't turn off our nerves, and we might still get nervous, but V-shaped thoughts give us enough room to shift to a being mode of mind rather than becoming anxious and falling into unproductive habits.

The bottom portion of the shape represents the perceived consequences of going outside our perceived margin of error. A-shaped thoughts have a large bottom portion because they project a threatening future, one filled with perceived consequences that we are unwilling to accept. Like the overly penalizing molten-lava death caused by even the slightest deviation from our overly narrow road, a future that is perceived as unmanageable and too threatening leads to fear and an avoidance of potential consequences.

As opposed to A-shaped thoughts, V-shaped thoughts have a narrow bottom portion because they project a future with more accurate, more manageable, and less threatening consequences that are more willingly accepted. As with regular roads, the projected future of a V-shaped thought isn't devoid of negative consequences. Instead, it contains minimal or manageable perceived threat, so our old brain won't see this future as something from which we have to protect ourselves. Thus, with these V-shaped thoughts, we can credibly permit ourselves to take calculated risks and play more freely.

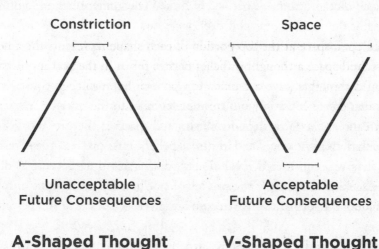

Constriction   **Space**

Unacceptable   **Acceptable**
Future Consequences   **Future Consequences**

A-Shaped Thought   V-Shaped Thought

There is another vital difference between A-shaped thoughts and V-shaped thoughts: how they impact our motivation, particularly when we come to choice points. A-shaped thoughts motivate us through fear and obligation; they tell us a story that motivates us to avoid mistakes, failure, discomfort, and uncertainty and essentially guarantee that we'll step back from choice points when we come to them.

On the other hand, V-shaped thoughts tap into and promote a fundamental human need to pursue progress toward meaningful experiences and objectives. They motivate us to chase the things we want, not in lieu of but in spite of things like failure and setbacks. V-shaped thoughts allow the discomfort and uncertainty that comes with performance. This shift is central to being motivated to play well and hit great shots versus being motivated to simply avoid performing poorly or hitting bad shots. It also highlights why the most stable source of confidence is your inner dialogue.

By having an image of what our thoughts look like, we can now use our inner dialogue to understand what words and phrases create A-shaped and V-shaped beliefs.

START AT THE TOP: CONSTRICTION OR SPACE

Experiencing some emotional discomfort related to our golf game may be normal and common, but that doesn't mean it's always beneficial or necessary, especially for extended periods of time. When emotional discomfort is ongoing, it deteriorates our golf experience, and when emotions are overly elevated, they disrupt our ability to play how we want to.

Psychologist Albert Ellis was a pioneer in psychology and the creator of some of the most effective cognitive-behavioral approaches for addressing beliefs that create constriction instead of space. Many decades on, Dr. Ellis's research and applied practices demonstrate that we often create most of our own constriction with rigid and irrational beliefs. His approach to addressing our beliefs was considered revolutionary during his time because it didn't involve seeking to unearth the origins of our beliefs and hashing through our childhood to explain why we cause ourselves to feel worse and get in our own way.

All events and experiences in our lives are filtered through our beliefs about them, making our interpretations of those events biased and subjective. We cannot change the events themselves. However, thinking about events differently changes our interpretations of those events, and that leads to us directly experiencing both external and internal events differently.

This was the contention that drove Dr. Ellis's work. He asserted that there are no external events that have any intrinsic value. Such events, like making a bogey or winning a tournament, have the exact intrinsic value we give to them. Thus, if we experience frustration or fear at a level that disturbs our ability to play freely, we are creating that constriction through our beliefs and thoughts. Here's what's really important: Dr. Ellis found that the more rigid and irrational our beliefs and thoughts, the less space we feel we have to maneuver within them. In contrast, the more flexible and rational our beliefs, the more cognitive and emotional space we have to think and act in ways that we want to.

As we've established, there is no "good" or "bad" without our thoughts and beliefs applying that judgment. There are the events and experiences of our lives themselves, and there are our beliefs telling us what those mean to us. Like mindfulness, Dr. Ellis's approach doesn't judge our beliefs and thoughts for how "good" or "bad" they are or how "right" or "wrong." Goodness, badness, righteousness, and wrongness are subjective, personal judgments *about* events and experiences from the doing mode of mind. The overlap with a mindful approach to observing our beliefs nonjudgmentally is part of why his approach is so effective. Instead of judging our beliefs with subjective conjecture, Dr. Ellis took the approach of intentionally evaluating our beliefs simply for how rational and beneficial they are for producing the types of feelings, behaviors, and results we desire.

Evaluating our thoughts for their rationality and usefulness creates space in the present in two ways. First, rationality is a measure of how factual our beliefs are. As humans, we are easily swayed by our emotions because we feel them directly. One of the most streamlined ways to cut through constricting thoughts and emotions generated from irrational beliefs is with objectivity. Our inner dialogue means more, makes clearer sense, and is more believable when what we say to ourselves is backed by objective evidence.

Second, we can use objective evidence to evaluate the direct impact a belief has on us and our performance rather than subjectively judging a belief for how "good" or "bad" it is. How a belief is directly impacting what we feel and what behaviors it produces allows us to assess how useful it is. If a belief is causing significant anxiety and impeding our ability to play freely, the tense and fearful swings produced by that belief are direct evidence of its futility. Like asking ourselves what a habit does for us, there's a simple and exacting credibility in our inner dialogue when we honestly evaluate whether what we believe is helping or impeding our pursuit of the type of golf we want to play.

As we examine our beliefs for how rational and beneficial they are, we'll start at the top of their shape, the area that represents our perceived margin for error. We're looking to understand the differences between thinking in ways that are constricting and thinking in ways that are spacious. By adapting the key fundamentals of Dr. Ellis's work, we'll look for specific words in our inner dialogue to identify those differences.

WHERE CONSTRICTION COMES FROM

When you feel frustration, anger, fear, and anxiety to the point where they inhibit your ability to play shots the way you want, you may have some A-shaped beliefs that revolve around irrational or unbeneficial key words and phrases. Here are the key words to listen for and be aware of: "have to," "need to," "must," "couldn't stand it if," "should," "shouldn't," "ought."

One of the most straightforward ways to evaluate a belief's rationality is to observe if it sees things we desire as absolute necessities. "Have to," "need to," "must," and "couldn't stand it if" constrict space by irrationally seeing things that can happen as things that *must* happen or *must not* happen. If we want to play well and be seen as a good player by others, we typically become nervous when results count. In such a case, our nerves will heighten our awareness and encourage us to focus on playing in the present moment. But if we earnestly believe that we *must* perform well above all and that we *have to* be seen as a good player by others, we will create considerable constriction for ourselves. We will unnecessarily leave ourselves with only two rigid and diametrically opposed options without any middle ground.

More than 250 scientific studies, many examining sport performances, have tested the effects of believing that something desired is an absolute necessity. About 95 percent of those studies show that people whose emotions significantly inhibit their ability to act confidently and freely have more irrational beliefs than those with functional emotional and behavioral responses. Instead of space in the form of shades of gray that one can maneuver within, absolute "must" beliefs shrink our perceived margin for error to an all-or-nothing scenario and create a trap loop with our confidence.

More recent research examining athletes specifically shows that irrational and inflexible beliefs are one of the strongest antecedents to performance anxiety that strongly predict choking under pressure.

Trap Loop of Unstable Confidence

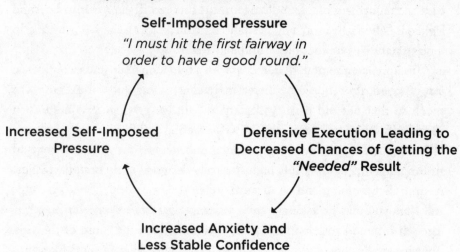

Self-Imposed Pressure
"I must hit the first fairway in order to have a good round."

Increased Self-Imposed Pressure

Defensive Execution Leading to Decreased Chances of Getting the "Needed" Result

Increased Anxiety and Less Stable Confidence

To see how irrational beliefs create constriction, consider the belief that "I must start my round by hitting the first fairway in order to have a good round." It may look silly on paper, but you'd be surprised how many professional golfers tell me this is a belief they bring to the first tee. The belief applies self-imposed pressure that we *must* produce a favorable result in order to stabilize confidence about the future of our round. That self-imposed pressure is already constricting the space to execute our first shot, increasing the chances that we'll hit our first drive trying *not to miss* the fairway rather than trying to hit a target in the fairway. The defensive swing *decreases* the chances of hitting the fairway, on which our entire round and stability of confidence are now relying. If somehow we do hit the fairway that we *must* hit, we're still left with the same self-imposed pressure and unstable confidence for the next shot—and every shot after that.

And if we don't hit the fairway that we believe we *must* hit, our confidence will become even more unstable, and we will put even more self-imposed pressure on our next shot to make up for the missed fairway. More self-imposed pressure leads to more constriction and an even more defensive swing, further decreasing the chances of hitting the green with our next shot. The loop goes on and on, continuing to constrict more with each shot until things get so bad, we accept our self-imposed fate and give up trying to force the ball onto the fairway, which usually leads to swinging freely long after our score-card and enjoyment of a round have already suffered. The more irrational and rigid our beliefs, the more reliant we become on an increasingly unstable trap loop to stabilize our confidence and play freely.

It's important to note that if we stay in a trap loop of unstable confidence long enough, it will become increasingly constricting and threatening—so much so that our old brain will start to perceive playing certain shots in certain situations as events worthy of triggering a full-on threat response. When our old brain perceives something to be dangerously constricting and threatening, it does what it is prehistorically designed to do best: try to eject us from that moment and on to a safer one.

Wait, you may be asking—*are you saying what I think you're saying?* Yep. The self-imposed trap loop of unstable confidence is the cause of the yips. The yips are our brain trying to play golf, especially delicate shots like chips and short putts, through what it perceives to be an event that is so constrict-ing and with a future perceived as so threatening that the old brain takes the young brain offline and communicates to our body to do whatever it takes to avoid what it perceives is a danger to us. In essence, the yips are a full-blown threat response fueled by anxiety until that anxiety becomes panic. Put sim-ply, it's our old brain trying to remove us from a shot it perceives as so con-stricting and threatening that it's safer to get through the shot as quickly as possible, not as well as possible.

That response, which for many golfers includes involuntary muscle twitches, manifests because our prefrontal cortex is offline and our old brain is operating on high-frequency and high-intensity brain waves, making it almost impossible for it to efficiently communicate to our body how to sequence our movements, apply the appropriate amount of force to a deli-cate shot, and to focus on an external target. The result is an ongoing cycle of tense, stabby strokes, and those tense, stabby strokes reinforce the panic because they provide the exact safety-first reward value that our old brain is expecting. The more we yip, the more likely we are to yip again. It's why the yips can quickly become a habit.

The yips are a triggered threat response that stem from a trap loop of unstable confidence getting more and more constricting and threatening. One of the most common reasons players continue to struggle with the yips is because they try to "fix" them by addressing their physical technique. In effect, they identify the symptoms of the yips and apply time, effort, focus, and resources to them without tackling the cause.

Trying to address the yips on a physical level instead of at the source is an ongoing and painful reminder to many players that there are no such things as a short memory or muscle memory. Our brain is specifically designed to overestimate threat and remember those threats, real or perceived. Therefore, trying to have a short memory and "just forget" about mistakes and failures is a surface-level approach and a fool's errand. We don't "just forget" bad shots. However, we can be mindfully aware of how we think about the shots we hit and how we respond to them.

Similarly, our muscles do not have memories. We can train them to be stronger, faster, and more flexible, but no matter how much we train them, muscles cannot create, store, or access memories or skills in any form. Muscles do *not* have neuropathic ability or memory cells. Information processing about the events of our past, present, and future happen in our brain based on how our psychological framework and our direct experiences are constructed. Physical practice and training are essential for learning skills and being able to execute them on the course, but our muscles themselves cannot do anything without being instructed to do so by our brain.

The reason all the practice in the world doesn't lead to our muscles simply executing skills on command is because only our brain can give that command. How it gives that command—and, at times, whether it gives that command at all—is determined by our core beliefs and the habits those beliefs learn and reinforce. Therefore, the most effective way to deal with the yips is to address them at the source, as a reinforced habit that is learned and continually reinforced by A-shaped patterns of thought that create self-imposed perceived constriction and threat.

Another way we constrict space and get stuck in the trap loop is by not accepting our current reality. Drawing from our mindfulness section, we already know that the words "should," "shouldn't," and "ought to" are subjective judgments from the doing mode of mind that make us feel worse. They constrict our perceived space in the present moment by highlighting the difference between where we are and where we would prefer to be. "Should," "shouldn't," and "ought to" beliefs are not only an ineffective strategy for avoiding emotional discomfort because they amplify it; they are also an even less beneficial strategy for handling whatever challenges and shots we face in our current reality as it is right now.

Judgments invariably lead to multitasking between our current reality as it is and an imaginary reality we think we *should* have. "Should-ing" ourselves is a surefire way to make things harder for us and will often take us off time. If we think about the present moment as a raindrop like we did in the "Awareness" section, we can clearly see that being present—that is, centered in our raindrop—is almost impossible when we are multitasking between a reality that exists in the present moment and one that doesn't exist at all.

Let's say we've missed a short par putt that we believe we *must* always make, and we're now on the tee at the next hole. We would further constrict our space to execute the next shot by telling ourselves that we *shouldn't* have missed the short putt on the previous hole and that we *should* have made par instead of bogey. Because we're on the tee box "should-ing" all over ourselves about missing a short putt, we're not fully present with the shot that we actually have in front of us.

Managing our thoughts and emotions by "should-ing" ourselves not only makes us feel worse; believing we *shouldn't* be experiencing whatever we are actually experiencing in the present moment also makes us less capable of addressing the task at hand.

Whether we think we *shouldn't* have missed a short putt that we believe we *must* always make doesn't change the fact that the putt was missed. So when we tell ourselves that we *should* be making every putt inside four feet, *should* be playing better, or *should* be more confident, we are making ourselves feel worse and now multitasking between our actual reality and the one we believe we *should* be in.

If we're not accepting of our current shot and level of ability, it's not beneficial for improving how we deal with the challenges that come from playing golf. In essence, a constricting approach to our thoughts and emotions is also a constricting and avoidant approach to whatever our current reality may be. Avoiding the current reality of a challenge we believe *shouldn't* be happening only takes us farther from being able to work through it and takes us deeper into the trap loop. The fastest route to progress is through acceptance of our current reality.

Here are a few examples of irrational, unbeneficial, and constricting top portions of some A-shaped beliefs.

- I must be certain that I can shoot good scores all the time.
- I can't ever miss putts inside ten feet.
- I must not be judged unfavorably by others.
- I need to feel comfortable and relaxed.
- I shouldn't be feeling nervous.
- I shouldn't be making this many bogeys.
- I ought to be making more birdies.

It's important to clarify the difference between an irrational belief that undermines stable confidence and a competitive constraint. When playing golf, we willingly agree to competitive constraints. If we want to make the cut at an event, we must shoot a score that makes the cut. If we want to beat our friends in a round, we must shoot a better score than they do.

To be clear, there are real parameters we must operate within in most areas of our lives, including golf. Our lives and golf have actual margins for error. There's plenty of room to drive freely on most roads, but we can't just drive anywhere and expect to get where we want to go. Similarly, in golf, we can't just hit the ball anywhere and expect to score well.

As we mindfully evaluate our beliefs, we're *not* looking to create unlimited space—because that would also be irrational and unbeneficial. Instead, we're looking to bring our perceived margin for error closer to the actual competitive constraints within which we compete.

MOVE TO THE BOTTOM: THREAT OR ACCEPTANCE

Optimism and pessimism are the lenses through which we view the events of our lives. Conceptually, these are more nuanced than just the common depiction of "the glass is half full or half empty." Optimism and pessimism are different approaches for how we explain the events of our lives to ourselves—what psychologists call our "explanatory style."

Martin Seligman is a psychology professor at the University of Pennsylvania and a pioneer of positive psychology, the branch of psychology focused on both individual and societal well-being. He's also the world's foremost expert on optimistic and pessimistic explanatory styles. Through several decades of research, Dr. Seligman has repeatedly shown that, due to our old brain's prehistoric design, our default response to adversity and distress is a pessimistic explanatory style. In a prehistoric world, taking a pessimistic approach to everything increased the odds of surviving longer.

Although we all have the same brain with pessimistic default settings, not everyone's a pessimist; not everyone continues explaining the events of their lives and seeing the future through a pessimistic lens. So, if everyone is born predisposed to pessimism, how is it that some people become optimistic? This is the question that guided Dr. Seligman's research, leading to a rich understanding of why many people shy away from challenges and pressure-filled moments while others persist through and embrace them.

In a series of studies, Dr. Seligman and his colleagues created impossible or inescapable conditions and gave people a task within those conditions. For example, some people were given a puzzle that was deliberately designed to be unsolvable. They then asked these people to complete the task and observed how they responded.

In each study, Dr. Seligman observed that two-thirds of people quickly and hopelessly quit the tasks, with many feeling anxious and defeated. However, one-third of people continued to pursue the impossible tasks with confidence and resilience. Using rigorously evaluated assessment measures, Dr. Seligman also measured whether the participants had pessimistic or optimistic explanatory styles. As you might expect, he found that pessimists gave up as soon as they felt even a hint of helplessness, while optimists persisted even though the tasks were indeed hopeless. The drastic differences in how people responded had to do with how they explained their failure to complete the same impossible task to themselves.

Those with a pessimistic explanatory style explained their failures as some combination of being permanent, pervasive, and personal. That is, they perceived not being able to complete the tasks as evidence that they would never complete the tasks—and that their inability to complete them was evidence of widespread inability in several areas of their life. They also explained that their long-term, pervasive inability was due to personal deficiencies or character flaws. For pessimists, failing to solve the task meant they would never be able to solve the task (permanent) and that they were incapable of solving other types of difficult tasks (pervasive) because they were the type of person who can't handle difficult tasks (personal).

A golfer with a pessimistic explanatory style might explain something like failing to maintain a Sunday lead on the back nine of a tournament as evidence that they will never have what it takes to hold onto a lead and that they are also incapable of handling other similar pressure-filled situations like winning a playoff or playing well when on the cut line. This pessimistic explanation of failing to maintain a lead and close a tournament undoubtedly makes the consequences of the experience more long-term, more widespread, and more personal than they really are.

Conversely, those in Dr. Seligman's studies with optimistic explanatory styles explained their failures as temporary, localized, and nonpersonal. That is, they saw not being able to complete a task as evidence that they were getting closer to being able to solve the task—and that their inability to complete a task was specific to that time and task, not a reflection of their ability to handle other difficult tasks at other times. Furthermore, they judged that their temporary and specific failure was due to a deficiency in a skill set that needed refining or a strategy that hadn't been learned yet, not a personal indictment of their talent or character.

A golfer with an optimistic explanatory style might explain failing to maintain a Sunday lead on the back nine of a tournament as evidence that they are getting closer to winning, that failing to win was the result of a few specific adjustments that can be improved, and that while failing is an unpleasant outcome, it's a reflection of applied effort, not a final conclusion about their ability or the fabric of their character.

It's likely that you've seen the difference in these explanatory styles in others or yourself. Let's look at a few examples of the bottom portion of A-shaped beliefs shaped by a pessimistic explanatory style:

- Making a single mistake means I'm assured to make more mistakes.
- Losing in a playoff means I'm incapable of ever winning a playoff.
- Failing means I'm unworthy of success.

- Starting my round less than perfectly means I won't play well for the rest of the round.
- Not being able to win another tournament means I'm a fluke.
- Being nervous means I can't play well.
- Other people judging me unfavorably means they're right about me.
- One bad tournament will ruin my entire season.

To be clear, there is always some risk involved with playing golf, and there are consequences for everything we do. In our lives and our performances, there are always chances that things might not work out the way we want. Failure is an option, and there may be some physical, financial, social, and emotional consequences to performance.

When competing, we agree to assume some degree of risk that we may fail and experience some undesired consequences. If we want to play tournament golf or a weekend skins game with our friends, we must compete against other capable golfers, and if we don't shoot the best score, we won't win.

If you're pursuing better golf, you will face significant uncertainty, make mistakes at times, encounter conditions that are beyond your current skill level, and likely face the judgment of other people. Those who are unwilling to persist when faced with these inevitable realities because of their pessimistic explanation for them will eventually be outperformed by those who explain those same challenges optimistically.

WHERE A THREATENING FUTURE COMES FROM

The real limitation of a pessimistic explanatory style is that it projects a threatening future. Such a simple truth is why learning an optimistic explanatory style is so valuable and why researchers in a range of fields are finding that optimism is one of the most important factors for building consistent performance over time and under pressure. The same findings are apparent neurologically in that perceived threat is also a state where our brain is running at a diminished cognitive capacity and on high-frequency brain waves that disrupt our brain's ability to effectively send signals to our body.

As we evaluate the explanatory style of our beliefs and thoughts, we're *not* looking to project a future and explain performance in a way where there are only favorable consequences or none at all. That would be irrational, delusional, and in direct opposition to the essence of what competition is about. Instead, we are developing a credible optimistic explanatory style that projects a future we are willing to accept. Like interest curiosity and connecting to our breath, acceptance is a mindful behavior driven largely by an optimistic explanatory style.

MINDFUL BEHAVIOR AND BETTER OPTION: ACCEPTANCE

Acceptance isn't a resignation to failure. We are not allowing ourselves to settle for less. Acceptance doesn't mean we don't care about our performance or the results we produce. Acceptance recognizes that the future may include results and experiences that we don't like, find uncomfortable, and won't be satisfied with but explains those possibilities in a way where we can credibly tell ourselves we can manage them and don't need to be protected from them.

Acceptance is a mindful behavior that grants us access to the present moment. It does so because it considers and receives *all* possible future outcomes. When we are aware of these possibilities and are willing to receive them, we can use them to step out of our comfort zones and be grounded in our current reality simply because the things we don't want to experience are no longer perceived as threats that *must* be avoided.

It is willing acceptance that allows us to stop trying to project the future and just see how it plays out. On a neurological level, when we allow the future to play out, our old and young brain are less surprised and threatened by the discrepancy between our expectations and how events actually play out. It bears repeating that when we think in ways that increase that perceived discrepancy and threat, we are more likely to create the frequency and intensity of brain waves that then disrupt our ability to play freely. Thus, it is our explanatory style that determines how much we *must* project the future or whether we can allow it to unfold.

The reason why pessimists, in one way or another, give up quickly and easily and opt for playing scared golf is because they believe the consequences of failure are more permanent, pervasive, and personal than in reality. For pessimists, the future is perceived as something worth being anxious about.

As Dr. Seligman points out, when faced with real challenges and pressure-filled moments, through a pessimistic lens we behave and compete in ways that avoid the calculated risks necessary for growth and success. However, through an optimistic lens, when faced with the same challenges, we behave and compete in ways that move us toward the experiences and results we want. The difference is a matter of acceptance.

ACCEPTANCE IN ACTION

George Gankas is one of the most influential golf coaches in the world, teaching both professional and amateur players. In a lesson with a young golfer, George talked about how a willing acceptance of the future improves the fluidity and rhythm of a putting stroke.

> So, when I'm missing . . . two- to three-footers, which happens once in a while, all of a sudden, your nerves start hitting and everything starts to get weird, okay? That's when you start missing more, okay? So, what I do is I let my players know that my trigger is "It's okay to miss." . . . [addressing a short putt] It's okay for me to miss this. If I get up here and I go, "Okay, it's okay to miss," and I miss, I'm okay with that.
>
> . . . But if it's not okay to miss, what happens? You get over this [short putt], you get real tight, and you start getting real flinchy— and then, all of a sudden, you don't know where your ball is going.
>
> So, what happens when it's okay to miss? There's no pressure. You just let it go. But when it's straight up "Okay, I *have* to make this, I *have* to make this"—your adrenaline pumps.
>
> . . . If you get all careful here and "*have* to make this," guess what? You tighten up, and you're not going to put your normal stroke on it. So what I want you to do is mentally get prepared and say, "It's okay to miss."
>
> —"GG Swing Tips Golf: GG's Simple Putting Tips—
> How to Putt on Target," August 14, 2019

Here, George is communicating the components of stable confidence. As knowledgeable as George is about all the finer techniques of putting, he clearly understands that allowing ourselves to make smooth putting strokes also requires space to execute them and a willing acceptance of a future where we may not get the result we want, even on short putts.

George encourages his students to understand that they don't *have* to make every putt because that A-shaped belief constricts the space they can give themselves in the present moment. At the same time, George is encouraging acceptance through an optimistic explanatory style of what it means to miss a short putt. Explaining a missed putt as something that is "okay" doesn't mean that his students shouldn't care about whether they make putts, that they should resign themselves to always missing short putts, or that they should be satisfied with not making short putts. It means that when they do miss a short putt from time to time, there don't have to be permanent, pervasive, and personal consequences that create the perception that missing a short putt is something threatening.

All the skills George teaches his students and that they painstakingly practice cannot be freely executed through A-shaped beliefs filled with "musts," "shoulds," and a pessimistic explanation of mistakes and failures. The acceptance that comes with an optimistic explanatory style is a mindful behavior. It decreases the perceived future threat of a mistake.

With an optimistic explanatory style, we give ourselves permission to fail. Such a notion is often received with great resistance, often as if it is blasphemy, especially for people in competitive performance realms. Many people falsely associate permission to fail with giving up or permanently settling for less. Let me be very clear: it's the permission to fail that allows us to take risks and pursue the things we really want more freely.

When we do not give ourselves permission to fail, we are in no uncertain terms asking our brain to multitask between pursuit of what we want and avoidance of what we don't. Remember, we suck at multitasking, so when we give our brain two objectives, both are compromised, and we get worse at what we're trying to pursue. Put simply, we can't be singularly committed to making a putt if we're also actively trying to avoid missing that putt. Here we see why it's almost impossible to be committed to any shot with a low level of acceptance.

And here's why understanding our prehistorically designed brain is vitally important. Remember, our brain's overriding function is to keep us alive. Specifically, it doesn't know whether missing a putt is a real threat or only a perceived one. So, when given the choice between pursuing what we want and avoiding what we perceive as threatening, the strength and speed of our old brain will take over and default to avoidance of the perceived threat, and we won't have a choice in the matter.

Acceptance includes us giving ourselves permission to fail. That permission to fail keeps us from multitasking between pursuit and avoidance when our brain is specifically designed to choose avoidance. The subtle but significant difference in perceived threat that comes with acceptance is largely why optimists are more resilient than pessimists are: they learn from failure, while pessimists learn to fear it. For this reason, more and more studies examining the explanatory styles of high performers are confirming that an optimistic explanatory style is one of a few key components that sits at the heart of mental toughness.

RESHAPING BELIEFS

WHERE CREDIBILITY COMES FROM

Before we start reshaping our beliefs, let's take a minute to note that building credible V-shaped thoughts is *not* about thinking more rigidly or thinking the same way in all situations. We are *not* looking to build a psychological framework that doesn't recognize nuance. In some situations, when the physical, financial, social, or emotional risk is too high, A-shaped thoughts, and the behaviors they help produce, may actually serve us better.

An important distinction of why Dr. Ellis's and Dr. Seligman's methods for evaluating our beliefs are so effective is because they explicitly consider the cost of failure. Each approach uses the fundamental guideline of asking ourselves, "What's the worst-case scenario?"

THE ABCS OF STABLE CONFIDENCE

Jamelle was twenty-two years old and had been working toward playing professional golf for most of her life. In the months preceding her first attempt to qualify for the LPGA Tour through the Tour's Q-Series, she'd been struggling to play well. Despite being one of the best amateur players in the world—and arguably the best collegiate golfer in the United States—her confidence had never been more unstable. With only a few weeks left before the start of the Q-Series tournaments, Jamelle had never been more frustrated and anxious in tournaments and practice rounds.

After a recent mini-tour event that hadn't gone well, Jamelle told me she felt like she was squandering an opportunity she had been working toward for years. She interpreted her failure in the event she'd just played as the final straw and as confirmation that her hopes of playing in the LPGA Tour were over.

"All my work over the last five years is going to be a waste. I have to make it to the LPGA Tour, but the way I'm playing, there's no chance," she told me.

In an attempt to rectify her situation, Jamelle was practicing more than ever. Even though she already had a lifelong swing coach, a collegiate coach, and national team coaches from her home country, she'd hired more private coaches and was questioning everything about her performance, from her swing and short game to her equipment. Understandably, Jamelle felt like she was at her wits' end and was deeply worried about the coming qualifying season.

"Jamelle," I said, "as best as you can, articulate your beliefs *about* the Q-Series and your current struggles."

Jamelle took a moment to organize her thoughts. "I have to make it to the Tour this year, or I won't ever make it to the Tour. Playing how I've been playing over the last few months just shows I'm not good enough."

There it was: the underlying A-shaped belief that had been generating Jamelle's inner dialogue, triggering and reinforcing unproductive habits, and destabilizing her confidence: "I must make the LPGA Tour on my first try, or I'm not good enough to ever make the LPGA Tour."

The consequences of Jamelle's struggles could have been quite different if she had been aware of and known how to evaluate her A-shaped beliefs *about* her struggles to make the LPGA Tour. Over the next few weeks, Jamelle and I worked together to shape more rational, beneficial, and optimistic beliefs about playing professional golf and her recent form in tournaments. We used a slightly modified form of the following method, pioneered by Dr. Ellis and further developed by Dr. Seligman, along with psychologists Steven Hollon, psychology professor at Vanderbilt University, and the late psychology professor Arthur Freeman.

The approach is a matter of ABC. **A** is the activating event we have experienced or may be experiencing in the future. "Activating event" is a term for an event or experience that is important to us. We can also think of an activating event as a triggering event in that it can be external or internal. In Jamelle's case, the activating event was the Q-Series.

B is our belief *about* the event. In Jamelle's case, her A-shaped belief was that she *must* qualify for the Tour on her first attempt, or else she would never make it to the LPGA Tour.

C is the natural consequences we experience as a result of our beliefs *about* the activating event or experience. In Jamelle's case, the natural consequences of her A-shaped beliefs about making the Tour were self-imposed constriction, frustration, anxiety, competing hesitantly and defensively, a continuing inner dialogue filled with A-shaped thoughts, unstable confidence, discouragement, decreased enjoyment of competing, and the fear of missing out on her dream of playing professional golf at the highest level.

Remember from our section on awareness that trying to change our thoughts by force is a habit from the doing mode of mind that doesn't work and just makes us feel worse. What you'll notice is that mindfully evaluating our beliefs using ABC is quite similar to mindfully mapping our habits—only now we are examining the beliefs themselves that create and reinforce our behaviors.

ABC is not a process of forcing ourselves to believe something different. Instead, it's a process of thinking differently *about* our beliefs and thoughts themselves by observing and evaluating them and what they do for us in a nonjudgmental way. In a sense, we are creating the opportunity for us to believe something more spacious and accepting by mindfully observing how an A-shaped belief is impacting our direct experience and golf.

To get a clearer view, let's look at Jamelle's ABCs, along with a few other examples of some ABCs common to many golfers.

Activating Event: Playing in Q-Series.
Belief: "I must make the LPGA Tour on my first try this year, or I'm not good enough to ever make the LPGA Tour."
Consequences: Increasing self-imposed pressure, frustration, anxiety, competing hesitantly and defensively, continued A-shaped

thoughts, unstable confidence, discouragement, dread of competing, and fear of the future.

Activating Event: Losing strokes on the last few holes.
Belief: "I shouldn't be dropping shots to finish a round. If I do, that means I can't ever close a round or hold a lead."
Consequences: Anxiety about the last few holes of a round, overswinging, second-guessing, dread about ruining a round in the last few holes, and being off time during the middle of a round.

Activating Event: Missing short putts.
Belief: "Missing short putts means I suck at putting."
Consequences: Fear of failure, defensive putting strokes, unstable confidence, anxiety about putting and failing, muscle tension, discouragement, and self-loathing.

Activating Event: Not performing well after winning a tournament or finding significant success.
Belief: "I have to always perform like I did when I was winning and most successful; otherwise, my wins and successes were a fluke."
Consequences: Unproductive expectations, self-imposed pressure, A-shaped inner dialogue, second-guessing, forcing shots, and anxiety.

Examining the ABCs above, we can see a few important patterns. First, all of the activating events are part of the competitive experience. If we choose to compete, there's no avoiding many of these events or similar events and experiences. Second, all the beliefs are irrational and unbeneficial. They either view something desired as an absolute necessity that we *must* have or are unaccepting of a current reality that *shouldn't* be happening, thus constricting space in the present. And they are pessimistic, explaining each event with some combination of long-term, widespread, and personal consequences, projecting a future that is perceived as threatening enough to avoid rather than seeing how it plays out. We can see why Jamelle wasn't able to give herself credible permission to play freely.

Third, we see that the natural consequences of the beliefs are unbeneficial. Each belief produces other A-shaped thoughts while triggering and reinforcing behaviors that impede and diminish the enjoyment of performance. They create either passivity and dejection or anxiety and self-imposed constriction. Here's an A-shaped belief with its irrational and pessimistic components alongside Jamelle's A-shaped belief.

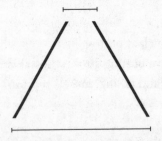

Irrational and Unbeneficial
"Have to," "Need to," "Must," "Should,"
"Shouldn't," "Ought to"

Pessimistic Explanatory Style
Permanent, Pervasive, Personal

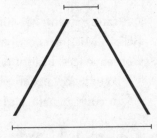

"I must make the LPGA Tour
on my first try this year
because if I don't . . .

. . . I'm not good enough to ever
make the LPGA Tour."

Once we are mindfully aware of our A-shaped beliefs, the next step is to think about the beliefs differently in ways that discredit them. In a sense, we are bringing interest curiosity to our A-shaped beliefs in a few specific ways. Thus, the most effective approach for reshaping them into V-shaped beliefs is to dispute them with evidence in a mindful but logical manner. Below are four important ways we can discredit our A-shaped beliefs and reshape them into credible V-shaped ones.

Evidence

The most convincing way to discredit an A-shaped belief is to prove that it is factually incorrect: we can simply ask ourselves, "Is this belief true?" More often than not, the answer is no. Since most of the time A-shaped beliefs irrationally underestimate the amount of space we have in the present moment, we generally have facts on our side.

Remember, our beliefs impact our direct experiences even when they are not at all true. So keep in mind that we're not asking ourselves if an

A-shaped belief *feels* true. We're not asking ourselves if someone else thinks it's true. And we're not asking ourselves what we believe *should* be true. We're asking if the belief itself is actually true, backed by factual evidence.

In Jamelle's case, she believed that she *needed* to make the LPGA Tour on her first try, or else she would never be good enough to make the Tour.

"Is this notion true?" I asked her. "In the history of golf, is it true that no one has ever made it to the LPGA Tour after failing to qualify on their first attempt?"

As you might guess, the answer was obviously no. A quick Google search revealed that in the history of the LPGA Tour, there have in fact been many players who earned their Tour card after failing on the first try, and sometimes on their second or third tries—some of whom have gone on to win LPGA tournaments and major championships. Another quick Google search revealed that many players have qualified for the LPGA Tour and then had to return to a qualifying tour before playing in the LPGA Tour again.

Through our discussion, Jamelle told me that she came to her belief because of what a coach had told her. Likely, the coach was well intentioned and trying to motivate her, but instead, Jamelle adopted the idea that she *had* to make the Tour on her first attempt without thinking twice about whether the idea was true. Like Santa or the Tooth Fairy, the idea ran around in her inner dialogue unchecked for long enough that it became a fully formed A-shaped belief despite not being true in any way whatsoever.

Another rule of thumb for assessing whether a belief is true is to consider if it's a written and official rule. For example, to win a tournament, you must shoot the lowest score or win in a playoff. That's a written rule we sign up for when we compete. It's a competitive constraint. But if a constraint isn't a rule, then it's an irrational and unnecessary self-imposed constriction.

For Jamelle, despite rifling through the rules of golf and the written qualifying requirements for the LPGA Tour, nowhere did she find a rule that prohibited players from the LPGA Tour if they didn't successfully qualify on the first attempt. It was a constraint she had adopted and unnecessarily imposed on herself.

There are no rules written anywhere that any of us must shoot good scores all the time or that other people need to have favorable opinions of us.

Asking ourselves, "Where is it written?" is a logical litmus test of a belief's rationality and utility. For example, we might ask ourselves, "Where is it written that I must hit the first fairway to have a good round? Where is it written that other people must have favorable opinions of me?" If it's not an actual rule, then it's not something we *have* to abide by and certainly not something we *must* believe.

With a few simple but intentional questions about whether an A-shaped belief was true, Jamelle was able to start mindfully and consciously discrediting her previously held convictions. She did so not through a storm of positive affirmations telling her that she was the best or that everything would just work out how she wanted, nor by trying to forcefully convince herself that she didn't care about playing on the LPGA Tour, but with actual direct evidence as to how irrational her A-shaped belief was.

Usefulness

Sometimes evaluating the impact of a belief on us and our performance is the most direct and procedural evidence for discrediting what we believe. Therefore, we can further discredit an A-shaped belief by asking ourselves, "Is this belief beneficial?"

With many A-shaped beliefs, the direct natural consequences of holding a belief matter as much as whether the belief is true. Jamelle's belief that she *needed* to make the LPGA Tour on her first try was demonstrably unbeneficial. It created self-imposed constriction, frustration, anxiety, discouragement, and a sense of dread when it came to competing in the upcoming Q-Series tournaments. Above all, the belief wasn't beneficial because it wasn't giving her credible permission to play freely and go for what she really wanted.

"What would you do if you found out that the golf ball you were using was impeding your ability to hit good golf shots and keeping you from enjoying the tournament golf you've been looking forward to most?" I asked Jamelle.

"I'd throw that ball out and test for a better one today. There's no reason to use a ball that doesn't work for me," she replied.

The same attitude most golfers take to their golf balls can also be applied to our beliefs. If the natural consequences of a belief aren't beneficial, you don't have to continue to use it. Like our established and long-standing habits, just because we have a belief, we have held it for a while, and it was beneficial in the past doesn't mean it's beneficial to us now. Mindfully considering the direct consequences of holding a belief gives procedural evidence of whether it's helping or hurting our golf game, and we can use that as evidence to let it go and upgrade it to something more beneficial, just like we would with our golf balls.

Contributing Factors

Very few things happen because of a single reason; events and outcomes have many contributing factors. Whether we perform well or poorly is often influenced to some degree by things like how rested we are, how well we've prepared, our mindset, our equipment, how difficult a golf course is, and how other competitors are performing. To discredit the pessimistic portion of an A-shaped belief, we can also ask, "Are there other contributing factors?"

Considering other factors isn't about being satisfied with poor performances. It's *not* about dodging responsibility for our thoughts and behaviors. Considering other factors is a credible acknowledgment that performance is impacted by a range of variables, many of which we cannot control. While we are the primary architects of our lives and performances, we are not the only thing that influences how we live and play. Taking ownership of our lives and performance means scanning for all possible causes, including those that are temporary, task-specific, and impersonal. Doing so gives us a more objective and therefore credible evaluation of what contributes to how we play and to our beliefs.

Jamelle offered a pessimistic view to explain her poor performance in the lead-up to the Q-Series and qualifying for the LGPA Tour: not being good enough. For her, not being good enough meant a permanent, either–or state of ability, a pervasive state applied to her ability in all rounds and under all conditions.

What Jamelle wasn't considering were more accurate and optimistic explanations. For instance, she wasn't considering that the A-shaped belief driving her struggles and unstable confidence could be discredited; thus, just holding onto the belief was short-term and changeable. Moreover, even if she wasn't *currently* good enough, that didn't mean she would *always* not be good enough. Not being good enough isn't the most enjoyable realization for any golfer, but it's a temporary, changeable, and nonpersonal state. What not being good enough really means is that we're not good enough *right now*—but with continued efforts to improve and with more stable confidence in the future, we might be.

Considering these factors also revealed that Jamelle's A-shaped belief was the specific cause of her poor performance—her swing, short game, and putting were more than adequate to score well while still having room for improvement. Her skill-related struggles were not nearly as widespread as her A-shaped belief suggested. And she could improve upon those specific areas with effective practice.

It was true that Jamelle wasn't performing well enough to make the LPGA Tour in that moment, but the start of the Q-Series was still a few weeks away. She could use that time to mindfully examine her beliefs, improve her skills, and learn new strategies for managing the challenges of Q-Series. Looking at the larger picture of contributing factors gives credible evidence that when we're not good enough, it doesn't mean that all areas of our game aren't good enough. It's much more likely that improving a few specific areas of our game with some well-directed effort will lead to significant improvement over time.

Mindful consideration of the many sources for Jamelle's recent struggles proved that there was a significant number of contributing factors that were changeable, specific to one or two areas of her game, and that were reflections of her current skill sets and knowledge; they were not her personal shortcomings as a person or a golfer. Like Jamelle, we can discredit the pessimistic explanations for poor performances and failure to get the results we want by considering all contributing factors. Doing so also allows us to take more ownership of our performances because it lets us constructively and objectively work toward getting better.

A significant danger of A-shaped beliefs is that they only see pessimistic explanations that, when considered, lead us to conclude that there's nothing we can do to get better, and therefore it's not worth even trying—thus giving away ownership of how we play. There's a reason why optimists are more resilient than pessimists. Considering all factors optimistically leads to hope and guided action. Optimists experience the same struggles as pessimists, but they explain those struggles in a way that leads to objective and more effective approaches to overcome them. So the same struggles that become mountains for pessimists are only molehills for optimists who consider all factors and facets, especially the optimistic ones, that impact our performances and failures. The reason optimists see the glass as half full is because they are credibly explaining the events of their lives to see the glass in that way.

Future Projections

Like in life, in golf things won't always go our way, especially as you ascend to the game's more competitive levels; if anything, as the level of competition increases, our chances of winning decrease because we start competing against more capable golfers. What allows those who are more successful and more consistent to compete freely is their willingness to accept the risk of failing. Reaching that acceptance means asking ourselves, "What does it mean if I don't perform well enough to get what I want? And what does that mean about me?"

For golfers with higher handicaps, playing golf through a pessimistic lens makes golf far less enjoyable because their current skill level ensures that mistakes and setbacks will happen, sometimes quite often. Taking those mistakes personally can make even a casual round of golf an infuriating or demoralizing experience. Over time, this pessimism can make practicing and trying to get better seem like a daunting task and not worth the effort. For those with lower handicaps, taking mistakes personally not only makes golf less fun but further amplifies mistakes and struggles under more competitive conditions. Therefore, regardless of our skill level, explaining mistakes, failures, and struggles pessimistically gives us a credible reason to prioritize avoiding future mistakes rather than pursuing success in the present moment.

Discrediting a pessimistic future and filling in uncertainty with optimism gives us the best chance to pursue the outcomes and experiences we want without multitasking by additionally avoiding the outcomes and experiences we don't want.

Let's look at how Jamelle discredited her A-shaped belief, as well as a few other examples.

Activating Event: Playing in Q-Series.
Belief: "I must make the LPGA Tour on my first try this year, or I'm not good enough to ever make the LPGA Tour."

Consequences: Increasing self-imposed pressure, frustration, anxiety, competing hesitantly and defensively, continued A-shaped thoughts, unstable confidence, discouragement, dread of competing, and fear of the future.

Discrediting:

Is this true?

It's not true. Many golfers have gone on to make professional tours and win tournaments after failing to qualify the first time around. Also, no rule says I can't make the Tour in future years, although it may be more difficult.

Is this beneficial?

Obviously not. Holding onto this belief is ruining my confidence, causing me to play defensively, and making me fear the idea of playing professional golf. It's also not making golf very fun for me.

What are all the contributing factors?

The most apparent factor is the way I'm thinking about qualifying. That's what's causing the lack of confidence and the dread of not making the Tour. Another factor is that I've surrounded myself with coaches who all have different inputs, which is confusing me. Both situations are changeable, specific, and nonpersonal.

What happens if you don't qualify for the LPGA Tour?

Not making the Tour would definitely suck. I've invested a lot of time and energy into this opportunity, and it's something that I really want. I'd be unsatisfied and disappointed if I didn't make the Tour—but not forever. I'll have chances to try again and play more golf in general. Not making the Tour also doesn't mean that I can't be successful in other tours or other areas of my life. And even though I will have failed to make the Tour, that won't mean that I am a failure as a person. It will mean that at least I had the guts to go for what I really want, even if there was a chance that I wouldn't get it.

Activating Event: Losing strokes on the last few holes.

Belief: "I shouldn't be dropping shots to finish a round. If I do, that means I can't ever close a round or hold a lead."

Consequences: Anxiety about the last few holes of a round, overswinging, second-guessing, dread about ruining a round in the last few holes, and being off time during the middle of a round.

Discrediting

Is this true?

It's not true. There's no rule anywhere that says if or where you should gain or lose strokes. Also, I've lost strokes at the end of a round before, so just because I feel like it shouldn't happen doesn't actually keep it from happening. What's more important is how I address playing the last few holes.

Is this beneficial?

No. If anything, it only increases my anxiety and leads to playing shots that are forced and scared, leading to more dropped shots.

What are all the contributing factors?

Nerves, thinking about the end of my round before I even get there, thinking about the times I've dropped shots to end a round before, my belief that I shouldn't be doing that, and not breathing effectively to be present at those times. All these areas can be improved with training.

What happens if you drop shots to end a match?

It'll mean that I dropped a few strokes, and while I would prefer not to, it's not a reflection of my entire round, just the last few shots that impact my final score. It's an area of my game that can be improved, and it doesn't mean that I'm personally incapable of closing a round.

Activating Event: Missing short putts.

Belief: "Missing short putts means I suck at putting."

Consequences: Fear of failure, defensive putting strokes, unstable confidence, anxiety about putting and failing, muscle tension, discouragement, and self-loathing.

Discrediting

 Is this true?

 It's not true. There's no rule anywhere that says missing a putt means you suck at putting. Even the best players in the world miss short putts. Putts are mutually exclusive events, and the only way for my confidence in future putts to be linked to a current putt is if I do that myself.

 Is this beneficial?

 No. It makes me anxious over putt shots, hurts my confidence, makes me dread short putts, and causes me to make forced, tense strokes that don't get the ball started on line, leading to more missed putts.

 What are all the contributing factors?

 The way I'm thinking about short putts is what's causing me to fear them, not the short putts themselves. Also, not all short putts are the same. Some four-foot putts are faster and have more breaks than some twenty-foot putts. The length of the putt is only part of what makes a putt difficult.

 What happens if you miss a short putt?

 It just means that I missed a short putt that I would have preferred to make. Missing a short putt counts just the same as missing a long putt. It just seems worse because I keep telling myself that I should never miss short putts. It'll cost me a stroke, but it'll only cost me more strokes if I think about it in ways that influence future putts.

Activating Event: Not performing well after winning a tournament or finding significant success.

Belief: "I have to always perform like I did when I was winning and most successful; otherwise, my wins and successes were a fluke."

Consequences: Unproductive expectations, self-imposed pressure, A-shaped inner dialogue, second-guessing, forcing shots, and anxiety.

Discrediting

 Is this true?

It's not true. Each round is its own round. Just because you play
    really well in one doesn't mean you will do the same in another
    one later. Nowhere in the rules does it say that you have to
    be at your best all the time. No one in the history of golf has
    performed at their best at every single tournament. Golf is a
    difficult sport, and just because you have had great success once
    doesn't mean that will always happen.

Is this beneficial?

It's not beneficial. It creates an unrealistic and rigid expectation. It
    causes me to devalue my past successes by trying to live up to
    them every time I compete. It causes anxiety and contributes to
    me playing shots defensively. It also makes playing less fun.

What are all the contributing factors?

I performed at my best to win a tournament, and I'm proud of
    that. However, if some things had gone somewhat differently, I
    may not have won. Many factors went into playing well in that
    event, and those same factors don't play out the same way in
    every event. I can only control my play style and how I think
    about my own career. I also see now that a lot of the pressure
    to live up to my past successes comes from my thoughts about
    what other people will think of me if I don't perform that well
    all the time.

What happens if you don't perform well after winning and past
    success?

Failure and success are a part of every competition, neither lasts
    forever, and neither defines all areas of your life. Performing
    poorly isn't satisfying, but it's also not the end of the world, and
    I don't need others' opinions to validate my success. Not being
    at my best doesn't make me a fluke. I earned that previous win
    and that success regardless of how well I play in any other
    tournament.

The ABCs of credibility begin with a mindful awareness of our A-shaped
beliefs, the events that test and expose those beliefs, and the consequences
of our beliefs. With that awareness, we can practically and systematically

discredit and dispute our irrational, unbeneficial, and pessimistic beliefs by thinking about them mindfully using facts, our own direct experiential evidence, and intentional questions. The last step is to effectively reshape our A-shaped beliefs into credible V-shaped beliefs. To do this, we simplify and streamline the ABCs we've already worked through.

It may also be helpful to think of V-shaped beliefs as mindful behaviors. To do so, start at the top, creating space in the present by taking a discredited, irrational, and unbeneficial *necessity* and making it an authentic intention. Here we acknowledge the things we authentically *want* without making them absolute necessities. Reshaping doesn't mean that we convince ourselves that we don't want or care about something. There's no credibility in telling ourselves lies about what we want. We can want something as much as we genuinely want it so long as we're mindful not to cross the line that makes it a necessity. So, if what we want is to play on tour, shoot under par, close a round better, or have our efforts lead to the results we want, we can freely allow ourselves to want those things. It's okay to want whatever we want to whatever degree we want it as long as wanting it doesn't pass the point of diminishing returns of a necessity.

Instead of a "should," "shouldn't," "ought to," "can't stand it if," "have to," "need to," or "must" at the top of an A-shaped belief, the top portion of a credible V-shaped belief consists of words or phrases like "want to," "would really like it if," "strongly prefer to," "would love it if," and "it would be great if." We create credible space in the present moment by allowing ourselves to acknowledge the things we want to pursue, but we are deliberate in not thinking about *needing* them rigidly and irrationally. "I have to start my round by hitting the first fairway" becomes "It would be really beneficial to hit the first fairway." The subtle difference between a rational, beneficial desire and an irrational, unbeneficial need gives us literal and figurative breathing room in the present moment to execute our skills.

Next, we move to the bottom to project a future that we may not like but are willing to accept by taking a discredited pessimistic explanation of the future and making it optimistic instead. We mindfully consider what the future means for us and about us if it doesn't work out the way we'd prefer. Simply, credible willingness to accept an uncertain future comes from optimistically considering the worst-case scenario. If the future includes the possibility of mistakes, failures, emotional discomfort, and judgments from others, we consider them—mindfully and optimistically.

Instead of explaining past, present, and future events as permanent, pervasive, and personal, as with an A-shaped belief, the bottom portion of a credible V-shaped belief explains events and future consequences as temporary, localized, and impersonal. We project a future that we are willing to accept by objectively using context and direct questions. "Failing means I'm never going to be good enough" becomes "Failing means there will be other chances," "I can improve in a few specific areas," or "Failing now is not the same as being a failure forever and as a person." Compared to a pessimistic explanatory style, an optimistic one decreases our perceived levels of threat and gives us more freedom to credibly permit ourselves to take calculated risks.

Here's what Jamelle's effectively reshaped belief looks like, along with some other examples of A-shaped and V-shaped thoughts that you may find helpful.

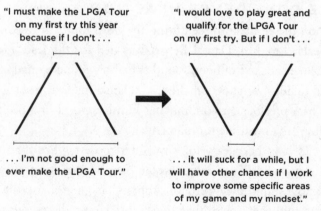

"I must make the LPGA Tour on my first try this year because if I don't . . .

. . . I'm not good enough to ever make the LPGA Tour."

"I would love to play great and qualify for the LPGA Tour on my first try. But if I don't . . .

. . . it will suck for a while, but I will have other chances if I work to improve some specific areas of my game and my mindset."

"I have to be perfect because if I'm not . . .

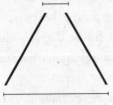

. . . I'm never going to be good enough."

"I must not miss any putt inside five feet because if I do . . .

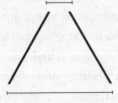

. . . I won't ever make any putts inside five feet."

"I shouldn't ever be hitting bad shots because if I am . . .

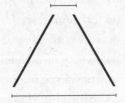

. . . I'm unworthy and incapable of success."

"I would love to be the top player on my team, but if I'm not . . .

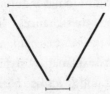

. . . it doesn't dictate how I'll play going forward or mean that I'm not good enough."

"I want to hit every fairway and every green, but when I don't . . .

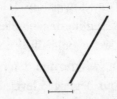

. . . it's only one shot. It's always possible to make birdie from the rough or get up and down."

"I would love to make every single putt, but when I don't . . .

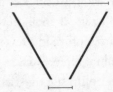

. . . it means that putting is really hard and that there are things I can do to get better. Just because a putt misses doesn't make it a bad putt."

STABLE CONFIDENCE IN ACTION

Standing on the eighteenth tee during the third round of the 2021 AT&T Pebble Beach Pro-Am, Daniel Berger was tied for the lead. He promptly blasted his tee shot out of bounds and ended his round by making a double bogey and falling two shots off the lead. Daniel made a mistake off the tee that cost him precious strokes, moving him backward in a pack of several players all vying to win the tournament.

It would have been easy for any golfer to destabilize their confidence after such a mistake. Many golfers would have berated themselves, ruminating about how stupid they were for dropping shots in that position. Others would have told themselves that they'd just blown the whole tournament and that they weren't the kind of golfer who can close a round and win a tournament.

Here's what Daniel Berger had to say in his post-round interview just moments after making a costly double bogey.

Well, I actually played pretty good—I mean, I obviously finished with a double, but, I mean, I'm still two shots out of the lead, so I feel pretty good about my chances going into tomorrow ... [If I] drop a few more putts, and it'll be a good week.

... I hit a bunch of really good golf shots. Today was really tough, you know. It was blowing fifteen, twenty all day. [I had a] bunch of putts that just barely missed, and ... it's a hard day when it blows at Pebble. So, you know, overall, I'm pretty happy. Obviously, I would like that swing back on the last hole, but I'm not going to let it ruin my week, for sure.

—TenGolf Television, "Daniel Berger: Saturday Flash Interview AT&T Pebble Beach Pro Am," February 13, 2021

Watching Daniel's body language and hearing the composure in his voice during the interview, it's clear that Daniel has stable confidence built on credible V-shaped beliefs. Daniel rationally and beneficially recognized an authentic intention not to have hit his tee shot out of bounds when he said, "Obviously, I would like that swing back on the last hole." But notice that he didn't say that he *must not* make those kinds of mistakes or that he *shouldn't* have hit a wayward drive. Instead of making himself feel worse and not accepting his current reality that he had just lost a few strokes on the last hole, he honestly acknowledged that he preferred not to make the mistake and accepted his current reality, even though it certainly wasn't what he wanted. He created space for himself by thinking about making a double bogey rationally and beneficially.

Daniel also explained the mistake optimistically. Instead of interpreting making double bogey as a long-term problem that would cost him the tournament, even with a round left to play, Daniel saw the mistake as a short-term setback, saying, "I'm still two shots out of the lead." He also explained the last hole as a specific mistake and not as a pervasive reflection of his round; the tee shot was just one mistake in a round where he'd "hit a bunch of really good golf shots." And at no point in his comments did Daniel explain his round or the eighteenth hole personally as evidence that he wasn't good enough to play.

In this interview, Daniel considered many contributing factors to objectively evaluate his round, not using the eighteenth hole as the only measure of his performance. He considered that he putted well: "[I had a] bunch of putts that just barely missed." And he considered the difficult conditions of the course that impacted his round: "Today was really tough, you know. It was blowing fifteen, twenty all day . . . it's a hard day when it blows at Pebble." He wasn't making excuses; he was considering a wider and more objective set of factors that contributed to his score, not just a single hole that didn't go well.

It's unlikely that when Daniel came to the eighteenth tee hole the next day needing a birdie to win or a par to force a playoff, he didn't think about how the hole had played out the day before. Most likely, he was also nervous about being in a position to win. Standing on the edge of the Oceanside tee box, he came to a choice point, a moment where he could either shy away and protect himself from making a mistake that would lose him the tournament or give himself permission to play freely in pursuit of the shots and results he wanted, knowing there was no guarantee that things would work out.

Given Daniel's V-shaped thinking, it's not surprising that he swung freely and split the fairway with a 276-yard drive. It's also not a surprise that, despite the Pacific Ocean awaiting an approach shot too far left, and deep rough, a tree, and bunkers awaiting an approach too far right, Daniel swung freely again and flushed a 3-wood with a 250-yard tight draw into the middle of the eighteenth green. Daniel's stable confidence wasn't the only factor that contributed to his final-round 7-under 65, but it was the only thing that could give him credible permission to freely execute his skills with the tournament on the line. As a bonus, Daniel also sunk a thirty-foot eagle putt to secure his fourth win on the PGA Tour and move up to thirteenth in the World Golf Ranking.

Most certainly, Daniel is an expertly skilled golfer who works incredibly hard to build his skills. But what allowed him access to those skills under pressure was a credible inner dialogue giving him permission to play freely, even when the results mattered greatly but were not assured.

GET TO THE ROOT

The A-shaped beliefs that destabilize confidence and make it most difficult to play freely revolve around our personal and subjective notions of being good enough, those that "validate" our efforts, and our thoughts about being judged by others. Given how we celebrate and idolize those we deem successful and how we often harshly judge those we deem failures, it's not surprising that we learn and biasedly confirm many of the A-shaped beliefs on these topics as we do, as they are tightly interwoven with our egos.

Perhaps you're wondering, "How will I know when I get to the belief(s) that are at the root of how stable, or unstable, my confidence is?" The general answer is that you'll know because you'll have a sense of clarity, a sense of "Oh. Yeah, that makes sense," so to speak. Or you'll feel a sense of emotional discomfort, a sense of "Oh—that's the thing I've been worried about and trying to avoid and that's been keeping me from giving myself permission to freely pursue what I want."

As you do your inner work, keep in mind that everyone is different and has different beliefs at the root of their psychological framework. Some people learn irrational, perfectionistic thinking and learn to consider desired outcomes as absolute necessities. For others who learn to judge other people and themselves harshly, their root beliefs are a layer or two down and more personal. It's not making a mistake they really worry about; it's their own harsh inner dialogue or others' judgments after a mistake that they explain pessimistically and destabilizes confidence.

So, as you do your inner work and your ABCs, you may need to peel back the layers of the onion and ask some difficult questions. What are the beliefs you have that may be keeping you from building stable confidence and playing more freely?

If you're finding it difficult to clarify the beliefs at the root, it's often helpful to consider the shapes of the beliefs you have revolving around the question "What if I give my best effort, and that's not enough?" In truth, this is *the* existential question and choice point that reveals how stable your confidence is—or isn't.

And to be very clear, no human can credibly avoid this question or the choice points that expose our answers to it. Inevitably, there will be times when our best efforts may not and will not be enough. Because our best efforts can't credibly guarantee success all the time, there is always the possibility within our current reality of giving all we have as best as we know how and still failing. Thus, we don't have the choice to avoid this fundamental question, and there are only two ways we can answer it—we can answer it mindfully on our own terms and with V-shaped consideration, or we can try to avoid the question and cover it up, trying to assure ourselves of comfort and certainty. With the latter option, the choice points where results matter the most will force our brain's default survival settings to answer the question, almost always in A-shaped thinking and denying permission to play freely and see how things shake out.

Every time I have worked with clients to address their beliefs about this question, their vulnerability and honesty have cultivated credible space, acceptance, and more stable confidence. However, being vulnerable and honest isn't always easy.

With respect and reverence for all my clients and their competitive experiences, another question I often ask is "What is it that you're really protecting yourself from?" Rather than letting them dance around beliefs that aren't getting to the root of their unstable confidence, I challenge them to mindfully think about their beliefs revolving around the choice points most important to them.

One unavoidable consequence of performance is the opinions of others. Golf at all levels is a social sport and thus exposes us to others' thoughts about our performances. Many players have difficulty giving themselves credible permission to play freely because they worry about other people judging them negatively. Their A-shaped beliefs mistakenly assert that other people's negative opinions *must* be true and *must* be more valuable than their opinions of themselves. The A-shaped belief at the root is not about how they explain their golf game but instead about how they explain the possibility of people's unfavorable opinions.

Any golfer can spend all day trying to convince themselves that other people won't have opinions of them and their game or that, if people do, their opinions will always be favorable. But no such reality can be credibly assured. The A-shaped belief keeping golfers from building stable confidence and competing freely is something along the lines of "Other people cannot think I'm a bad golfer because if they do, I will therefore be a bad golfer since their opinions are correct."

Here's something important to note about beliefs that create fear of people's opinions, or FOPO. Humans are social creatures; we need connection to other people. Thus, others' opinions *about* us do matter to a certain degree in our lives—it would be almost impossible to build and maintain meaningful relationships with others without them. It's a psychosocial need for every human to develop what's called our "social self," the part of us that tries to manage the impressions we make on other people and cares about whether that impression lands favorably. Having a developed social self helps us to know how to act around others in ways that build meaningful and healthy connections, the types that allow us to grow and enjoy the things we do together, like golf.

However, when we believe that people *must* have favorable opinions of us, our social self becomes overly invested in others' opinions to the point that we worry and become fearful. When this A-shaped belief colors our experiences, including our golf experience, it creates a habit that keeps us from valuing and accepting ourselves. In essence, we come to value others' opinions of us more than being authentic. The habit also creates the perception that people's opinions about us are far more important than they actually are, and it makes it difficult to build stable confidence.

Of course, there is no rule that says other people *must not* have certain opinions of us. People naturally form opinions, but rarely do we have an accurate assessment of them. Even if we do, we can't control those opinions. It's not a matter of *if* others have opinions about us and our performance; it's a matter of what we believe *about* those opinions and what value we give to them.

For many golfers, believing that others *must* have favorable opinions of them creates significant constriction. These golfers also explain others' unfavorable opinions about their performances as facts. To them, "being a bad golfer" is a permanent state that will pervasively impact their future performances, and it is a deeply personal conclusion. Only when we challenge ourselves to mindfully examine what we are really protecting themselves from, like others' opinions, will our inner dialogue become credible enough to give us permission to play more freely.

Your life and your golf game are yours and yours alone. You don't have to ask yourself difficult questions if you don't want to. There's no rule mandating such self-exploration, and it's not helpful to go digging around for beliefs that don't exist just for the sake of digging. But for those who really want to fully explore their potential, perform better, and enjoy golf more, grappling with difficult questions and getting to the root beliefs in your psychological framework are the fastest ways to do so.

The inner work takes time, consistency, and repetition. Research shows that based on how our brain is designed, our brain needs to perceive five spacious and acceptable events or experiences to dilute the influence of one perceived constricting and threatening event or experience. Since how we perceive events and experiences is determined by the shape of our beliefs, consistently reshaping our beliefs will lead to thinking about events and experiences differently and ultimately having a different, and more beneficial, direct experience with them.

Just like grooving a golf swing, refining a putting stroke, or building a healthy lifestyle, the inner work is ongoing. Stable confidence requires consistent attention over time. For many of my clients, mindfulness training, mapping habits, and doing the ABCs are as consistent parts of their golf game as practicing, strengthening, conditioning, and calibrating equipment.

It also bears mentioning that as you do the inner work, you're also allowed to seek perspectives from people you trust, a performance consultant like myself, or even a mental-health professional. Often, having someone who is trained to listen and help to nonjudgmentally organize our thoughts and source beliefs can be an invaluable guide through the inner work.

Here are some blank ABCs for you to use on your own. Use the structures, descriptions, and examples described previously to guide you as needed.

Activating Event:

Belief:

Consequences:

Discrediting
    Is this true?

Is this beneficial?

What are all the contributing factors?

What happens if you do/don't?

Effectively Reshape:

Credible V-shaped belief:

Activating Event:

Belief:

Consequences:

Discrediting
Is this true?

Is this beneficial?

What are all the contributing factors?

What happens if you do/don't?

Effectively Reshape:

Credible V-shaped belief:

GETTING TO THE ROOT AND STEPPING OUT OF THE TRAP LOOP

What's important to understand about being in the trap loop of unstable confidence created by A-shaped beliefs is that there's no amount of good shots that can play you out of a trap loop for good, even for the best players in the world. Ben Hogan is widely considered one of the best golfers of all time. He won sixty-four times on the PGA Tour and won nine majors—and even *he* wasn't good enough or successful enough to escape the trap loop of unstable confidence by simply playing better. Here's what he had to say about how unstable his confidence was despite how good he was and how well he played.

> In the seasons before the war, as I learned more and more about the golf swing and how to play golf, I enjoyed increasing success on the tournament circuit. Nevertheless, I never felt genuinely confident about my game until 1946. Up to that year, while I knew once I was on the course and playing well that I had the stuff that day to make a good showing, before a round I had no idea whether I'd shoot a 69 or a 79. I felt my game might suddenly go sour on any given morning. I had no assurance that if I was a little bit off my best form, I could still produce a respectable round. My friends on tour used to tell me that I was silly to worry, that I had grooved a swing and had every reason to have confidence in it. But my self-doubting never stopped. Regardless of how well I was going, I was still concerned about the next day and the next day and the next day.

Hogan's detailed description of being in the trap loop of unstable confidence is something many players can relate to. We can see that he had brief, unstable stints when he would feel confident after playing well on the course.

But even when he would put together a good round, his boost in confidence would be temporary at best, and the trap loop would start all over again; he felt like his performance was teetering on a razor's edge day in and day out. As he notes, there was no level to which he could groove his swing, amount of success on the course, or number of positive affirmations that could create stable confidence. Not surprisingly, even the great Ben Hogan experienced significant and continued self-doubt and anxiety because he was trying to build confidence from the same unstable sources that most golfers do: comfort, certainty, and outcomes—none of which can be assured nor required to play good golf.

It wasn't until Hogan mindfully considered how he was thinking *about* a specific A-shaped belief at the root of his inner dialogue that his confidence stabilized. Hogan explains:

> In 1946, my attitude suddenly changed. I honestly began to feel that I could count on playing fairly well each time I went out, that there was no practical reason for me to suddenly "lose it all." I would guess what lay behind my new confidence was this: I stopped trying to do a great number of difficult things perfectly because it had become clear in my mind that this ambitious over-thoroughness was neither possible nor advisable . . .
>
> —Ben Hogan's *Five Lessons: The Modern Fundamentals of Golf*, pages 113

Hogan tells us that his inner dialogue had newfound credibility *not* because he had created a sense of comfort, certainty, and self-assurance that he would play well and get the outcomes he wanted. This credibility came from directly addressing an A-shaped belief about perfection, a belief that looked something like "I must play perfectly in order to be confident that my game won't fall apart." It was the A-shaped belief that was creating constriction and perceived threat for Hogan and, ultimately, the self-doubt and anxiety he was experiencing. No matter how well he played, how much success he had, and how many people told him he *should* be confident, Hogan's confidence didn't stabilize until he addressed the root belief *about* his golf game, which finally allowed him credible space in the present moment and acceptance of an uncertain and imperfect future. Only then was he able to step out of the trap loop and play more freely, something any golfer can do with a mindful awareness and a willingness to do the inner work.

COMMON A-SHAPED BELIEFS AT THE ROOT OF PERFORMANCE

The challenges that come with performance have a way of testing our psychological framework and exposing the areas where our beliefs undermine our confidence and efforts toward growth. We all have our own learned A-shaped beliefs that impact our lives and performances. However, there are a few A-shaped beliefs so commonly held that they have been identified, observed, and researched rigorously in many performance realms. For anyone looking to play more consistently and enjoy their performances more, it's important to be aware of and understand two of these specific A-shaped beliefs: one related to the relationship between talent and effort, and the other pertaining to the relationship between us and our craft.

UNDERSTANDING TALENT AND EFFORT

Culturally, we have a real love affair with talent. We talk about it all the time. We hear about it everywhere related to just about everything. Every year, organizations in professional sports, college recruiting, academic admissions, and the corporate world continue to invest massive amounts of resources into finding talented people. Such a strong emphasis on talent leads to questions of who has it and how to best develop it. Thanks to an economic boom in sports and some well-designed research, we now understand more about talent than ever before. Through countless research studies, scientists have explored talent through multiple lenses like intelligence measures, genetic codes, family history, and biomechanical analyses of elite performers.

All this research is intended to identify talent and predict as early and accurately as possible who will be the highest achievers. These goals aren't surprising when you consider how valuable they might be for organizations. But, of course, you don't have to be a researcher to know that talent definitely exists and comes in several forms.

We can hear talent: if you're watching *American Idol*, it doesn't take long to identify who the most talented singers are. We can see talent: you don't have to know much about basketball to see that LeBron James is an enormously talented player. And for less than an hour of your time, you can have a trained professional test your IQ and tell you exactly how intellectually talented you are.

Although these observations answer some obvious questions about talent, they leave complex questions unanswered. For instance, how is it that so many people with objectively high measures of talent and all the resources needed to be successful still fail to reach their potential? At the same time, why do others who have less talent and fewer resources turn out to be remarkably successful?

The more we look into these types of questions, the more we see that achievement and long-term success are, in many ways, byproducts of a relationship between talent and effort—and not everyone has equal amounts of either. Talent is the rate at which you increase your skill by applying effort. One thing we know for sure about talent is that it is not equally distributed; some people can increase their skills faster than others can, and some learn quicker than others, particularly in certain areas. For example, some people have more talent for a sport like golf, or even for a certain skill set within a craft, like ball striking over putting.

In truth, each of us has differing amounts of talent across an array of domains. If we're looking at the relationship between talent and how skills are developed, talent is clearly the sexier of the ingredients. Everyone would take more talent if they could, myself included—even though talent is highly overrated.

Don't get me wrong; talent is extremely valuable, but talent is overrated because, when it comes to long-term success and a fulfilling relationship with our respective crafts, how we apply effort matters more than talent does. Even though talent is the sexier ingredient contributing to achievement, talent alone is a terrible predictor of future success.

Talent is part of what leads to achievement, but we overestimate it by focusing only on what's obvious about it. Colleges and universities use standardized tests, the NFL uses results from the pre-draft Combine, and college coaches flock to recruiting rankings. Yet there's no significant evidence to suggest that any of these measures of talent predict future success with any measurable certainty. More recent research examining a variety of areas—including athletics, fine arts, academics, and business—found that talent more strongly predicted two other things.

First, people who are more talented don't always show up or keep showing up. Angela Duckworth is a professor of psychology at the University of Pennsylvania and the world's foremost expert on grit, which she defines as passion and perseverance toward long-term goals. Dr. Duckworth is quick to point out that talent and effort aren't tied together. In study after study, she finds that when she measures proxies for talent, such as intelligence or athleticism, there is no correlation between talent and effort. Put simply, just because you have talent doesn't mean you'll actually show up to use it. In more recent studies, Dr. Duckworth actually found a negative correlation between talent and effort, meaning that, over time, those with more talent are more likely to quit than those with less talent.

There's no shortage of people born with plenty of talent to be good at something. But it's important for us to remember that everyone starts at the

The Learning Curve

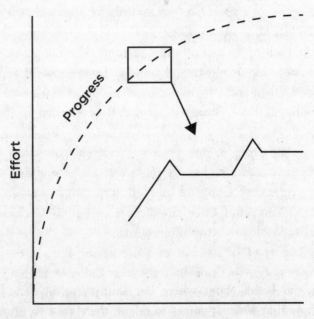

bottom of the learning curve; no one is born already knowing how to be good at something. In reality, we don't know how many golfers are able to compete at the highest levels. Only those who put in the effort to show up and keep showing up to develop their skills actually find out how good they can become.

Dr. Duckworth also found that talented people won't necessarily do the things required to get better. A common characteristic of those who achieve at a high level is that they continually put in effort to improve. They constantly look for opportunities to make progress, so they're invested in both the quantity and quality of their efforts.

Because we tend to notice and celebrate people after they're deemed successful, a common and dangerous misconception is that simply being talented is a straight line to success. But in reality, if we observe how people become successful, we see that progress is nonlinear and is comprised of a series of steps along the learning curve.

Specifically, when we invest continued effort to develop our skills, we see periods when performance improves, sometimes quite rapidly. Improvement is then followed by periods of decline in performance as we learn new and more complicated skills. These lulls are then followed by plateaus in performance as we figure out how to master and integrate those newly acquired skills.

We can see that each step toward improvement requires more time and more effort for smaller and smaller increments of progress. So while it's clear why committed effort is more valuable than talent alone, it's also clear why that commitment can be difficult.

Putting in the quantity and quality of effort required to get better, even in small and seemingly inconsequential ways, can be arduous. But, rather than talent alone, those tiny increments of progress earned through effort are what add up over time and ultimately lead to excellence. Just having talent doesn't mean we'll actually do anything with it. The activating agent for talent, and a vital ingredient for achievement, is effort, which counts twice: once for acquiring skills, and once for applying skills.

And what drives effort? You guessed it: our psychological framework—specifically, our belief about where our ability comes from. Decades of research show that when it comes to talent, there are two primary beliefs about where talent comes from. Carol Dweck is a professor of psychology at Stanford University and a pioneer in the field. Through several decades of research, she found that these two opposing beliefs about talent create radically different experiences and results.

On the one hand, there is the belief that talent is a fixed trait: whatever level of talent you are born with cannot be changed. Either you have the talent required or you don't. A person who believes this would likely agree with statements like "Some people are just naturals" and "You have a certain amount of talent, and that's that." Those with this belief have what Dr. Dweck refers to as a "fixed mindset."

On the other hand, there is a belief that talent is something that is grown—something that can be developed through effort. A person who believes this would agree with statements like "No matter who you are, you can get better" and "Hard work and dedication lead to success." Those with this belief have what Dr. Dweck refers to as a "growth mindset."

When studying people's core beliefs across a wide variety of ages and competitive settings, she discovered that people with a fixed mindset and those with a growth mindset have vastly different priorities. The top priorities for those with a fixed mindset are to always look good and at all costs; above all, they must never look bad. With these priorities, their approach to performance is to avoid difficult tasks and avoid taking calculated risks that might show that they aren't as good as they want to seem.

A fixed mindset is another A-shaped belief that creates an unproductive habit of entangling our ego with our performance and long-term growth. Those with a fixed mindset also learn to become overly concerned with other people's opinions of them and their performance: those opinions are seen as another metric to confirm or deny whether they do or don't have enough talent. This concern can easily turn into a fear of peoples' opinions because believing that those opinions are true has the potential to reflect and confirm the fear of not being talented enough. Over time, competing becomes more about protecting our ego and maintaining an image of being talented than actually getting better and performing well. Needless to say, confidence is unstable for those with a fixed mindset.

Conversely, for those with a growth mindset, the top priorities are to always learn and get better—and at all costs. With these priorities, the approach to performance becomes actively seeking and engaging in tasks and taking calculated risks that allow for one's skills to be tested. Instead of ego protection and image maintenance, a growth mindset forms healthy ego strength and a genuine humility that allows us to be immersed in our efforts within our craft.

As you can probably guess, the priorities for those with a growth mindset are incredibly useful for making progress and building stable confidence. When we also consider that those with a growth mindset learn to value the two strongest predictors of future success—delayed gratification and effort—it's not surprising why those with a growth mindset are significantly more resilient than those with a fixed mindset, who tend to value ease and emotional comfort.

Ease and comfort aren't inherently bad values, but they're ineffective for developing and applying skills and performing under difficult conditions. Although some people make success look easy and comfortable, climbing the learning curve and performing at a high level when we come to choice points are anything but. They both require tremendous effort that involves stretching our comfort zones over and over again.

Given their priorities and values, those with a fixed mindset devote their focus to other people's opinions because high praise fulfills their priorities to look good and avoid looking bad. The problem is that these priorities and values channel focus away from executing skills in the present moment and toward things that can't be controlled.

But for those with a growth mindset, their priorities and values act as a funnel that narrows their focus to the present moment and to controllable performance elements. It's not that having a growth mindset means not caring about scores or winning tournaments; it means focusing on effort that leads to results and improves performance and the chances of actually reaching those results.

Moreover, for people with a growth mindset, failure is a healthy and valuable reminder that our most authentic and fulfilling pursuits don't come easily and that long-term success rarely comes inside of our comfort zone. With a growth mindset, success that comes too easily is a sign that the bar is perhaps too low and not testing their current skill level or challenging them to improve.

On a basic level, those with a growth mindset actively seek out opportunities to test their skills because such opportunities give them information about how to get better and produce better results. However, for those with a fixed mindset, testing skills in difficult conditions is perceived as threatening because these people seek validation. Such a difference highlights that the fundamental problem with having a fixed mindset is that things are guaranteed to get really difficult. No one goes through any extended period without failing, making mistakes, and suffering setbacks. Eventually, we're all going to run into challenges that exceed our current skill level, and we'll fail, potentially looking bad and feeling uncomfortable. Those with a fixed mindset, who are unwilling to risk failure and suffer from unstable confidence, are effectively unprepared for such inevitable circumstances.

Even more problematic are the deeper beliefs that a fixed mindset develops. When we believe that talent is innate and cannot be changed, applying real effort is seen as a bad thing—in other words, if you have talent, you *shouldn't* need to apply much effort. This is one of the most dangerous beliefs anyone can have and is one of the main reasons why so many talented people and promising young athletes fail to reach or even pursue their potential.

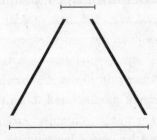
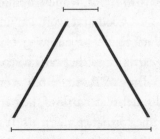

"I shouldn't have to try this hard, and I must not fail because . . .

"I must not struggle or fail because if I do . . .

. . . it would mean that I'm not talented enough or special."

. . . it confirms that I'm not talented enough."

The A-shaped belief that "I shouldn't have to apply effort, and if I do, that means I'm not talented or special" is irrational. But in a fixed mindset, ease and success are seen as necessities to confirm a personal identity of being talented, special, intelligent, or any other trait believed to be innate. The belief is highly unbeneficial because it encourages people, especially those with a lot of talent, to do things with as little effort as possible. This causes them to develop habits where they'll coast along until they eventually reach steps on the learning curve beyond their current skill level. Those steps will require them to apply real effort, but they won't be able to because they won't have developed the cognitive or emotional capacity to do so. What those with fixed mindsets fear is the possibility of applying effort without any excuses for failure and then still failing. To them, their best effort not being good enough is perceived as permanent, pervasive, and acutely personal.

However, those with a growth mindset develop deeper beliefs that perceive effort as the fuel for growth, thus building their capacity to step outside of their comfort zones. Those with a growth mindset rationally see success as a preference and not a necessity to confirm how talented they are or how good they can become. A growth mindset is beneficial because it promotes learning to enjoy hard work, embraces emotional discomfort, and allows us to compete freely because it explains both failure and success credibly and optimistically. Failure isn't necessarily enjoyable for those with a growth mindset, but it's viewed rationally and optimistically; failure becomes valuable feedback for improving, not a threat to be avoided.

As you can imagine, these different beliefs about where talent comes from lead to drastically different experiences. Nearly one hundred studies show that while users of each mindset experience both positive and negative emotions, those with a fixed mindset experience a wider range of negative emotions more often and more intensely than do those with a growth mindset. Moreover, neural-imaging studies also show neuroplastic changes in the brain based on which mindset we ascribe to. The brain areas associated with grief, fear, and discomfort are more developed in people with a fixed mindset, compared to the areas of the brain associated with task immersion, patience, and learning that are more developed in those with a growth mindset.

In a fixed mindset, we see ourselves as either having the amount of talent required or not having it, and that's all we get. And if we believe that we have enough fixed talent, we *must* not experience real struggle or failure because we will perceive both through a pessimistic lens, giving us credible reasons to give up when things inevitably become challenging. If having to apply effort and failing causes considerable emotional disturbance and confirms that you aren't what you thought you were, you'll learn habits to fear and avoid effort and struggle.

Herein lies the reasons that those with a fixed mindset create trap loops, lack resilience, find it intensely difficult to perform under pressure, and weed themselves out as the level of competition increases long before it actually exceeds the limits of their potential.

Earlier in this section, we discussed how important even the smallest tweaks are for evolving how we think. Those tweaks are most evident when comparing the differences between a fixed and growth mindset. In a recent study, researchers tested whether a mindset change could impact college students placed in remedial math classes because they had not yet mastered basic high-school math. In the study, half of the students were given a short article to read detailing how the brain learns knowledge and skills through continued effort and deliberate practice. After the students read the article, researchers then asked those students to simply summarize what they'd read. Students who read and summarized the article got better grades and dropped out of their math classes half as often as the other students who were given a different article on an unrelated topic. Reshaping a fixed mindset into a growth mindset through this simple tweak led to more resilience, more learning, and better outcomes—the same pattern I see with golfers over and over again.

What's clear is that during a golf career, regardless of how talented someone is, every golfer will reach many points where the challenges they face are outside of their current skill level. Those points might be moving up a level of competition, experiencing new and more difficult competitive conditions, dealing with injuries, doing the inner work, or navigating the increased scrutiny that comes with success.

When these inevitable points are reached, our beliefs are the driving force for how triggering these events will be to us and for what behaviors we'll have learned to respond to them with. It's been my observation that those with a fixed mindset get weeded out shortly after they reach the points where their current level of talent alone isn't enough to move them forward. More accurately, they weed themselves out at these points because their belief about their ability leaves them woefully unprepared for the increasing demands of moving up the learning curve.

Conversely, it's been my observation that when golfers with a growth mindset reach the same points, they meet those challenges with an open mind, a willingness for change, and a readiness to put forth the effort to improve.

The same events do not trigger unproductive behaviors, and, more often than not, those with a growth mindset continue to persist when challenged—and even when frustrated. They do so not because they can just will themselves to or because they were blessed at birth but because their psychological framework about where their ability comes from allows them to.

The good news is that it's never too late to examine and reshape our psychological framework, which means that we can always develop a growth mindset. Mark Manson is a best-selling author with a better understanding of core beliefs than that of many psychologists. Mark expertly articulates that the power of a growth mindset lies in believing that talent is developed with effort, which leads to a rich passion for improvement. Mark points out that for those who develop exceptional levels of ability, their passion for improvement stems from a belief that they are, in fact, not talented enough to get by on talent alone and that effort is the key to improvement. This is an anti-entitlement approach to growth and performance.

Mark's observation is supported by decades of research in a variety of fields, including medicine, academics, business, athletics, and skilled labor, all of which shows that people who become great at any given craft become great in large part because they recognize that they aren't already great, an acknowledgment psychologists call "professional self-doubt." Contrary to the belief that people who are great believe they are great, many don't; often, they see themselves as average, even mediocre, but believe that with continued effort they can improve their levels of mastery for any craft.

Whenever I give a workshop that includes a discussion of fixed and growth mindsets, I'm invariably asked, "But what about natural talent? What about savants and prodigies?" These are fair questions. Innate ability does matter to a degree. If you're born with the genetic code to be 6' 9", that would certainly be more advantageous for playing professional basketball than having a genetic code that limits your physical growth to 5' 6." Innate ability does play a role in our performance, but even for naturals, prodigies, and savants, that role is far more limited than meets the eye.

Several decades of research examining expert performers show that natural talent has its strongest influence when learning new skills at the base of the learning curve. However, the influence of natural ability rapidly and continuously weakens with each successive step up that learning curve. In fact, the vast majority of research studies examining the trajectory of expert performers show that natural talent is one of the least predictive factors of expert-level ability. The most predictive factors of expert performance and how quickly we can climb the learning curve are the degree to which and effectiveness of how we train our body, mind, and craft.

Observing expert performers and the role of natural ability also discredits the argument that there are such things as "naturals," like natural-born winners, natural-born closers, or those born to be golfers, lawyers, or anything else. Prior to his passing, K. Anders Ericsson was the world's foremost expert on how experts practice, a form of practice called "deliberate practice." Dr. Ericsson pointed out that the obvious flaw in the argument for the existence of naturals is that we only label people as naturals *after* they've demonstrated their ability in an accomplished way. Retroactively describing people as naturals is only more evidence that "being a natural" isn't what leads to expert-level performance. If people were born with a natural talent to be something, we would know that far sooner than by the time they become it. There have been countless studies examining our genetic codes, and none has ever identified or isolated genes that reliably predict long-term success anywhere near the predictive power of developing a growth mindset and practicing deliberately. When asked about what leads to expert-level ability, Dr. Ericsson clearly stated that elite performers develop their ability through years of dedicated effort and deliberate practice, improving step by step over an extended period of time and without shortcuts.

What's clear from Dr. Dweck's and Dr. Ericsson's research is that one of the most deep-seated and enduring beliefs about human performance is that natural talent plays a leading role in determining ability. What's also clear from their research is that those who grow their abilities and ultimately reach expert-level performance do so not from natural ability but from consistent effort and deliberate practice.

Another perhaps more urgent reason to develop a growth mindset is that a fixed mindset and its overvaluing of natural ability leads to an inhibiting confirmation bias. When we believe that talent and natural ability determine a person's limits for growth and success, that belief leads to the assumption that if we aren't good at something right away, we should give up and try something else because there is no real success with it in our future. This

A-shaped belief about talent and natural ability makes it easy to quit on our-selves and others long before we've applied effort for long enough to find out how good we can be at any given craft. To put it plainly, the belief encourages us to quit on ourselves and others if things don't come easily—and if things do come easily, it only furthers a fixed mindset that will undermine our con-fidence and efforts over time. Overvaluing innate ability and natural talent only serves to give us an easy reason to quit or to promote other A-shaped beliefs. It makes it more difficult to get better and holds us back when we come to choice points within our lives and performance.

Failure, setbacks, struggles, and even doubt are normal stepping stones as we climb the learning curve and approach higher levels of performance. Growth and the success it leads to require struggle—it's not a matter of *if* struggle will happen, but *when*. Whether we move through those bumps and challenges, see them as valuable experiences and feedback, and use them to continue to grow is *not* a matter of innate ability. It's a matter of whether we have a fixed or growth mindset about our ability that drives our efforts, or lack thereof.

Like any other A-shaped belief, a fixed mindset can be credibly reshaped. Here's an example, using our ABCs with some specific direction that you might consider for moving from a fixed mindset to a growth mindset.

> **A**ctivating Event: Struggle (like having to apply considerable effort to get better and not seeing progress for an extended period of time) or failure (like losing a tournament when in contention).
>
> **B**elief: "Talent is a fixed trait, and I either have enough of it or I don't. I must not struggle or fail because that would mean I don't have enough talent to be successful."
>
> **C**onsequences: Fear of failure, anxiety, avoidance of applying effort, decreased resilience, ego-first approach to performance, more A-shaped beliefs about effort and failure, discouragement, and giving up easily.
>
> **D**iscrediting:
> Is this true?
> It's not true. To dispute this factually, I recommend researching the life of anyone you think has had resounding success. Then ask

yourself if that person's success came more from natural ability
or from a lifetime of intentionally applied effort.

Is this beneficial?

It's not. Consider the consequences listed above.

What are all the contributing factors?

If you did your research on a person who you think has had
resounding success, consider all the factors that played into
their success and which ones were the most influential.

What happens if you struggle or fail?

What does it mean when we struggle and fail? Are these events
permanent, pervasive, and personal indictments of our fixed
level of ability? Or are they temporary, task-specific, and
nonpersonal reflections of our current level of ability that can
be improved with well-informed effort?

Effectively Reshape:

Credible V-shaped belief:

I have some level of talent, and the level of my ability is unknown
but grows with effort over time. I would love to see how good I
can be, and when I struggle and fail, that gives me feedback for
how I can improve my efforts and get better.

DECOUPLING SELF AND CRAFT

First, it was Maya, the multiple-time Olympic champion, multiple-time
national champion, and multiple-time World Cup champion who experienced intense fear of failure and fear of success. Despite her history of success, she felt crushed by fear to the point where she was having bouts of panic
before and during competition. Then it was Vicente, the professional golfer
who was burnt out, dreading and hating the sport he grew up loving more
than anything. Still in the prime of his career, he was on the verge of walking
away from the game that had become torturous to him. Then there was the
pop star Iris, who had several best-selling albums, a dozen Grammy awards,
and more than eighty million social-media followers. She had never been
more successful in her life, but she was now feeling intense emotional letdown. She was objectively one of the most successful people in her industry

and one of the most famous people on the planet—yet she felt miserable about herself.

These are not the only clients of mine who have felt stuck in the ruts of fear, burnout, and unhappiness. Their experiences are some of the most common for athletes and performers pursuing any craft. The common thread between their experiences was a particular A-shaped belief, one even more dangerous than a fixed mindset. They believed that their performances and the outcomes they produced were direct measures of their self-worth and value as a person, a belief I refer to as a coupling of self and craft.

There are few things that we as humans hold more dearly than our sense of who we are as a person. Coupling of self and craft is an A-shaped belief that sounds and looks like a variation of "I have to perform well to be important," "I must be a success to feel good about myself," "I have to do extraordinary things to be an extraordinary person," and "I must not fail because, if I do, that means I'm a bad person and a failure." On a fundamental level, the belief reduces who we are to what we do, forming a conditional relationship with our craft based on conditions that cannot be met. It's one of the most common but most damaging beliefs for anyone looking to thrive and enjoy what they do.

Coupling of self and craft is quite common because it has evolutionary and cultural origins. Thousands of years ago, when humans lived in tribes and everyone's safety and survival depended on others, those who were not valuable to the tribe were typically cast out and left to fend for themselves. Being left alone without protection and help from others was essentially a death sentence. So we humans developed a fear of being unworthy of our tribe to ensure our safety and survival. Proving our value and worth to ourselves and others with what we did and produced assured our place in the safety of the tribe. As humans, we are hardwired to live and work in tribes, and we'll go to great lengths to avoid letting down other members of our tribes. Therefore, believing that our self-worth and value as a person is defined by what we do begins as an ingrained evolutionary survival mechanism. It was incredibly valuable for a world filled with reasons to put survival first. For thriving in the modern world, however, this belief is a hindrance and is even dangerous at extreme levels.

Another reason a coupling of self and craft is so prevalent is that, culturally, we tend to celebrate and adore people more for their external accomplishments than for who they are as people, including ourselves. We celebrate in awe the tiny percentage of performances that end in a trophy ceremony far more than we notice and celebrate the work those people put in when no one was watching to reach those moments. We describe high achievers as special, heroic, legendary, and worthy champions based on their impressive accomplishments, yet we rarely consider who those people are behind and away from those accomplishments. Moreover, we typically second-guess, scrutinize, and negatively judge those who try and then fail. We attribute their failures to personal character flaws like being unworthy, not having the right pedigree, and lacking the natural ability to handle pressure. Based on how we culturally admonish and devalue people when they try and fail, while at the same time idolizing those we deem successful, it's not a stretch to see why we might develop a belief that we should judge ourselves in the same rigid and conditional ways. All around us, we see that our performance measures our self-worth and value, a belief learned through our direct experiences.

When we're younger, our early successes and failures happen at a time when we're still forming our identities. At these times, as with any time, it's normal and healthy to feel good about our efforts and ourselves when we experience success. It's also normal to feel some disappointment about trying and failing. At a young age, these normal and functional emotions connected to our successes and failures can easily be highlighted and intensified by how other people respond to them, especially adults. When we accomplish something, like getting an A on a test or shooting a new personal-best score in a tournament, we're typically met with praise. In contrast, when our efforts aren't deemed good enough, we often won't get praise but see that others who performed better than us will. This false association begins to link our identity and emotional state to whatever we learn are "adequate" levels of success and failure.

When we don't yet have a sense of who we are, we can easily get attached to anything that gives us that sense, and the easiest path to that are the things we're good at. However, things we're good at are often the least productive and most dangerous sources of self and identity. Instead of naturally discovering who we are for ourselves, our craft starts to take on that work, and a conditional relationship is forged. We see this most prominently in those who experience easy and early success in a given craft.

Easy and early success is both a gift and a curse. The upside is that it shows we have some level of ability to move up the learning curve and provides us a means to feel good about ourselves. When we're on the bottom of the learning curve, where progress comes faster and more easily, coupling ourselves to our craft works and makes us feel good about ourselves. The downside is that, while latching our identity and self-worth to early success works for generating confidence and feeling good about ourselves, it also builds the expectation that success *should* always come quickly and easily and that we *should* always feel good about ourselves through that success. Not surprisingly, the expectations that we *should* be able to quickly and easily produce results and that those results *should* continue to make us feel good about ourselves are met less and less as we climb the learning curve and as we experience more struggle and failure. An A-shaped belief that was once a source of confidence in a set of quick and easy conditions will later serve to undermine confidence as conditions and competition become more difficult and success becomes harder to achieve.

Even more of a downside is that coupling our identity and emotional state to our successes and failures begins to groove a conditional relationship with our craft, one built on conditions that can't always be met because we are using external measures to fill an internal space. For example, we may come to believe that we can only be happy if we play well enough to earn that happiness. When those conditions aren't met, we're left with a fear of failure, burnout, and being unfulfilled no matter how successful we become. Ultimately, coupling our self with our craft makes it difficult to find fulfillment in any craft we pursue as we ascend the learning curve.

Intense levels of fear and anxiety come from having to protect our self-worth and value as a person through our performance. If who we are as a person is at stake every time we compete, the result is a trap loop of self-induced pressure. This kind of trap loop erodes confidence and motivation based on the belief that we can only feel good about ourselves if we get the results we desire. Failing makes us feel bad about ourselves, which, for some people, can turn into self-loathing. Self-loathing is a particularly painful habit. Once you've coupled yourself to your craft, the only way to avoid that level of emotional discomfort is to avoid mistakes and failure altogether. Since mistakes and failure are necessary ingredients for progress and unavoidable parts of life and sport, we learn to fear our craft based on the conditions we've created. Our craft becomes the vessel for our deeply personal emotional discomfort.

Another layer of emotional discomfort born from coupling your self with your craft is a perpetuated fear of other people's opinions—the FOPO mentioned earlier. Just like with a fixed mindset, others' opinions of us can become scary and threatening when we build this sort of relationship with our craft. Those opinions have the potential to reflect and confirm our fears that we are not good enough, that we are unworthy, undeserving, and unvaluable—but as we established earlier, those opinions are rarely accurate, rarely account for context, and are subjective judgments. They hold little or no power over us personally unless we believe that they do. Other people's opinions can be mistakenly taken as facts and not for what they are: just people's thoughts *about* us. Those opinions of us do have some impact on our lives, but rarely do they have weight and impact anywhere near what we perceive. We learn to overvalue and fear other people's opinions when we believe they truthfully confirm our worst fears about ourselves.

Instead of allowing you to compete freely and confidently execute skills in the present moment, a coupling of self and craft destabilizes any semblance of confidence. There is no perceived space in the present moment when what we *need* is to perform well to feel good about ourselves and when the consequences of both failure and success are seen as permanent, pervasive, and deeply threatening to us personally.

A fear of success isn't really a fear of success—it's a fear of not being able to *maintain* that success, which is seen as another form of failure. And if we believe that not being able to maintain success is just another form of failure, then we will also fear success by fearing failure. Coupling ourselves to our craft also creates a belief that reaching success narrows the margin for future success. The more successful we are, the smaller the perceived margin for error becomes to deem ourselves successful. This is why many people will sabotage their opportunities for success, sometimes intentionally, in an attempt to avoid a more narrow margin to protect themselves from the emotional pain of failure. For those who have coupled self and craft, there is no outcome that isn't feared. Failure confirms we're unworthy and unvaluable, and success makes perceived failure more likely in the future.

By now we can see that Maya, the multiple-time Olympic champion, feared both failure and success. Based on the conditional relationship she had built with her craft, she feared failing because, to her, that meant she was undeserving and unvaluable. Simultaneously, the more successful she became, the more she feared failing because failing to maintain her success meant she was a failure and was thus, again, undeserving and not valuable. Coupling herself to her craft created a trap loop that not only made it immensely more difficult for Maya to pursue the results she believed she *needed*; it also meant that getting those results would change nothing. If anything, performing well only served to increase her constriction while also making her perceived future appear more threatening. No matter her performance results, they tightened the trap loop her A-shaped belief had created.

The trap loop of *needing* to perform well to feel good about ourselves is also the fastest route to burnout. It's worth noting that overtraining and burnout are not the same. Overtraining is when you train and compete long and intensely enough for your mind and body to become fatigued and not function as efficiently; the remedy for overtraining is effective rest and recovery. Comparatively, burnout is a psychological and emotional state where we learn to dread, even hate, engaging with our craft. Burnout results from being in a trap loop of fear, decreased performance, and emotional discomfort for long enough that we become averse to our craft. As we climb the learning curve and the level of competition gets more challenging, coupling of self and craft further fuels a fear of failure, which causes us to perform more defensively, stunting any progress. It doesn't take a psychologist to realize that continually interacting with something that we fear, don't enjoy, and see no progress with will lead to a certain level of repulsion.

Trying not to make any mistakes in competition only leads to more mistakes and failure. Protecting our self-worth has a particularly distasteful flavor. And doing so repeatedly will eventually turn an activity that we love doing, like playing golf, into a miserable experience. There is no amount of rest and time away from any craft that will remedy burnout. The only remedy for burnout is to address it at the root by decoupling ourselves from our craft.

As long as our self-worth and value are coupled to our craft, burnout will remain, and we'll continue to become entrenched in the trap loop.

The rub behind the trap loop created by a coupling of self and craft is that even experiencing success doesn't free us from the trap. Even when we achieve what we believe is *needed* to validate our self-worth and value, we're still left with emotional letdown. External validation cannot fulfill us internally because we can't control sources of external validation, and the more we rely on them, the more we build a tolerance to them.

If we could control sources of external validation—like scores, awards, social-media followers, and praise from others—we would always get them in the exact amounts at the exact times we feel we *need* them. The trap loop created by coupling self and craft is our failed attempt to control the things we think we *need* to feel validated. But it doesn't control any source of external validation, which is why we become more anxious and burnt out the longer the loop goes on.

Sources of external validation also have an ever-shortening shelf life. At first, shooting a certain score or getting a compliment from someone will make us feel validated and good about ourselves for a while. But soon enough, the amount of time that we feel validated will begin to shorten. What once made us feel good about ourselves for a week will later only last for a few days, or a few hours, or even a few minutes. More than a handful of times, clients have told me that the validation they felt winning an Olympic gold medal faded away even before they stepped off the podium.

The more we rely on external sources of validation, the more we become dependent upon those sources to keep making us feel the same level of validation. Shooting a certain score or winning a tournament might initially make us feel worthy and valuable, but it won't be long before we start feeling that we need a better score and even more wins to feel the same sense of worth and value. My pop-star client Iris has won more Grammy awards than she can hold in her arms at one time, and her social-media followers account for 1 percent of the entire earth's population. But even that wasn't enough for her to feel validated. Only a year prior, Iris had been feeling great about having a million followers on social media and recording her first album, and every minute of every day, she had people telling her how wonderful she was. She also had the awards, money, and fame to support their claims. But the more awards, money, fame, and praise she received, the more she needed them to feel content about herself.

Believing that external sources measure our self-worth is the psychological equivalent of guzzling salt water to quench our thirst: the more of it we drink, the more dehydrated and thirstier we become. The emotional letdown that comes with increasing external success is a painful and costly lesson that reminds us that there is no amount of external success from what we do that can fulfill an internal space of who we are.

To be very clear, performing at a high level requires us to be personally invested in our performance. For us to grow and learn, it is normal, healthy, and necessary for us to at times feel unsatisfied by our efforts, be uncomfortable, and be honest with what we feel about our successes and failures. But coupling of self and craft goes beyond personal investment because it reaches a point where we are not emotionally safe in our own relationship with the thing we do and it becomes the primary barrier to performance and enjoyment.

Decoupling ourselves from our craft involves defining our performance as something that we are personally invested in but not personally defined by. It's a continuous process that works by reversing the order of doing and being. Instead of *doing* more to *be* more, allowing ourselves to prioritize *being* frees us from the coupled self-and-craft trap loop.

When we are decoupled from our craft, we allow ourselves to *be* more grounded, *be* more accepting, *be* more optimistic, *be* more authentic and compassionate with ourselves and others—to shift into a *being* mode of mind more and to *be* attuned and connected to the many layers of our identities instead of reducing our identities to a singular, external source.

There's a misconception that we must hold our self-worth hostage to maintain our edge and be motivated. However, research examining what motivates high performers instead shows that those with higher levels of self-acceptance and higher levels of acceptance for failure also report deeper levels of intrinsic motivation. For them, failure isn't perceived as a deterrent to future growth and enjoyment. People who decouple themselves from their craft aim just as high as those who live and die by their performances. The key difference is that those who are decoupled from their craft don't fear bad performances and as a result don't lose motivation to pursue performing well when the inevitable possibility of bad performances is presented.

As the saying goes, we are human beings, not human doings. Having a malleable sense of self that isn't held hostage by what we do but is instead self-determined is a cornerstone of resilience and stable confidence. Contrary to the common and unbeneficial belief that we perform at our best and enjoy our craft more by doing things that validate our personal worth, allowing ourselves to *be* leads to a better and more fulfilling relationship with our craft and frees us to pursue doing what we want. The more we allow ourselves to be and let what we do flow from there, the more we will experience the astounding credibility and authenticity that comes from being ourselves without relying on something or someone else to validate us.

Like any other A-shaped belief, a coupling of self and craft can be credibly reshaped or mapped as a habit with some repetition and persistence. Using our ABCs and mapping our habits, you'll find some specific direction that you might consider for prioritizing being over doing.

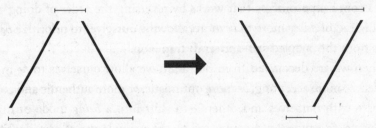

"I have to perform well, and I must not fail because if I do . . .

"Failure and success are a part of life and sport. I want to perform well and would prefer not to fail. But whether I succeed or fail . . .

. . . that means I'm unworthy, undeserving, unvaluable, and a bad person."

. . . I'm still the same person, no more or less valuable to myself."

Activating Event: Success or failure.

Belief: "I have to perform well to be important; I must be a success to feel good about myself; I have to do extraordinary things to be an extraordinary person. I must not fail because, if I do, it'll mean that I'm a bad person and a failure. I must maintain success because, if I don't, it'll mean that I'm a fluke and a failure."

Consequences: Fear of failure, fear of success, fear of others' opinions confirming my fears about myself, anxiety, a trap loop of destabilizing confidence, burnout, emotional letdown, discouragement, a reliance on external validation, and decreased performance quality.

Discrediting

Is this true?

It's not true. To dispute this factually, I recommend looking for athletes who do not couple themselves to their craft and examining how they perform over time and under pressure. You might also ask yourself, "Where is it written that I must perform well to feel okay?"

Is this beneficial?

It's not—consider the consequences listed above. Use your own negative experiences produced by coupling self and craft as direct evidence of how unbeneficial it is.

What are all the contributing factors?

What are all the factors that people can use to define themselves? Is it just one thing, like performance? Or are there many factors?

What happens if you succeed or fail?

What does it mean when we are successful and yet fail? Is failure a permanent, pervasive, personal indictment? Or is it a temporary, task-specific, and nonpersonal reflection of our current level of ability that can be improved with well-informed effort?

Effectively Reshape:

Credible V-shaped belief: Performance is something I choose to do and is not who I am. It's okay to be personally invested in my performance without using it as a measure of self-worth and value.

For many people, it's also helpful to map a coupling of self and craft as a habit.

Coupling of Self and Craft Habit

Trigger: Failure and success, among many other internal and external triggers.

Behavior: Coupling of self and craft.

(Outdated) Reward: Feeling like I'm "doing something" to be valuable.

Result:

What does it feel like to engage in this behavior?

1. It makes me feel anxious, scared, unfulfilled, frustrated, etc.
2. What am I getting from this behavior? (Or, what does this behavior do for me?)

    Unstable confidence, more uncertainty, fear of failure, burnout, a deepening dependence on external validation, learning to hate the game I love, unhappiness.

Recognize—Coupling myself to my craft by defining myself by results.

Accept—Yep, that's the trap loop I've created that feels awful and creates anxiety.

Interest—"Hmm, how interesting that I believe that measuring myself as a person based on what I do and produce will make me more confident and happy and will help me enjoy playing golf more, when all it does is the exact opposite and only gets worse the more I continue this habit."

Now—Ground myself with some connected breaths and allow myself to be present and to compete the best I can and just see what happens.

SUPPORTING SOURCES OF STABLE CONFIDENCE

When it comes to building stable confidence, the order of operations matters because our beliefs are the strongest determinant for what we perceive as triggering, which behaviors turn into habits, and how those behaviors are reinforced. For these reasons, our beliefs are the most influential component of our psychological framework and impact the stability of our confidence the most. However, *after* reshaping our beliefs, we can also further support the stability of our confidence by being aware of where we fill our need for control, defining our success, and understanding the sources of motivation we draw from most.

IMPORTANT VERSUS VALUABLE

Control is essential and a significant factor for building stable confidence. Seeking control is rational and beneficial for everyone. Seeking control becomes irrational and unbeneficial, however, when we seek to control things that we can't, or when we don't seek control in the places where it can be found.

When we feel like we don't have control, our perceived space in the present moment shrinks. Think about how constricting it is when you don't feel like you have any control. Conversely, when we feel like we do have control, the perceived space in the present moment expands. Moreover, seeking to control things that cannot be controlled fuels a pessimistic view of the future because the future will seem like a place where we have no control. However, when we focus our energy and efforts toward what we can control in the present, it projects a future filled with more of the same, which is a future that is more willingly accepted. Therefore, where we seek to fill our need for control matters. And the more control we have, the more it will support stable confidence.

The reason we seek to control things that cannot be controlled is to be more confident and avoid anxiety. The idea is that if we can control everything about our lives and our performances, there will be nothing to worry about, and we'll have all the space in the world and a perfectly acceptable future because we'll be in control of both. We strengthen this irrational and unbeneficial belief by holding onto another belief—that if we just try harder and exert more willpower to control things like outcomes and other people's opinions, everything will turn out the way we want. The problem is that this gives us the exact opposite effect instead.

Where we decide to seek control relies heavily on our belief system about control, what psychologists refer to as "locus of control." People with an external locus of control believe their lives and performances depend highly on things like luck, fate, or destiny. People with an internal locus of control believe they have complete control over what happens to them now and in the future.

Effectively filling our need for control and agency in our lives and our performance is about finding the right balance between an external and internal locus of control. When our locus of control is too external, we don't seek control where it can be found, like the present moment, the actions we choose to take, and the shots we choose to play. When we ascribe fully to an external locus of control believing that "whatever's meant to be will be," we miss opportunities available to us to exert influence. As a result, we gain little or no control over our lives and performance. Thus, an overly external locus of control provides almost no control and undermines our confidence.

At the same time, when our locus of control is too internal, we seek control where there is none, like in the past, the future, other people's actions, or the outcomes of our performance. When we ascribe fully to an internal locus believing "I have control over everything," we waste our time and energy giving away control and, again, feel like we have little or no control over our lives and performance.

Researchers studying a range of performance types have repeatedly found that people who develop a "bi-locus of control" feel less anxiety and exert more influence over their own lives. For those with a bi-locus of control, finding the right balance means recognizing how their relationship with their thoughts, decisions, and behaviors can impact their chances for success, but it also means recognizing how external factors, like someone else's performance, can play a role too. In short, we find the most control and have the most influence over our lives and performances not from a completely external or completely internal locus of control but from a balance of the two. One of the more effective ways to find the right balance, a bi-locus of control, is to consider what's *important* versus what's *valuable*.

Many things in our performances that cannot be controlled are important to us. For just about every golfer, scores, tournament outcomes, other people's opinions, awards, rankings, and earning money are all important. But seeking to control them isn't valuable because they cannot be directly controlled. Focusing our time, energy, and effort seeking to control these performance elements only leads to feeling out of control, frustrated, and anxious. It's perfectly okay to recognize how important outcomes and other things we can't control are to us; the key lies in recognizing that seeking to control them isn't helping our chances of getting them, nor does it actually give us more influence over our performance.

Focusing our time, energy, and effort on controllable elements of our lives and performance effectively fills our need for control, thus building stable confidence and directly and positively impacting our actions. To that degree, the more important outcomes are to us, the more important it is for us to focus our energy and efforts on the elements of performance where control is actually found. The more important winning is to us, the more valuable it is to be mindful of what mode of mind we're in and to be present with our performance as it's happening. The more important future results are to us, the more valuable it is to focus on learning and being consistent with our efforts. The more important outcomes are to us, the more valuable it is to adopt a growth mindset and decouple ourselves from our craft. The more important control is to us, the more valuable it is to develop a bi-locus of control and habits that lead to control. The more important competing freely is to us, the more valuable it is to seek control where it can actually be found so that our need for control supports stable confidence.

By separating each area we seek to control into what's important (but not controllable) and what's valuable (because it's controllable), we receive direct feedback for developing a bi-locus of control.

THE BEST OR *YOUR* BEST

Not long ago, I received a call from a World Golf Hall of Fame player, Kenji. After a long career on the PGA Tour and as a current member of the PGA Tour Champions, Kenji's confidence was becoming increasingly unstable, and he wasn't sure whether he wanted to continue to play professional golf. In earlier seasons of his career, Kenji had won many tournaments, including a few majors, but while he was still a card-carrying member of the Champions tour, he was now over the age of sixty and facing the stark reality that winning was much more difficult for him now than at any other time in his life.

As I asked Kenji more about what was impacting his confidence and his decision about whether to retire, Kenji revealed that he still loved playing professional golf as much as ever but was considering retirement from the game because he didn't consider himself successful enough to be confident.

"Let me get straight to the point. I'm just not successful anymore, and that makes me think it's time to retire. It's just that I really don't want to," Kenji told me. "What do you think I should do?"

"Kenji, I would never tell you how you should think about your career, and I would certainly never tell you when it's time to retire," I replied. "But

I am curious about something that may be helpful to you. Can I ask you a direct question?

"By all means," Kenji said.

"Kenji, how do you define success?"

After a moment of careful consideration, Kenji replied, "Honestly, I don't think I've ever thought about it."

Golf isn't a binary experience. It's not merely good or bad, fun or not fun. It's not just victory or defeat, nor is it entirely worthwhile or a total waste. Reducing it to one thing or another grossly overlooks how nuanced, layered, and multidimensional we are as humans and how many different experiences there are within the challenges of playing golf.

Although most people equate success in golf with scores, wins, awards, money, and prestige, clearly not every golfer desires these things as the only markers of success. However, many golfers adopt these definitions of success because they are commonly held and celebrated by others. When we adopt definitions of success from other people without considering what we really want, our golf experience becomes outsourced and therefore less personalized. On the surface, we tell ourselves and others that we want certain things, but those things may not be what moves us on a more meaningful level.

By adopting the stock versions of success without considering our own definition of success, we give away a degree of control in our golf experience. Often, the experience becomes less fulfilling. I've often had clients describe how there's a certain disconnect and dissonance produced by continually training and competing based on someone else's ideas of what the golf experience should be and not what they themselves want it to be.

There is no right or wrong definition of success, but there are more authentic definitions of it for each of us. Instead of adopting a one-size-fits-all approach, there's a significant level of credibility that comes with being honest about what we really want. We know this because there are many champions in every sport with championship titles, awards, respect, adoration from others, and all the money in the world—yet many are still unhappy and unfulfilled in their sports experience. Simultaneously, many people have never won a championship or an award, have never made a dime playing golf, and are remarkably unknown but are still happy and sincerely fulfilled in their golf experience. Therefore, the most accepted measures of success don't apply to everyone in the same ways.

An important question for us to ask ourselves is, "How do you define success?" If you are really trying to be *the* best, that's okay. If what you really want is to be *your* best and see what that ultimately leads to, that's also okay. What's essential is reflecting on and answering this question in a self-determined and honest way because each end of the spectrum comes with its own challenges and opportunities.

For those who authentically want to be the best, that pursuit comes with particular challenges to wrestle with. At times, trying to be the best tends to invite comparison to others, reliance on uncontrollable outcomes, scrutiny from others, more perfectionistic thinking, and ego-engagement with your golf experience. At the most competitive levels of golf, the definition of success narrows considerably because people's livelihoods are often at stake and winning is an unavoidable metric for success. None of these things are wrong or bad, but they are challenges that can make performing more difficult at times and make golf less enjoyable if they are not things we are authentically pursuing.

Often, parents of young athletes will ask me what the secret to greatness is because they want their child to become the best. Most parents are discouraged when I reply that there is no secret to excellence, and, even if there was, I certainly don't know it. Those parents typically become even more disheartened when I tell them that if they knew what I know about pursuing being the best, they probably wouldn't push their child toward it. Furthermore, if their child knew what the pursuit of being the best entails, their child probably wouldn't choose it, either. What we often overlook when we celebrate people who are elite and reach the pinnacle of any given domain is that reaching those heights comes at a significant cost.

There is a dark side to pursuing being the best as a definition of success. It is a venture requiring significant personal, social, financial, emotional, and physical sacrifice. Even for those who genuinely want a chance to be the best, the sacrifice required is still burdensome at times. And make no mistake about it: to be successful enough to be the best at anything, you will fail more often and more publicly even as you get better. Even those with the most robust and accepting relationships with failure and others' opinions are not immune to them. As we've addressed at length, feeling frustrated and disappointed when our efforts don't produce the results we want is normal. However, continued anxiety and unwillingness to accept failure, scrutiny, and the emotional discomfort that come with both is one of the primary reasons many people stop pursuing elite-level performance. For many people, the effort, discomfort, and sacrifices are not worth it.

What I've also learned from many of my clients—and from a deep body of research examining the lives of those who have either reached the peaks of their respective crafts or done something that very few people have ever done, like summiting Mount Everest or traveling to outer space—is that being the best and doing something that very few people have ever done fashions an experience and life difficult for others to relate to. Pursuing being the best and perhaps actually becoming the best is often a lonely place where you are celebrated and judged by many but truly loved and understood by few.

Again, there is nothing wrong with honestly wanting to be the best. And being the best isn't always a burdensome pursuit or a lonely accomplishment, especially when we're honest with ourselves about what we want. Trying to be the best also gives us ample opportunity to learn, grow, push ourselves past what we thought we were capable of, meet new people, and take exciting risks. In truth, it can lead to an amazing life. The pursuit comes with baked-in challenges and a life that is assured to be unbalanced, but those challenges are part of what makes unlocking human potential so stimulating, even exhilarating, for those who pursue them authentically.

At the same time, defining success as being *your* best also comes with its own challenges. Pursuing being your best can make it easier to get caught up in performance naiveté, where we become so engrossed in mastery of our own skills and methodologies that we don't observe and learn from what other people are doing. We can easily become unaware of competitive and global standards, overlook new methodologies and strategies, and lose sight of how enjoyable it is to pursue and produce improved outcomes. After all, a process-orientation's strength is that it provides more control over our performance and skill execution, promoting better results. Performance naiveté can transform being immersed in our process into ignorance or apathy when being our best isn't measured by some level of industry standards.

What's clear is that pursuing being your best and doing so relentlessly while also loving the process and looking for external knowledge allows us to grow at a faster pace and unlock important skillsets. It also explores our craft's nuances without an ultimate and rigid end goal, encouraging sustainable effort and passion. We can pursue being our best at any moment, and doing so will lead to the type of growth where getting better and producing better results are not surprising.

Being *the* best and being *your* best are bookends on the spectrum of the golf experience. They highlight that there is more than one way to define success and build a golf experience. It's also important to note they aren't the only options; in fact, there are many ways to define success. What's greatly valuable for supporting stable confidence is authentically defining what success means to us, whatever that may be. As a reminder, we all have the need and ability to exert influence over our own lives. Adopting someone else's version of success without considering our own thoughts on the matter gives away control and destabilizes confidence. We are pursuing something that is not of our own design when we give away our influence. For those who genuinely pursue their authentic versions of success, the sacrifices required are a toll willingly paid. In contrast, for those who follow someone else's version of success, the same sacrifices may make the pursuit more of a chore than a passion.

Whether you define success as spending time with friends at your local club, winning a major championship, or anything in between, be honest with yourself. Consider the larger picture of your golf experience and not just the phase you're in currently.

Take some time to consider these questions. Honest answers to these questions will give you more influence over your own golf experience.

- How do you define success for yourself in your golf experience?
- What would the pursuit of this kind of success entail?
- What might be the costs and sacrifices of that pursuit?
- What would be the best ways to use your time, energy, effort, and resources to pursue your definition of success?
- What habits would impede or facilitate this definition of success?
- What beliefs would you need to evaluate and potentially reshape to pursue this definition of success?

- How would you measure whether you've reached your definition of success?
- Are you willing to put forth the effort required for long enough to have a chance at reaching your definition of success?

Finally, keep in mind that part of what makes defining your own success credible is the fact that your definition of success can change. Like in life, our golf experience has many seasons to it. Just because you defined success in one way for a while doesn't mean that your definition can't evolve. It's been my observation that most of the world's best performers' definitions of success and relationship with their crafts change throughout their careers. Many begin with one type of intense pursuit early in their careers. That pursuit later evolves into getting the most out of their golf experience while they still can, whatever that means to them.

Though Kenji and his career had evolved, his definition of success had not. It wasn't until he spent some time authentically redefining what success was to him that he began to find more stable confidence and enjoyment in the twilight of his career.

There is no rule in golf that defines personal success in your golf experience for you. Great scores, winning, and awards are essential measures of success that help push the boundaries of such a demanding sport, but they are not the only measures of success. The more we take honest ownership of how we define success, the more personalized and authentic the golfing experience becomes—and the more credibility there will be when we give ourselves permission to pursue the things we want.

FIREWORKS AND BONFIRES

In the "Awareness" section, we discussed flow state, the optimal state of human functioning characterized by a sense of effortlessness of action and skill execution, deep immersion in the task at hand in the present moment, a complete detachment of ego, intrinsic motivation without goal striving, and intense enjoyment of whatever we are doing. Although there are external factors that influence the likelihood of entering flow state, there is nothing stronger than our own psychology for moving us closer to, or farther away from, flow state.

By going beneath the surface, we can see how cultivating a being mode of mind, developing productive habits, and building a V-shaped psychological framework makes executing skills easier, helps immerse us in the present moment, and allows us to detach our ego from our performance. To clarify, ego attachment comes from the personal conclusions of a pessimistic explanatory style.

We don't need to be in flow state to perform well. However, understanding and training awareness, habits, and our psychological framework brings us closer to the optimal state of human functioning. This leads to better and more enjoyable performances.

But what about that other element of flow state, the part about intrinsic motivation without goal striving? What does that even mean? I'm so glad you asked. Motivation is another important area of our psychology. It's often discussed but also often only understood on a surface level.

One of the most common misconceptions about motivation is that we either are or aren't motivated. But humans don't operate like on/off switches: motivation for humans is more layered and nuanced. As humans, we are always motivated. It's a matter of what we're motivated to do and not do—specifically, which sources of motivation we're relying on most.

Sources of motivation fall under two broad categories: extrinsic and intrinsic. Extrinsic sources of motivation come from external sources. Money, awards, praise from others, and outcome goals are examples of extrinsic sources of motivation. They motivate us by providing something external to obtain and possess. Intrinsic motivation is internally driven. Intrinsic motivation, the kind experienced during flow state, motivates us to engage with something simply because doing so provides us a level of personal fulfilment. Intrinsic motivation is what motivates us to engage with something for no other reason than because we want to.

It's important to understand that no human is only extrinsically or only intrinsically motivated. Both sources of motivation are powerful. In fact, just about everything we do, including playing golf, involves us being motivated by both extrinsic and intrinsic sources.

As powerful as both sources are, extrinsic and intrinsic motivation are not equals. In fact, when it comes to learning productive habits, long-term growth on the learning curve, performance under pressure, and enjoyment of any given craft, nearly a century of research on human motivation shows that intrinsic motivation is the more powerful and enduring source. As an analogy, we can think of extrinsic motivation as a firework and intrinsic motivation as a bonfire. Both provide light and heat. However, the light and heat of a bonfire is more enduring and valuable than the quick flash and bang of any firework.

As you're probably starting to deduce, the reason intrinsic motivation is a fundamental characteristic of flow state is because it lends stronger and more sustainable support to stable confidence. You may also be realizing that there is a superficial nature to extrinsic sources of motivation. This isn't to say that extrinsic motivation is bad or fake. However, a dependence on external sources makes it more difficult to sustain motivation over time and typically takes us farther from flow state, especially in competitive conditions. This brings us to our last myth: that success requires us to have a choke hold on our goals.

MYTH: SUCCESS REQUIRES A CHOKE HOLD ON GOALS

Many of our social institutions, performance cultures especially, tell us that to be motivated and successful, we must strive to obtain future goals, like making a certain amount of money, winning a tournament, or shooting a certain score. While there is a large body of research showing that achieving goals makes us feel good, with boosts to motivation and confidence, that same research shows that the boosts that come from reaching goals are short-lived.

You can string together short-lived boosts by creating another goal to achieve, and then another, and then another, but there is a downside to a dependence on boost after boost. These boosts, which are bursts of dopamine, must be created constantly with new goals, which, by definition, are desired future-based outcomes. Like external validation, another source of extrinsic motivation, goals cannot be controlled and have an ever-shrinking shelf life, and we build a tolerance to them. Because of their extrinsic, superficial nature, the more we rely on goals to be motivated and confident, the more we develop a dependent relationship with them.

Here again we see the trap loop leading to not just unstable confidence but also unstable motivation that relies on external sources to create something internal. More and more, golfers of all skill levels are telling me just how exhausting and unfulfilling it is to chase goals when the purpose of reaching a goal is to continually summon some level of motivation and confidence. Such an unending trap loop is why reaching even the loftiest of goals cannot create sustained motivation for difficult pursuits or stable confidence, even for the best and most accomplished players in the world.

If you're thinking that a trap loop where we *must* reach our goals to stay motivated and be confident enough to reach the next goal reeks of A-shaped thinking, you're right. Researchers examining people's motivation continue to find that the more extrinsic sources of motivation we depend on, the less intrinsically motivated we are. Plainly speaking, the more we depend on fireworks for light and warmth, the more reliant on fireworks we become, and, in turn, our bonfires become less bright and less warm. This is true even when, and in most cases *especially* when, we actually reach the goals we strive for.

It's not just researchers who are shedding light on the myth about having a choke hold on goals. Some of the most successful people in the world are literally telling us why extrinsic motivation with goal striving isn't a characteristic of flow state and why the choke hold can't sustain motivation.

Each episode of the *Finding Mastery* podcast is hosted by performance-psychology expert Michael Gervais. Guests of the podcast are some of the world's best athletes, industry leaders, top scientists, elite military personnel, tech moguls, astronauts, and others who have ascended to the top of their respective crafts. In hundreds of episodes of conversations, Dr. Gervais has interviewed his guests about an array of topics, including how they motivate themselves in some of the most challenging and competitive environments in the world.

Ben Houltberg, the director of research at the Performance Science Institute at the University of Southern California, analyzed common and meaningful messages between Dr. Gervais and his guests. He found that when the world's best performers were beholden to future-based outcome goals, these goals significantly disrupted their ability to be immersed in the present moment; led to inconsistent effort, especially when faced with challenges; and led to a fear of taking calculated risks. Put simply, an attentional and emotional choke hold on future-outcome goals makes it harder for people to perform because it takes them out of the present moment, makes their efforts inconsistent, and destabilizes their confidence.

What some of the best performers in the world are telling us about being overly dependent on goals makes sense. Goals, by their very nature, can only exist in the future; therefore, if we are attentionally and emotionally dependent on them, we are going to have one eye on the future, keeping us from being fully immersed in the present moment as our performance is happening. Being focused on even the loftiest of goals, like shooting a personal-best score or winning a major, means we're multitasking between a future goal and whatever the shot at hand is. Just as a reminder, multitasking makes us dumber and less proficient at whatever tasks we're juggling.

It's also not surprising that a choke hold on extrinsic goals leads to inconsistent effort. The amount of time and effort required to improve as we get closer to the top of the learning curve is immense. The more we rely on extrinsic motivators, the more we *need* them to stay motivated. But over time, being compelled by the wagging finger of a trap loop with goals tends to make practicing, training, traveling, and even playing in the most prestigious tournaments in the world more of an obligation than a passion. Even for the best players in the world, reaching their most desired goals doesn't maintain motivation, and therefore their efforts, in a sustainable way.

Performance sciences continually show that lasting success is built upon a stable foundation that prioritizes *intrinsic* sources of motivation, health, well-being, and general life satisfaction, *not* extrinsic sources. While people can perform well and produce impressive outcomes chasing goals and external validation, those successes tend to happen earlier on the learning curve and only for short periods of time. Because those stints of success are dependent upon being motivated by extrinsic sources, they break down quickly and easily, usually lasting only a few weeks, a few months, or, at most, a few years. The simple reason for their short-lived success is because the power of extrinsic motivation is inherently inconsistent and diminishes as the demands on the learning curve continually increase. Put simply, fireworks don't have consistent enough light or heat for sustained success. Sustained success requires consistent effort, and consistent effort requires sustained motivation, the kind that extrinsic sources can't provide.

Taking a closer look at goals, it also makes sense how being overly beholden to them destabilizes confidence. When we become attentionally and emotionally beholden to goals, it becomes easy to start thinking about them through A-shaped beliefs, especially a fixed mindset and a coupling of self and craft. Outcomes can't be controlled; therefore, no goal is ever absolutely assured to be reached. So, if we start to believe that we *must* reach our goals in order to avoid perceived permanent, pervasive, and personal consequences, it's not a surprise that we would feel constriction and threat at the possibility that our goals may not be met. That constriction and threat makes it far more likely that we'll be protective of our goals instead of giving ourselves credible permission to take the risks required to achieve them. Here we see why extrinsic motivation with goal striving isn't a characteristic of flow state and why intrinsic motivation without goal striving is.

Being in a trap loop of unstable confidence dependent on reaching goals also comes at a significant personal cost to us. Several studies examining high achievers found that one of the most common threads among high achievers who struggle with injury and illness, both physical and psychological, is that they are consistently pushing for, and attentionally and emotionally dependent on, future goals for the purpose of validating their efforts or themselves personally. That same research also revealed that striving toward outcome goals for the purpose of meeting a *need* for external validation most strongly predicted burnout.

To be very clear, goals in and of themselves are not a bad thing. They can be helpful for providing us direction and serve as a frame of reference for evaluating our performance. And in truth, everyone is motivated to reach certain outcomes in their lives, and there's nothing wrong with that. There's a significant body of research suggesting that having meaningful goals and making progress toward them is in fact a psycho-emotional need for every human.

But what's also clear is that chasing goals as your sole or primary source of motivation has significant and costly pitfalls. Dependence on any form of extrinsic motivation isn't a formula for being present, applying consistent effort, or supporting stable confidence, all of which are required for long-term growth and success. In fact, researchers are finding more and more that the most successful people in the world are less reliant on and motivated by goals than ever.

Those same studies that showed the pitfalls of being overly beholden to goals also found that high achievers who cultivate a relationship with their craft that does *not* depend on *needing* to reach outcome goals, specifically as the primary source of motivation and confidence or for validation, have longer, more fulfilling, and more successful careers.

I'll repeat that just in case you breezed past it: a dependent relationship with goals is *not* a requirement for success. One more time: high achievers who are *not* beholden to extrinsic sources of motivation and are more intrinsically motivated have longer, more enjoyable careers and are more successful. These findings are consistent in a diverse set of performance realms, including business, art, medicine, and athletics.

In Dr. Houltberg's analysis of conversations between Dr. Gervais and some of the best performers in the world, podcast guests reported performing closer to their best and being more motivated when they were specifically beholden to thoughts, words, and actions that centered around personal values, not around future-based outcome goals. Specifically, he found that when the world's top performers were oriented toward their values, they were more immersed in the present moment, applied more consistent effort, and took the calculated risks required for success, however success was defined for them.

MINDFUL BEHAVIOR AND BETTER OPTION: PERSONAL VALUES

Personal values are guiding principles for our thoughts, words, and actions. They are not a description of our best selves. They are not a different version of us. Personal values are a succinct articulation of what matters most to us, especially when faced with challenging conditions and choice points.

Throughout our lives, we establish a hierarchy of values for ourselves, often without even knowing it. Without a hierarchy of values, we would have immense difficulty in situations that present us with several options for what we can decide to do. In truth, without a hierarchy of values, we would be painfully confused at important choice points.

Harvard professor, psychologist, and best-selling author Susan David points out that the traditional definition of values tends to see them as rigid notions of right or wrong. Instead of seeing values as a set of inflexible and judgmental rules, she offers an updated conceptualization. Specifically, she reminds us that values are powerful because, in many ways, they are another mindful behavior in that:

- Values are freely chosen, not imposed by others.
- Values are ongoing, not fixed.
- Values guide us by creating space. They are not constricting.
- Values promote acceptance of our current reality, internal and external.
- Values guide tangible action in the present moment toward what we want to do.
- Values are not a comparison to others. They are about what's meaningful to us personally.

As with our beliefs and habits, it's not a matter of *if* we have values; it's a matter of whether we have intentionally identified them for ourselves. We often share the same or similar values with many people, especially those we are closest to and spend the most time with. But values are not universal. The values that are intrinsically motivating and that support stable confidence for one person may not do so in the same way for someone else. Thus, it's important for us to evaluate our values mindfully.

Best-selling author Mark Manson offers pragmatic guidelines for mindfully evaluating how useful or problematic our values are. Slightly adapted to fit much of what we've discussed, he explains that useful values are rational, beneficial, and immediately accessible.

Some examples of useful values are honesty, effort, groundedness, patience, curiosity, creativity, acceptance, intention, persistence, competitiveness, and humility. As you can tell, there is significant continuity between many of these useful values and other mindful behaviors. Each of these values is rational, beneficial, and internally driven, which makes them immediately accessible and available for us to act upon at any moment, regardless of circumstances.

For example, being honest with ourselves rationally reflects our current reality. It's also beneficial because honesty lends credibility to our beliefs and inner dialogue. Honesty is also something we have control over; we can choose to be honest in any circumstance, even when it's difficult to do so. When we're honest, we gain control over how we choose to respond to whatever our current reality may be without needing any extrinsic sources to fall into place.

Some examples of problematic values include ease, comfort, certainty, avoidance, other people's opinions, blanket positivity, external validation, absolutes, and always being right. Here again we see the overlaps between problematic values, the doing mode of mind, and unproductive habits.

Each of these problematic values is irrational, unbeneficial, and not always accessible. For example, avoidance is an irrational value because we can't always avoid the things we feel we must. Mistakes, failure, judgments from other people, our own thoughts, triggers, and emotional discomfort happen regardless of how much we try to avoid them. Avoidance as a value is also unbeneficial because, by avoiding things like effort, discomfort, uncertainty, criticism, and failure, we limit our growth, increase anxiety, and avoid the risks required to be successful. Avoidance is also something we can't immediately access or control. In fact, the more we want to grow and succeed, the harder it is to avoid the things we wish to not experience but can't control.

What we value becomes what we focus on. This link is the foundation for why useful values are a better option than goals for sustaining motivation and supporting stable confidence.

Because useful values are immediately accessible and actionable, they channel our focus to the present moment. At the same time, useful values are an intrinsic motivator that support consistent effort for long-term pursuits. Aligning with useful values promotes a fundamental shift in the direction of our motivation from extrinsic to intrinsic because they reflect freely chosen, genuine interests rooted in personal purpose rather than an obligation. Such a vital shift is sometimes subtle but matters for even the simplest behaviors that impact the consistency of our efforts, including the habits we learn and reinforce.

In a series of studies, researchers found that two people with the same goal, such as losing weight, making more money, or passing a test, perceived and reacted to the same decisions with differing levels of effort depending on the source of their motivation. Specifically, intrinsic motivation sourced from personal values predicted conscious and intentional decision-making when considering the best course of action.

Conversely, studies also showed that being motivated extrinsically actually ramped up the likelihood and intensity with which participants would become triggered because it made them experience—you guessed it—deprivation and constriction. Herein lies one of the reasons a dependence on goals as a sole source of motivation tends to undermine self-control and make us more susceptible to reinforcing unproductive habits that lead to inconsistent effort.

Useful values are also a credible source of support for stable confidence. Several studies show that when we are connected to what we value most, the gap between how we feel and how we ultimately act begins to lessen. In studies asking people to reflect on important decisions in their lives, people reported that following their values as opposed to following their feelings led to less second-guessing and fewer regrets. This means that when making decisions based on personal values, we don't have to feel comfortable or certain to give ourselves credible permission to take calculated risks.

Taking action toward the things we want, and doing so based on what we authentically value, is intrinsically motivating. Put simply, just because we may think and feel X, we can still focus on and do Y because doing Y is deeply meaningful to us, and that feels good. And if you recall from our section on habits, our brain is designed to learn, reinforce, and be motivated to repeat behaviors that feel good.

Being able to think and act differently from how we may feel is an intensely empowering support for V-shaped beliefs, which is why study after study in a variety of different areas continue to show that having clarity of what matters to us personally leads to more fulfillment, greater learning, better overall health, more fulfilling relationships, and more consistent performance.

Moreover, studies examining people's motivations behind courageous behaviors found that people who demonstrated consistent composure and courage when faced with adversity had clear personal values supporting a belief system that emphasized effort. Cynthia Pury, a professor in the College of Behavioral, Social and Health Sciences at Clemson University, specializes in the cognition of anxiety and fear. In a series of studies, she and her colleagues found that being oriented toward personal values significantly supported courageous behaviors both general, like standing up for a friend, and personal, like competing in front of other people. This means that people intrinsically motivated by useful personal values that reinforce already established V-shaped beliefs are more composed and confident under pressure and act braver than people who are not.

Even with our deepest passions, there's a natural waxing and waning of motivation. Like everything else we've discussed in the book, values do not make those pursuits easier or mean that we'll always feel magically motivated. Instead, values make us better equipped to deal with challenges.

For the pursuits in our lives that are most important to us, long-term growth is far less about dazzling bursts of effort here and there and far more about being able to maintain the pace of effort over time. Mastering any craft is far less about intensity on any single day than it is about discipline over the course of weeks, months, and years.

When we set meaningful goals, it can be easy for us to try to rush the process of getting better because we want our goals to be achieved immediately. It's this choke hold on goals that focuses us too far into the future and tempts us with shortcuts, life hacks, and quick fixes. After they fizzle out, we end up right back where we started.

Researchers from Harvard University, Northwestern University, and the University of Pennsylvania all found that the more people emphasized goals for daily motivation, especially goals based on measurable outcomes, the more irrational their risk-taking was, the more likely they were to engage in unethical behavior, and the more they reported a *lack* of motivation. It wasn't having goals that led to these effects—it was having a choke hold on those goals.

Values, by their intrinsic nature, complement our goals by promoting longevity of groundedness, consistency of effort, and calculated risk-taking because they allow our goals to exist and be important to us while also keeping us beneficially detached from them. That detachment allows us to use the present moment to focus on what needs to be done to get better, and that keeps us motivated and grounded. Research also shows that when we detach from our goals, we get more consistent streams of dopamine because we will naturally break a big goal down into smaller chunks of tangible action. Moreover, a consistent stream of dopamine motivates us in ways that are not hyper-dependent on success and failure to sustain motivation.

Since so much of life and golf is about the process, it makes sense that we need more than goals to keep us motivated and confident. It's not surprising that people with clear, useful personal values are more grounded, give more consistent effort, and take more calculated risks in challenging situations simply because their thoughts, words, and actions are continually drawn from credible, personally meaningful, and intrinsic sources.

To begin identifying what useful values are personally meaningful to you, consider these questions.

- What are the handful of words that matter most to you?
- Who are the people who have had the most positive impact on your life? What do/did they stand for?
- When you're playing and competing at your best, what values are guiding you?
- When you faced the most difficult challenges of your life or golf game, what values guided you through those times?
- Regardless of your score, what values make you fulfilled with how you've played on a golf course?

Consider the goals you have for yourself and your golf game:

- What values would help consistently motivate you to apply effort toward your goals?
- What values would help you be grounded more often as you pursue your goals?
- What values would support building stable confidence to take the calculated risks required to move toward and achieve your goals?

As you take some time to consider useful values, keep in mind that we don't need a laundry list of them. What you're looking for is a handful of values that are most authentic to you and will guide your focus to the present moment, consistently motivate your efforts, and support your V-shaped beliefs.

Of course, identifying and evaluating which values are useful and authentic to you is only part of what's required for values to be a better option. Once we are clear on our values, those values only become valuable to us when we play and live by them. It's one thing to know your values and another to put them into action.

There are many ways we can put our values into action. However, research continually shows that building a consistent approach to effectively marrying goals and values tends to follow a rudimentary structure.

1. Clarify your goal(s).
   What are your desired outcomes?
2. Clarify the effort/actionable steps that make achieving the goal most likely.
   What would you have to consistently do/train/learn/develop/etc.—physically, strategically, and psychologically—to give you the best chance at getting better and achieving your clarified goal(s)?
3. Release your choke hold on outcomes. Mostly forget about your goal(s).
   Remember, this doesn't mean that you don't care about your goals; this step actually shows that you do care about them.
4. Clarify your values and use them to guide your actions.
   What are your values? What would it look like to immerse yourself into your practice, play, training, etc. through your values?
5. Use failures, mistakes, setbacks, worry, anxiety, frustration, and disappointment as triggers to reorient with your values to drive your efforts.
   Also, use successes, progress, growth, excitement, confidence, and fulfilment as triggers to reorient with your values to drive your efforts.
   Trigger: Natural ups and downs of the learning curve.
   Behavior: Orient with what's most meaningful and intrinsically motivating to you.
   Reward: Groundedness, more consistent effort, more stable confidence, and a better chance of reaching your goal(s) at some point.
6. Focus on productive daily action and less on the outcomes of any single day.

If you have meaningful goals for yourself and your golf game, that's great. I know I have mine, and I know it feels good to reach them. Ambition and striving for better outcomes are highly motivating forces for us so long as we can detach from them emotionally and attentionally to invest in consistent, meaningful, and values-directed effort toward pursuing them.

Having goals and dreams about what you can do is inspiring. Everyone loves fireworks. Like fireworks shows, those moments of accomplishment, the moments that we reach our goals, are wonderful—of that there is no doubt. But those moments are just that: moments. They do not endure forever, and eventually they come to pass. They provide light and heat, but, like every moment of our lives, they are fleeting. Personal values offer us something that burns brighter and hotter for longer in the time between fireworks shows. Values go beneath the surface to a place where goals, even the loftiest ones, cannot because they connect us to that which makes doing what we're doing more meaningful in every moment, not just in the moments where we do or don't accomplish a goal.

There's no reason we can't launch some fireworks and stoke a bonfire at the same time. Outcomes and goals matter to everyone, but they do not have to be the be-all and end-all that our motivation and golf game teeter upon. In truth, it is a psycho-emotional need for us as humans to have and make progress toward meaningful pursuits. However, it is not a psycho-emotional need for us to actually reach the ends of those meaningful pursuits to get better, be successful, and be deeply fulfilled.

We only get to play golf for a limited time, whether that's on a professional tour or having the occasional casual round. If we take a moment to mindfully consider our golfing experience and what we value most for ourselves, it makes sense to use that time and whatever opportunities that come with it in ways that will culminate in something personally meaningful more than just something we do to string one accomplishment to the next.

Closing Thoughts

As you take the information in this book and put it to use, allow me to leave you with some parting thoughts. It has been my observation in the last several years of working with athletes and performers at all skill levels that the most fulfilling moments in our lives are not the easiest nor the most comfortable and almost always involve some levels of uncertainty and vulnerability. These moments are lived on a razor's edge, filled with choice points where we come face to face with opportunities to pursue what we want while facing the possibility that our best efforts may not be enough to get what we want when we want it. Those moments don't always work out, and others are often competing for many of the same things we are. Quite frankly, even when we give ourselves credible permission to take those leaps, there's still no guarantee of success. The only thing that avoiding failure, holding ourselves back, and getting in our own way does, however, is guarantee regret.

However, when we limit the amount of self-imposed interference we place on our performance by understanding our brain, forging a being-mode-of-mind relationship with our inner experience, developing productive habits, and building stable confidence, we gain more control over how we pursue the things we decide we really want. In a simple way, that's what growth, competing under pressure, resilience, and enjoyment are truly built upon.

Talented people are everywhere, but rarely are the best athletes and performers in the world necessarily the most talented. Instead, they're the ones who build their psychology from beneath the surface. They're the ones who ride the razor's edge, and when they come to choice points, they continually permit themselves to go for what they want when others can't or won't.

You might have noticed that I've challenged many of the common methods that are taught pertaining to building mental toughness. The primary reason for this is because most of the common methods that prevail in many areas of performance, including golf, still revolve around the idea of avoiding or distracting ourselves from things that we find fearful, challenging, uncertain, and uncomfortable. If I have written this book even semi-competently, you will understand now that any psychology professional who is even remotely capable knows that life is inherently challenging, uncomfortable, and uncertain. Sport is purposely designed to expose our underdeveloped areas—physical and psychological. Seeking comfort and certainty and trying to avoid that which we fear by distracting ourselves, telling ourselves not to think, or by coddling ourselves with positive affirmations is by far the least effective approach to building mental toughness: it makes us weaker, not stronger.

The way we develop all the attributes that we associate with mental toughness and continued persistence toward what we want is not to avoid that which challenges us, is uncertain, and makes us uncomfortable. Psychological strength comes from understanding our psychology and building a relationship with all of ourselves, from how our brain works, to our own thoughts and feelings, to our habits, all the way to how we've constructed our psychological framework.

It is my hope that this book has given you a comprehensive look at what's beneath the surface so that you too, regardless of your skill level, can continue to grow, enjoy the game, and play better golf when it matters to you. That being said, nothing that I've presented is a quick fix or trick designed to make you more comfortable, make you more certain, help you avoid things that can't be avoided, coddle you, or make you immune to the challenges that come with life and golf. Instead, everything in this book is designed to help you understand your psychology and use it to play more of the golf you want—not because it's quick and easy but because it's worth it.

Acknowledgments

Golf Beneath the Surface has been a labor of love for me over the last few years, but it would not have been possible without the help and expertise of so many others. Many thanks to all the researchers whose work has informed this book and is continually committed to improving the lives and performances of others. My most sincere thanks to the multitude of professional, collegiate, and amateur golfers, instructors, coaches, and industry leaders within golf and psychology who read early versions of this book and provided me with critical feedback and peer review to make sure it would serve readers as best as it can. Finally, thank you to my editors Lilith Dorko, Ryan Harrington, Camille Cline, Lydia Choi, and Vy Tran and to the entire team at BenBella Books for their courage, honesty, and willingness to invest in a book that challenges the status quo for performance psychology offered to golfers. Above all, thank you to the love of my life, my wife, Allison, who supported me while I read and wrote and then reread and rewrote again and again for the last three years. I love you.

References

YOUR BRAIN

Berti Ceroni, Giuseppe, Cecilia Neri, and A. Pezzoli. "Chronicity in major depression: A naturalistic prospective study." *Journal of Affective Disorders* 7, no. 2 (1984): 123–32. doi:10.1016/0165-0327(84)90030-2.

Brewer, Judson, Patrick D. Worhunsky, Jeremy R. Gray, Yi-Yuan Tang, Jochen Weber, and Hedy Kober. "Meditation experience is associated with differences in default mode network activity and connectivity." *Proceedings of the National Academy of Sciences* 108, no. 50 (November 2011): 20254–59. doi:10.1073/pnas.1112029108.

Broadhurst, P. L. "Emotionality and the Yerkes-Dodson Law." *Journal of Experimental Psychology* 54, no. 5 (1957): 345–52. doi:10.1037/h0049114.

Cahill, Larry, Bruce Prins, Michael Weber, and James L. McGaugh. "Beta-adrenergic activation and memory for emotional events." *Nature* 371 (October 1994): 702–4. doi:10.1038/371702a0.

Chernev, Alexander, Ulf Böckenholt, and Joseph Goodman. "Choice overload: A conceptual review and meta-analysis." *Journal of Consumer Psychology* 25, no. 2 (April 2015): 333–58. doi:10.1016/j.jcps.2014.08.002.

Eagleman, David. *Incognito: The Secret Lives of the Brain.* New York: Vintage Books, 2012.

Eagleman, David. *The Brain: The Story of You.* New York: Vintage Books, 2017.

Eysenck, H. J. "A dynamic theory of anxiety and hysteria." *Journal of Mental Science* 101, no. 422 (January 1955): 28–51. doi:10.1192/bjp.101.244.28.

Fogarty, Robin, and Brian Pete. *Metacognition: The Neglected Skill Set for Empowering Students.* Bloomington, IN: Solution Tree Press, 2020.

Freeman, Kelly, David S. Goldstein, and Charles R. Thompson. *The Dysautonomia Project: Understanding Autonomic Nervous System Disorders for Physicians and Patients.* Sarasota, FL: Bardolf & Company, 2015.

Goleman, Daniel. *Emotional Intelligence,* 25th anniversary ed. London: Bloomsbury, 2020.

Halford, Scott G. *Activate Your Brain: How Understanding Your Brain Can Improve Your Work—and Your Life.* Austin, TX: Greenleaf Book Group Press, 2015.

Hallinan, Joseph T. *Why We Make Mistakes: How We Look Without Seeing, Forget Things in Seconds, and Are All Pretty Sure We Are Way Above Average.* New York: Broadway Books, 2010.

Hofman, Michel A. *Evolution of the Human Brain: From Matter to Mind.* Cambridge, MA: Academic Press, 2019.

Jackson, Susan A. "Factors influencing the occurrence of flow state in elite athletes." *Journal of Applied Sport Psychology* 7, no. 2 (1995): 138–66. doi:10.1080/10413209508406962.

Lopes da Silva, Fernando. "Neural mechanisms underlying brain waves: From neural membranes to networks." *Electroencephalography and Clinical Neurophysiology* 79, no. 2 (August 1991): 81–93. doi:10.1016/0013-4694(91)90044-5.

Moini, Jahangir, and Pirouz Piran. *Functional and Clinical Neuroanatomy: A Guide for Health Care Professionals.* Cambridge, MA: Academic Press, 2020.

Muse, Lori A., Stanley G. Harris, and Hubert S. Feild. "Has the inverted-U theory of stress and job performance had a fair test?" *Human Performance* 16, no. 4 (2003): 349–64. doi:10.1207/S15327043HUP1604_2.

Obler, Loraine K., and Deborah Fein. *The Exceptional Brain: Neuropsychology of Talent and Special Abilities.* New York: Guilford Press, 1988.

Peters, Steve. *The Chimp Paradox.* London: Ebury Publishing, 2020.

Rock, David. "What inequality does to your brain." *Huffington Post*, January 10, 2012. https://www.huffpost.com/entry/psychology-of-inequality_b_1075227.

Sukel, Kayt. *The Art of Risk: The New Science of Courage, Caution, and Chance.* Washington, DC: National Geographic Society, 2016.

Whitwam, Ryan. "Simulating 1 second of human brain activity takes 82,944 processors." *ExtremeTech*, August 5, 2013. https://www.extremetech.com/extreme/163051-simulating-1-second-of-human-brain-activity-takes-82944-processors.

Yerkes, Robert M., and John D. Dodson. "The relationship of strength of stimulus to rapidity of habit-formation." *Journal of Comparative Neurology and Psychology* 18, no. 5 (November 1908): 459–82. doi:10.1002/cne.920180503.

AWARENESS

Aherne, Cian, Aidan P. Moran, and Chris Lonsdale. "The effect of mindfulness training on athletes' flow: An initial investigation." *The Sport Psychologist* 25, no. 2 (2011): 177–89. doi:10.1123/tsp.25.2.177.

Baltzell, Amy L., ed. *Mindfulness and Performance.* Cambridge University Press, 2016.

Baumeister, Roy F., and Todd F. Heatherton. "Self-regulation failure: An overview." *Psychological Inquiry* 7, no. 1 (1996): 1–15. doi:10.1207/s15327965pli0701_1.

Beck, Judith S. *Cognitive Behavior Therapy: Basics and Beyond.* New York: Guilford Press, 2011.

Bennett-Goleman, Tara. *Emotional Alchemy: How the Mind Can Heal the Heart.* New York: Three Rivers Press, 2001.

Biber, David D., and Rebecca Ellis. "The effect of self-compassion on the self-regulation of health behaviors: A systematic review." *Journal of Health Psychology* 24, no. 14 (December 2019): 2060–71. doi:10.1177/1359105317713361.

Brach, Tara. *Radical Acceptance: Embracing Your Life with the Heart of a Buddha*. New York: Bantam Dell, 2003.

Brewer, Judson. *Unwinding Anxiety: New Science Shows How to Break the Cycles of Worry and Fear to Heal Your Mind*. New York: Avery, 2021.

Brewer, Judson. *The Craving Mind: From Cigarettes to Smartphones to Love—Why We Get Hooked and How We Can Break Bad Habits*. New Haven, CT: Yale University Press, 2017.

Brewer, Judson, Patrick D. Worhunsky, Jeremy R. Gray, Yi-Yuan Tang, Jochen Weber, and Hedy Kober. "Meditation experience is associated with differences in default mode network activity and connectivity." *Proceedings of the National Academy of Sciences* 108, no. 50 (November 2011): 20254–59. doi:10.1073/pnas.1112029108.

Bühlmayer, Lucia, Daniel Birrer, Philipp Röthlin, Oliver Faude, and Lars Donath. "Effects of mindfulness practice on performance-relevant parameters and performance outcomes in sports: A meta-analytical review." *Sports Medicine* 47, no. 11 (November 2017): 2309–21. doi:10.1007/s40279-017-0752-9.

Costa, Joana, and José Pinto-Gouveia. "Experiential avoidance and self-compassion in chronic pain." *Journal of Applied Social Psychology* 43, no. 8 (July 2013): 1578–91. doi:10.1111/jasp.12107.

Csikszentmihayli, Mihaly. *Flow: The Psychology of Optimal Experience*. New York: Harper & Row, 1990.

Damasio, Antonio. *Descartes' Error: Emotion, Reason, and the Human Brain*. New York: Penguin Books, 2005.

David, Susan. *Emotional Agility: Get Unstuck, Embrace Change, and Thrive in Work and Life*. New York: Avery, 2016.

David, Susan. "The Gift and Power of Emotional Courage." Filmed November 2017 in New Orleans, LA. TED video, 16:49. https://ed.ted.com/lessons/iaTNUBwR.

Davidson, Richard J., Jon Kabat-Zinn, Jessica Schumacher, Melissa Rosenkranz, Daniel Muller, Saki F. Santorelli, Ferris Urbanowski, Anne Harrington, Katherine Bonus, and John F. Sheridan. "Alterations in brain and immune function produced by mindfulness meditation." *Psychosomatic Medicine* 65, no. 4 (July 2003): 564–70. doi:10.1097/01. psy.0000077505.67574.e3.

Ekman, Paul, and Richard J. Davidson, eds. *The Nature of Emotion: Fundamental Questions*. New York: Oxford University Press, 1994.

Fallon, Marise. "The Differential Effects of Three Mindfulness Techniques on Indicators of Emotional Well-being and Life Satisfaction." Master's diss., University of Tasmania, 2014. https://eprints.utas.edu.au/22456/13/whole-fallon-thesis%20ex%20pub%20mat. pdf.

Feldman, Christina. *The Buddhist Path to Simplicity: Spiritual Practice for Everyday Life*. New York: Metro Books, 2006.

Flett, Jayde A. M., Harlene Hayne, Benjamin C. Riordan, Laura M. Thompson, and Tamlin S. Connor. "Mobile mindfulness meditation: A randomised controlled trial of the effect of two popular apps on mental health." *Mindfulness* 10, no. 5 (2018): 863–76. doi:10.1007/S12671-018-1050-9.

Gardner, Frank L., and Zella E. Moore. *The Psychology of Enhancing Human Performance: The Mindfulness-Acceptance-Commitment (MAC) Approach.* New York: Springer Publishing Company, 2007.

Gremer, Christopher, and Kristin Neff. *Teaching the Mindful Self-Compassion Program: A Guide for Professionals.* New York: Guilford Press, 2019.

Gschwandtner, Adelina, Sarah Jewell, and Uma S. Kambhampati. "Lifestyle and life satisfaction: The role of delayed gratification." *Journal of Happiness Studies* 23 (2022): 1043–72. doi:10.1007/s10902-021-00440-y.

Harris, Russ. *The Happiness Trap: How to Stop Struggling and Start Living.* Boston: Trumpeter, 2008.

Hayes, Steven C. "Why meditation might not be working for you." *Psychology Today*, February 8, 2022. https://www.psychologytoday.com/us/blog/get-out-your-mind/202202/why-meditation-might-not-be-working-you.

Hayes, Steven C., and Kirk D. Strosahl. *A Practical Guide to Acceptance and Commitment Therapy.* New York: Springer, 2004.

Hölzel, Britta, James Carmody, Mark Vangel, Christina Congleton, Sita M. Yerramsetti, Tim Gard, and Sara W. Lazar. "Mindfulness practice leads to increases in regional brain gray matter density." *Psychiatry Research: Neuroimaging* 191, no. 1 (January 2011): 36–43. doi:10.1016/j.pscychresns.2010.08.006.

Jackson, Susan A. "Factors influencing the occurrence of flow state in elite athletes." *Journal of Applied Sport Psychology* 7, no. 2 (1995): 138–66. doi:10.1080/10413209508406962.

Justice, Izzy. *GYRA Golf: Golf's 1st Mental Scorecard.* Bloomington, IN: iUniverse, 2020.

Kashdan, Todd B. "Psychological flexibility as a fundamental aspect of health." *Clinical Psychology Review* 30, no. 7 (November 2010): 865–78. doi:10.1016/j.cpr.2010.03.001.

Katahira, Kenji, Yoichi Yamazaki, Chiaki Yamaoka, Hiroaki Ozaki, Sayaka Nakagawa, and Noriko Nagata. "EEG correlates of the flow state: A combination of increased frontal theta and moderate frontocentral alpha rhythm in the mental arithmetic task." *Frontiers in Psychology* 9 (March 2018). doi:10.3389/fpsyg.2018.00300.

Kaufman, Keith A., Carol R. Glass, and Timothy R. Pineau. *Mindful Sport Performance Enhancement: Mental Training for Athletes and Coaches.* Washington, DC: American Psychological Association, 2018.

Killingsworth, Matthew A., and Daniel T. Gilbert. "A wandering mind is an unhappy mind." *Science* 330, no. 6006 (November 2010): 932. doi:10.1126/science.1192439.

Kroll, Keith, ed. *Contemplative Teaching and Learning: New Directions for Community Colleges (Number 151).* Hoboken, NJ: Jossey-Bass, 2010.

Langer, Ellen J. *Mindfulness.* Cambridge, MA: Perseus Books, 1989.

Lazar, Sara W., George Bush, Randy L. Gollub, Gregory L. Fricchione, Gurucharan Khalsa, and Herbert Benson. "Functional brain mapping of the relaxation response and meditation." *NeuroReport* 11, no. 7 (May 2000): 1581–85.

Lazar, Sara W., Catherine E. Kerr, Rachel H. Wasserman, Jeremy R. Gray, Douglas N. Greve, Michael T. Treadway, Metta McGarvey, et al. "Meditation experience is associated with increased cortical thickness." *NeuroReport* 16, no. 17 (November 2005): 1893–97. doi:10.1097/01.wnr.0000186598.66243.19.

Lippelt, Dominique P., Bernhard Hommel, and Lorenza S. Colzato. "Focused attention, open monitoring and loving kindness meditation: Effects on attention, conflict monitoring, and creativity—A review." *Frontiers in Psychology* 5 (2014): 1083. doi:10.3389/fpsyg.2014.01083.

Lopes da Silva, Fernando. "Neural mechanisms underlying brain waves: From neural membranes to networks." *Electroencephalography and Clinical Neurophysiology* 79, no. 2 (August 1991): 81–93. doi:10.1016/0013-4694(91)90044-5.

Lyubomirsky, Sonja, and Susan Nolen-Hoeksema. "Effects of self-focused rumination on negative thinking and interpersonal problem solving." *Journal of Personality and Social Psychology* 69, no. 1 (1995): 176–90. doi:10.1037/0022-3514.69.1.176.

MacBeth, Angus, and Andrew Gumley. "Exploring compassion: A meta-analysis of the association between self-compassion and psychopathology." *Clinical Psychology Review* 32, no. 6 (August 2012): 545–52. doi:10.1016/j.cpr.2012.06.003.

Mak, Lauren E., Luciano Minuzzi, Glenda MacQueen, Geoffrey Hall, Sidney H. Kennedy, and Roumen Milev. "The default mode network in healthy individuals: A systematic review and meta-analysis." *Brain Connectivity* 7, no. 1 (February 2017): 25–33. doi:10.1089/brain.2016.0438.

Mani, Madhavan, David J. Kavanagh, Leanne Hides, and Stoyan R. Stoyanov. "Review and evaluation of mindfulness-based iPhone apps." *JMIR mHealth and uHealth* 3, no. 3 (August 2015): 82. doi:10.2196/mhealth.4328.

Marasigan, Portia R. "Using brief cognitive restructuring and cognitive defusion techniques to cope with negative thoughts." *Social Values and Society*, no. 4 (2019): 11–14. doi:10.26480/svs.04.2019.11.14.

Mehl, Matthias R., Simine Vavire, Nairán Ramírez-Esparza, Richard B. Slatcher, and James W. Pennebaker. "Are women really more talkative than men?" *Science* 317, no. 5834 (July 2007): 82. doi:10.1126/science.1139940.

Moawad, Heidi. "What are alpha brain waves and why are they important?" *Healthline*, October 9, 2019. https://www.healthline.com/health/alpha-brain-waves.

Muthukumaraswamy, Suresh D. "High-frequency brain activity and muscle artifacts in MEG/EEG: A review and recommendations." *Frontiers in Human Neuroscience* 7 (2013): 138. doi:10.3389/fnhum.2013.00138.

Nalbant, Ahmet, and Fatih Yavuz. "Getting out of language cocoon: Cognitive defusion." *Journal of Cognitive-Behavioral Psychotherapy and Research* 8, no. 1 (2019): 58–62. doi:10.5455/JCBPR.33709.

Neff, Kristin D., Phoebe Long, Marissa C. Knox, Oliver Davidson, Ashley Kuchar, Andrew Constigan, Zachary Williamson, Nicolas Rohleder, István Tóth-Király, and Juliana G. Breines. "The forest and the trees: Examining the association of self-compassion and its positive and negative components with psychological functioning." *Self and Identity* 17, no. 6 (2018): 627–45. doi:10.1080/15298868.2018.1436587.

Neff, Kristin D., and Elizabeth Pommier. "The relationship between self-compassion and other-focused concern among undergraduates, community adults, and practicing meditators." *Self and Identity* 12, no. 2 (2013): 160–76. doi:10.1080/15298868.2011.64 9546.

Neff, Kristin D., Stephanie S. Rude, and Kristin L. Kirkpatrick. "An examination of self-compassion in relation to positive psychological functioning and personality traits." *Journal of Research in Personality* 41 (2007): 908–16. doi:10.1016/j.jrp.2006.08.002.

Neff, Kristin D., and Roos Vonk. "Self-compassion versus global self-esteem: Two different ways of relating to oneself." *Journal of Personality* 77, no. 1 (February 2009): 23–50. doi:10.1111/j.1467-6494.2008.00537.x.

Nolen-Hoeksema, Susan. *Women Who Think Too Much: How to Break Free of Overthinking and Reclaim Your Life*. New York: St. Martin's Press, 2003.

Papageorgiou, Costas, and Adrian Wells. "Positive beliefs about depressive rumination: Development and preliminary validation of a self-report scale." *Behavior Therapy* 32, no. 1 (2001): 13–26. doi:10.1016/S0005-7894(01)80041-1.

Phillips, Wendy J., and Donald W. Hine. "Self-compassion, physical health, and health behavior: A meta-analysis." *Health Psychology Review* 15, no. 1 (March 2021): 113–39. doi:10.1080/17437199.2019.1705872.

Privette, Gayle. "Peak experience, peak performance, and flow: A comparative analysis of positive human experiences." *Journal of Personality and Social Psychology* 45, no. 6 (1983): 1361–68. doi:10.1037/0022-3514.45.6.1361.

Raichle, Marcus E., Ann Mary Macleod, Abraham Z. Snyder, William J. Powers, Debra A. Gusnard, and Gordon L. Shulman. "A default mode of brain function." *Proceedings of the National Academy of Sciences* 98, no. 2 (February 2001): 676–82. doi:10.1073/pnas.98.2.676.

Ravizza, Kenneth. "Body Scan Mindfulness Practice." MP3 file. Los Angeles.

Ring, Christopher, Andrew Cooke, Maria Kavussanu, David McIntyre, and Rich Masters. "Investigating the efficacy of neurofeedback training for expediting expertise and excellence in sport." *Psychology of Sport and Exercise* 16 (January 2015): 118–27. doi:10.1016/j.psychsport.2014.08.005.

Rosenberg, Larry. *Breath by Breath: The Liberating Practice of Insight Meditation*. Boston: Shambhala Publications, Inc., 1998.

Rude, Stephanie S., Richard M. Wenzlaff, Bryce Gibbs, Jennifer Vane, and Tav Whitney. "Negative processing biases predict subsequent depressive symptoms." *Cognition and Emotion* 16, no. 3 (2002): 423–40. doi:10.1080/02699930143000554.

Russell, William D. "An examination of flow state occurrence in college athletes." *Journal of Sport Behavior* 24, no. 1 (March 2001): 83–107.

Segal, Zindel V., John D. Teasdale, and J. Mark G. Williams. "Mindfulness-based cognitive therapy: theoretical rationale and empirical status." In *Mindfulness and Acceptance: Expanding the Cognitive-Behavioral Tradition*, edited by Steven C. Hayes, Victoria M. Follette, and Marsha M. Linehan, 45–65. New York: Guilford Press, 2004.

Sevinc, Gunes, Britta K. Hölzel, Jonathan Greenberg, Tim Gard, Vincent Brunsch, Javeria A. Hashmi, Mark Vangel, Scott P. Orr, Mohammed R. Milad, and Sara W. Lazar. "Strengthened hippocampal circuits underlie enhanced retrieval of extinguished fear memories following mindfulness training." *Biological Psychiatry* 86, no. 9 (November 2019): 693–702. doi:10.1016/j.biopsych.2019.05.107.

Stulberg, Brad. *The Practice of Groundedness: A Transformative Path to Success That Feeds—Not Crushes—Your Soul.* New York: Penguin Random House, 2021.

Watkins, Ed, and Simona Baracaia. "Why do people ruminate in dysphoric moods?" *Personality and Individual Differences* 30, no. 5 (April 2001): 723–34. doi:10.1016/S0191-8869(00)00053-2.

Wegner, Daniel M. *The Illusion of Conscious Will*, New Edition. Cambridge, MA: MIT Press, 2017.

Wegner, Daniel M., David J. Schneider, Samuel R. Carter, and Teri L. White. "Paradoxical effects of thought suppression." *Journal of Personality and Social Psychology* 53, no. 1 (1987): 5–13. doi:10.1037/0022-3514.53.1.5.

Williams, Mark, John Teasdale, Zindel Segal, and Jon Kabat-Zinn. *The Mindful Way through Depression.* New York: Guilford Press, 2007.

Xiang, Ming-Qiang, Xiao-Hui Hou, Ba-Gen Liao, Jing-Wen Liao, and Min Hu. "The effect of neurofeedback training for sport performance in athletes: A meta-analysis." *Psychology of Sport and Exercise* 36 (May 2018): 114–22. doi:10.1016/j.psychsport.2018.02.004.

Yoshida, Kazuki, Daisuke Sawamura, Yuji Inagaki, Keita Ogawa, Katsunori Ikoma, and Shinya Sakai. "Brain activity during the flow experience: A functional near-infrared spectroscopy study." *Neuroscience Letters* 573 (June 2014): 30–34. doi:10.1016/j.neulet.2014.05.011.

HABITS

Aherne, Cian, Aidan P. Moran, and Chris Lonsdale. "The effect of mindfulness training on athletes' flow: An initial investigation." *The Sport Psychologist* 25, no. 2 (June 2011): 177–89. doi:10.1123/tsp.25.2.177.

Arnsten, Amy F. T. "Stress signaling pathways that impair prefrontal cortex structure and function." *Nature Reviews Neuroscience* 10, no. 6 (June 2009): 410–22. doi:10.1038/nrn2648.

Arnsten, Amy F. T. "Stress weakens prefrontal networks: Molecular insults to higher cognition." *Nature Neuroscience* 18, no. 10 (October 2015): 1376–85. doi:10.1038/nn.4087.

Arnsten, Amy F. T., Murray A. Raskind, Fletcher B. Taylor, and Daniel F. Connor. "The effects of stress exposure on prefrontal cortex: Translating basic research into successful treatments for post-traumatic stress disorder." *Neurobiology of Stress* 1 (January 2015): 89–99. doi:10.1016/j.ynstr.2014.10.002.

Baltzell, Amy L., ed. *Mindfulness and Performance.* Cambridge University Press, 2016.

Baumeister, Roy F., and Todd F. Heatherton. "Self-regulation failure: An overview." *Psychological Inquiry* 7, no. 1 (1996): 1–15. doi:10.1207/s15327965pli0701_1.

Blanchard, Tommy C., Benjamin Y. Hayden, and Ethan S. Bromberg-Martin. "Orbitofrontal cortex uses distinct codes for different choice attributes in decisions motivated by curiosity." *Neuron* 85, no. 3 (February 2015): 602–14. doi:10.1016/j.neuron.2014.12.050.

Brach, Tara. "Feeling overwhelmed? Remember RAIN." *Mindful*, February 7, 2019. https://www.mindful.org/tara-brach-rain-mindfulness-practice/.

Brewer, Judson. "Feeling is believing: The convergence of Buddhist theory and modern scientific evidence supporting how self is formed and perpetuated through feeling tone (*vedanā*)." *Contemporary Buddhism* 19, no. 1 (2018): 113–26. doi:10.1080/14639947.20 18.1443553.

Brewer, Judson. "Mindfulness training for addictions: Has neuroscience revealed a brain hack by which awareness subverts the addictive process?" *Current Opinion in Psychology* 28 (August 2019): 198–203. doi:10.1016/j.copsyc.2019.01.014.

Brewer, Judson. *Unwinding Anxiety: New Science Shows How to Break the Cycles of Worry and Fear to Heal Your Mind*. New York: Avery, 2021.

Brewer, Judson, Kathleen A. Garrison, and Susan Whitfield-Gabrieli. "What about the 'self' is processed in the posterior cingulate cortex?" *Frontiers in Human Neuroscience* 7 (2013). doi:10.3389/fnhum.2013.00647.

Brewer, Judson. *The Craving Mind: From Cigarettes to Smartphones to Love—Why We Get Hooked and How We Can Break Bad Habits*. New Haven, CT: Yale University Press, 2017.

Brewer, Judson, Sarah Mallik, Theresa A. Babuscio, Charla Nich, Hayley E. Johnson, Cameron M. Deleone, Candace A. Minnix-Cotton, et al. "Mindfulness training for smoking cessation: Results from a randomized controlled trial." *Drug and Alcohol Dependence* 119, no. 1–2 (December 2011): 72–80. doi:10.1016/j. drugalcdep.2011.05.027.

Brewer, Judson, Patrick D. Worhunsky, Jeremy R. Gray, Yi-Yuan Tang, Jochen Weber, and Hedy Kober. "Meditation experience is associated with differences in default mode network activity and connectivity." *Proceedings of the National Academy of Sciences* 108, no. 50 (November 2011): 20254–59. doi:10.1073/pnas.1112029108.

Bühlmayer, Lucia, Daniel Birrer, Philipp Röthlin, Oliver Faude, and Lars Donath. "Effects of mindfulness practice on performance-relevant parameters and performance outcomes in sports: A meta-analytical review." *Sports Medicine* 47, no. 11 (November 2017): 2309–21. doi:10.1007/s40279-017-0752-9.

Chernev, Alexander, Ulf Böckenholt, and Joseph Goodson. "Choice overload: A conceptual review and meta-analysis." *Journal of Consumer Psychology* 25, no. 2 (August 2014): 333–58. doi:10.1016/j.jcps.2014.08.002.

David, Susan. *Emotional Agility: Get Unstuck, Embrace Change, and Thrive in Work and Life*. New York: Avery, 2016.

Davidson, Richard J., Jon Kabat-Zinn, Jessica Schumacher, Melissa Rosenkranz, Daniel Muller, Saki F. Santorelli, Ferris Urbanowski, Anne Harrington, Katherine Bonus, and John F. Sheridan. "Alterations in brain and immune function produced by mindfulness meditation." *Psychosomatic Medicine* 65, no. 4 (July 2003): 564–70. doi:10.1097/01. psy.0000077505.67574.e3.

Davis, James M., Simon B. Goldberg, Kelly S. Angel, Rachel H. Silver, Emily A. Kragel, and Delaney J. Lagrew. "Observational study on a mindfulness training for smokers within a smoking cessation program." *Mindfulness* 8, no. 6 (December 2017): 1698.

Engber, Daniel. "Everything is crumbling." *Slate*, March 6, 2016. http:// www.slate.com/articles/health_and_science/cover_story/2016/03/

ego_depletion_an_influential_theory_in_psychology_may_have_just_been_debunked.
html.

Flett, Jayde A. M., Harlene Hayne, Benjamin C. Riordan, Laura M. Thompson, and Tamlin S. Connor. "Mobile mindfulness meditation: A randomised controlled trial of the effect of two popular apps on mental health." *Mindfulness* 10, no. 5 (2018): 863–76. doi:10.1007/S12671-018-1050-9.

Galla, Brian M., and Angela L. Duckworth. "More than resisting temptation: Beneficial habits mediate the relationship between self-control and positive life outcomes." *Journal of Personality and Social Psychology* 109, no. 3 (September 2015): 508–25. doi:10.1037/pspp0000026.

Garrison, Kathleen A., Juan F. Santoyo, Jake H. Davis, Thomas A. Thornhill, Catherine E. Kerr, and Judson Brewer. "Effortless awareness: Using real time neurofeedback to investigate correlates of posterior cingulate cortex activity in meditators' self-report." *Frontiers in Human Neuroscience* 7 (2013). doi:10.3389/fnhum.2013.00440.

Garrison, Kathleen A., Dustin Scheinost, R. Todd Constable, and Judson Brewer. "BOLD signal and functional connectivity associated with loving kindness meditation." *Brain and Behavior* 4, no. 3 (May 2014): 337–47. doi:10.1002/brb3.219.

Gruber, Matthias J., Bernard D. Gelman, and Charan Ranganath. "States of curiosity modulate hippocampus-dependent learning via the dopaminergic circuit." *Neuron* 84, no. 2 (October 2014): 486–96. doi:10.1016/j.neuron.2014.08.060.

Hayes, Steven C., and Kirk D. Strosahl. *A Practical Guide to Acceptance and Commitment Therapy*. New York: Springer, 2004.

Hofmann, Wilhelm, and Lotte F. Van Dillen. "Desire: The new hot spot in self-control research." *Current Directions in Psychological Science* 21, no. 5 (October 2012): 317–22. doi:10.1177/0963721412453587.

Janes, Amy C., Michael Datko, Alexandra Roy, Bruce Barton, Susan Druker, Carolyn Neal, Kyoko Ohashi, Hanif Benoit, Remko van Lutterveld, and Judson Brewer. "Quitting starts in the brain: A randomized controlled trial of app-based mindfulness shows decreases in neural responses to smoking cues that predict reductions in smoking." *Neuropsychopharmacology* 44, no. 9 (August 2019): 1631–38. doi:10.1038/s41386-019-0403-y.

Justice, Izzy. *GYRA Golf: Golf's 1st Mental Scorecard*. Bloomington, IN: iUniverse, 2020.

Killingsworth, Matthew A., and Daniel T. Gilbert. "A wandering mind is an unhappy mind." *Science* 330, no. 6006 (November 2010): 932. doi:10.1126/science.1192439.

Kringelbach, Morten L., and Edmund T. Rolls. "The functional neuroanatomy of the human orbitofrontal cortex: Evidence from neuroimaging and neuropsychology." *Progress in Neurobiology* 72, no. 5 (April 2004): 341–72. doi:10.1016/j.pneurobio.2004.03.006.

Lally, Phillippa, Cornelia H. M. van Jaarsveld, Henry W. W. Potts, and Jane Wardle. "How are habits formed: Modelling habit formation in the real world." *European Journal of Social Psychology* 40, no. 6 (July 2009): 998–1009. doi:10.1002/ejsp.674.

Langer, Ellen J. *Mindfulness*. Cambridge, MA: Perseus Books, 1989.

Lazar, Sara W., George Bush, Randy L. Gollub, Gregory L. Fricchione, Gurucharan Khalsa, and Herbert Benson. "Functional brain mapping of the relaxation response and meditation." *NeuroReport* 11, no. 7 (May 2000): 1581–85.

Lazar, Sara W., Catherine E. Kerr, Rachel H. Wasserman, Jeremy R. Gray, Douglas N. Greve, Michael T. Treadway, Metta McGarvey, et al. "Meditation experience is associated with increased cortical thickness." *NeuroReport* 16, no. 17 (November 2005): 1893–97. doi:10.1097/01.wnr.0000186598.66243.19.

Litman, Jordan A. "Curiosity and the pleasures of learning: Wanting and liking new information." *Cognition and Emotion* 19, no. 6 (2005): 793–814. doi:10.1080/02699930541000101.

Litman, Jordan A. "The COPE inventory: Dimensionality and relationships with approach- and avoidance-motives and positive and negative traits." *Personality and Individual Differences* 41, no. 2 (July 2006): 273–84. doi:10.1016/j.paid.2005.11.032.

Litman, Jordan A. "Interest and deprivation factors of epistemic curiosity." *Personality and Individual Differences* 44, no. 7 (May 2008): 1585–95. doi:10.1016/j.paid.2008.01.014.

Litman, Jordan A. "Relationships between measures of I- and D-type curiosity, ambiguity tolerance, and need for closure: An initial test of the wanting-liking model of information-seeking." *Personality and Individual Differences* 48, no. 4 (March 2010): 397–402. doi:10.1016/j.paid.2009.11.005.

Litman, Jordan A. "Curiosity: Nature, Dimensionality, and Determinants." In *The Cambridge Handbook of Motivation and Learning*, edited by K. Ann Renninger and Suzanne E. Hidi, 418–42. Cambridge University Press, 2019.

Litman, Jordan A., Tiffany L. Hutchins, and Ryan K. Russon. "Epistemic curiosity, feeling-of-knowing, and exploratory behaviour." *Cognition and Emotion* 19, no. 4 (2005): 559–82. doi:10.1080/02699930441000427.

Litman, Jordan A., and Paul J. Silvia. "The latent structure of trait curiosity: Evidence for interest and deprivation curiosity dimensions." *Journal of Personality Assessment* 86, no. 3 (2006): 318–28. doi:10.1207/s15327752jpa8603_07.

Lopes da Silva, Fernando. "Neural mechanisms underlying brain waves: From neural membranes to networks." *Electroencephalography and Clinical Neurophysiology* 79, no. 2 (August 1991): 81–93. doi:10.1016/0013-4694(91)90044-5.

Lyubomirsky, Sonja, and Susan Nolen-Hoeksema. "Effects of self-focused rumination on negative thinking and interpersonal problem solving." *Journal of Personality and Social Psychology* 69, no. 1 (1995): 176–90. doi:10.1037/0022-3514.69.1.176.

Marasigan, Portia R. "Using brief cognitive restructuring and cognitive defusion techniques to cope with negative thoughts." *Social Values and Society*, no. 4 (2019): 11–14. doi:10.26480/svs.04.2019.11.14.

Mayr, Ulrich, and Reinhold Kliegl. "Task-set switching and long-term memory retrieval." *Journal of Experimental Psychology: Learning, Memory, and Cognition* 26, no. 5 (2000): 1124–40. doi:10.1037/0278-7393.26.5.1124.

Milyavskaya, Marina, and Michael Inzlicht. "What's so great about self-control? Examining the importance of effortful self-control and temptation in predicting real-life depletion and goal attainment." *Social Psychological and Personality Science* 8, no. 6 (2017): 603–11. doi:10.1177/1948550616679237.

Monsell, Stephen, and Jon Driver, eds. *Control of Cognitive Processes: Attention and Performance XVIII*. Cambridge, MA: MIT Press, 2000.

Nolen-Hoeksema, Susan. *Women Who Think Too Much: How to Break Free of Overthinking and Reclaim Your Life*. New York: St. Martin's Press, 2003.

Novaco, Raymond W. "Anger and psychopathology." In *International Handbook of Anger: Constituent and Concomitant Biological, Psychological, and Social Processes*, edited by Michael Potegal, Gerhard Stemmler, and Charles Speilberger, 465–97. New York: Springer, 2010.

O'Doherty, John P., Morten L. Kringelbach, Edmund T. Rolls, J. Hornak, and C. Andrews. "Abstract reward and punishment representations in the human orbitofrontal cortex." *Nature Neuroscience* 4, no. 1 (2001): 95–102. doi:10.1038/82959.

Papageorgiou, Costas, and Adrian Wells. "Positive beliefs about depressive rumination: Development and preliminary validation of a self-report scale." *Behavior Therapy* 32, no. 1 (2001): 13–26. doi:10.1016/S0005-7894(01)80041-1.

Privette, Gayle. "Peak experience, peak performance, and flow: A comparative analysis of positive human experiences." *Journal of Personality and Social Psychology* 45, no. 6 (1983): 1361–68. doi:10.1037/0022-3514.45.6.1361.

Raichle, Marcus E., Ann Mary Macleod, Abraham Z. Snyder, William J. Powers, Debra A. Gusnard, and Gordon L. Shulman. "A default mode of brain function." *Proceedings of the National Academy of Sciences* 98, no. 2 (February 2001): 676–82. doi:10.1073/pnas.98.2.676.

Rescorla, Robert A. "Variation in the effectiveness of reinforcement and nonreinforcement following prior inhibitory conditioning." *Learning and Motivation* 2, no. 2 (May 1971): 113–23. doi:10.1016/0023-9690(71)90002-6.

Resnick, Brian. "Why willpower is overrated." *Vox*, January 2, 2020. https://www.vox.com/science-and-health/2018/1/15/16863374/willpower-overrated-self-control-psychology.

Rogers, Robert D., and Stephen Monsell. "The costs of a predictable switch between simple cognitive tasks." *Journal of Experimental Psychology: General* 124 (1995): 207–31. doi:10.1037/0096-3445.124.2.207.

Rosenberg, Larry. *Breath by Breath: The Liberating Practice of Insight Meditation*. Boston: Shambhala Publications, Inc., 1998.

Rubinstein, Joshua S., David E. Meyer, and Jeffrey E. Evans. "Executive control of cognitive processes in task switching." *Journal of Experimental Psychology: Human Perception and Performance* 27 (2001): 763–97. doi:10.1037/0096-1523.27.4.763.

Segal, Zindel V., John D. Teasdale, and J. Mark G. Williams. "Mindfulness-based cognitive therapy: theoretical rationale and empirical status." In *Mindfulness and Acceptance: Expanding the Cognitive-Behavioral Tradition*, edited by Steven C. Hayes, Victoria M. Follette, and Marsha M. Linehan, 45–65. New York: Guilford Press, 2004.

Sevinc, Gunes, Britta K. Hölzel, Jonathan Greenberg, Tim Gard, Vincent Brunsch, Javeria A. Hashmi, Mark Vangel, Scott P. Orr, Mohammed R. Milad, and Sara W. Lazar. "Strengthened hippocampal circuits underlie enhanced retrieval of extinguished fear memories following mindfulness training." *Biological Psychiatry* 86, no. 9 (November 2019): 693–702. doi:10.1016/j.biopsych.2019.05.107.

Small, Dana M., Robert J. Zatorre, Alain Dagher, Alan C. Evans, and Marilyn Jones-Gotman. "Changes in brain activity related to eating chocolate: From pleasure to aversion." *Brain* 124, no. 9 (September 2001): 1720–33. doi:10.1093/brain/124.9.1720.

Sollisch, Jim. "Multitasking makes us a little dumber." *Chicago Tribune*, August 10, 2010. https://www.chicagotribune.com/opinion/ct-xpm-2010-08-10-ct-oped-0811-multitask-20100810-story.html.

Stice, Eric, Sonja Spoor, Cara Bohon, Marga G. Veldhuizen, and Dana M. Small. "Relation of reward from food intake and anticipated food intake to obesity: A functional magnetic resonance imaging study." *Journal of Abnormal Psychology* 117, no. 4 (November 2008): 924–35. doi:10.1037/a0013600.

Stulberg, Brad. *The Practice of Groundedness: A Transformative Path to Success That Feeds—Not Crushes—Your Soul.* New York: Penguin Random House, 2021.

Tangney, June Price, Patricia E. Wagner, Deborah Hill-Barlow, Donna E. Marschall, and Richard Gramzow. "Relation of shame and guilt to constructive versus destructive responses to anger across the lifespan." *Journal of Personality and Social Psychology* 70, no. 4 (1996): 797–809. doi:10.1037/0022-3514.70.4.797.

Thanarajah, Sharmili Edwin, Heiko Backes, Alexandra G. Difeliceantonio, Kerstin Albus, Anna Lena Cremer, Ruth Hanssen, Rachel N. Lippert, et al. "Food intake recruits orosensory and post-ingestive dopaminergic circuits to affect eating desire in humans." *Cell Metabolism* 29, no. 3 (March 2019): 695–706. doi:10.1016/j.cmet.2018.12.006.

Tops, Mattie, and Maarten A. S. Boksem. "'What's that?' 'What went wrong?' Positive and negative surprise and the rostral–ventral to caudal–dorsal functional gradient in the brain." *Frontiers in Psychology* 3 (2012). doi:10.3389/fpsyg.2012.00021.

University of Hertfordshire. "Self-acceptance could be the key to a happier life, yet it's the happy habit many people practice the least." *ScienceDaily*, March 7, 2014. www.sciencedaily.com/releases/2014/03/140307111016.htm.

Vanhamme, Joëlle, and Dirk Snelders. "The role of surprise in satisfaction judgements." *Journal of Consumer Satisfaction, Dissatisfaction and Complaining Behavior* 14 (2001): 27–45.

Vrticka, Pascal, Lara Lordier, Benoît Bediou, and David Sander. "Human amygdala response to dynamic facial expressions of positive and negative surprise." *Emotion* 14, no. 1 (2014): 161–69. doi:10.1037/a0034619.

Watkins, Ed, and Simona Baracaia. "Why do people ruminate in dysphoric moods?" *Personality and Individual Differences* 30, no. 5 (April 2001): 723–34. doi:10.1016/S0191-8869(00)00053-2.

Wegner, Daniel M. *The Illusion of Conscious Will*, New Edition. Cambridge, MA: MIT Press, 2017.

Williams, Mark, John Teasdale, Zindel Segal, and Jon Kabat-Zinn. *The Mindful Way through Depression.* New York: Guilford Press, 2007.

Yeung, Nick, and Stephen Monsell. "Switching between tasks of unequal familiarity: The role of stimulus-attribute and response-set selection." *Journal of Experimental*

Psychology: Human Perception and Performance 29, no. 2 (2003): 455–69. doi:10.1037/0096-1523.29.2.455.

Yoshida, Kazuki, Daisuke Sawamura, Yuji Inagaki, Keita Ogawa, Katsunori Ikoma, and Shinya Sakai. "Brain activity during the flow experience: A functional near-infrared spectroscopy study." *Neuroscience Letters* 573 (June 2014): 30–34. doi:10.1016/j. neulet.2014.05.011.

FRAMEWORK

Arkes, Hal R. "Costs and benefits of judgment errors: Implications for debiasing." *Psychological Bulletin* 110, no. 3 (1991): 486–98. doi:10.1037/0033-2909.110.3.486.

Bandura, Albert. *Self-Efficacy: The Exercise of Control.* New York: W.H. Freeman and Company, 1997.

Bandura, Albert, Nancy E. Adams, and Janice Beyer. "Cognitive processes mediating behavioral change." *Journal of Personality and Social Psychology* 35, no. 3 (1977): 125–39. doi:10.1037/0022-3514.35.3.125.

Beatty, Joy E., Jennifer S. A. Leigh, and Kathy Lund Dean. "Finding our roots: An exercise for creating a personal teaching philosophy statement." *Journal of Management Education* 33, no. 1 (February 2009): 115–30. doi:10.1177/1052562907310642.

Bénabou, Roland, and Jean Tirole. "Self-confidence and personal motivation." *Quarterly Journal of Economics* 117, no. 3 (August 2002): 871–915. doi:10.1162/003355302760193913.

Berger, Daniel. "Daniel Berger: Saturday flash interview AT&T Pebble Beach Pro Am." TenGolf, February 13, 2021. YouTube video, 2:03. https://youtu.be/chONcKCm2i4.

Boileau, Laurence, Patrick Gaudreau, Alexandre Gareau, and Melodie Chamandy. "Some days are more satisfying than others: A daily-diary study on optimism, pessimism, coping, and academic satisfaction." *British Journal of Educational Psychology* 91, no. 1 (March 2021): 46–62. doi:10.1111/bjep.12346.

Breines, Juliana G., and Serena Chen. "Self-compassion increases self-improvement motivation." *Personality and Social Psychology Bulletin* 38, no. 9 (September 2012): 1133–43. doi:10.1177/0146167212445599.

Carver, Charles S., and Michael F. Scheier. "Optimism, Pessimism, and Self-Regulation." In *Optimism & Pessimism: Implications for Theory, Research, and Practice*, edited by Edward C. Chang, 31–51. Washington, DC: American Psychological Association, 2001.

Cesario, Joseph, and Melissa M. McDonald. "Bodies in context: Power poses as a computation of action possibility." *Social Cognition* 31, no. 2 (2013): 260–74. doi:10.1521/soco.2013.31.2.260.

Cohen, Elliot D. *Caution: Faulty Thinking Can Be Harmful to Your Happiness.* Trace-Wilco Publishers, 1994.

Colvin, Geoff. *Talent is Overrated: What Really Separates World-Class Performers from Everybody Else.* New York: Portfolio, 2008.

Connelly, F. Michael, and D. Jean Clandinin. "On narrative method, personal philosophy, and narrative unities in the story of teaching." *Journal of Research in Science Teaching* 23, no. 4 (1986): 293–310. doi:10.1002/tea.3660230404.

Cuddy, Amy. *Presence: Bringing Your Boldest Self to Your Biggest Challenges*. New York: Hachette, 2015.

DiMeglio, Steve. "Daniel Berger ends AT&T Pebble Beach Pro-Am in grand style for fourth PGA Tour win." *Golfweek*, February 14, 2021. https://golfweek.usatoday.com /2021/02/14/daniel-berger-eagle-18-wins-att-pebble-beach-pro-am/.

Dweck, Carol S. "Can personality be changed? The role of beliefs in personality and change." *Current Directions in Psychological Science* 17, no. 6 (2008): 391–94. doi:10.1111/j.1467-8721.2008.00612.x.

Dweck, Carol S. *Mindset: How You Can Fulfill Your Potential*. London: Constable & Robinson, 2012.

Ehrlinger, Joyce, Ainsley L. Mitchum, and Carol S. Dweck. "Understanding overconfidence: Theories of intelligence, preferential attention, and distorted self-assessment." *Journal of Experimental Social Psychology* 63 (March 2016): 94–100. doi:10.1016/j. jesp.2016.11.001.

Ellis, Albert. *How to Stubbornly Refuse to Make Yourself Miserable About Anything—Yes, Anything!* New York: Citadel Press, 2006.

Ellis, Albert. *How to Control Your Anxiety Before It Controls You*. New York: Citadel Press, 1998.

Epstein, David. *The Sports Gene: Talent, Practice and the Truth About Success*. London: Vintage Publishing, 2014.

Eysenck, Michael W. "Anxiety, Cognitive Biases, and Beliefs." In *Emotions and Beliefs: How Feelings Influence Thoughts*, edited by Nico H. Frijda, Antony S. R. Manstead, and Sacha Bem, 171–94. Cambridge University Press, 2000.

Feldman, Stanley. "Structure and consistency in public opinion: The role of core beliefs and values." *American Journal of Political Science* 32, no. 2 (May 1988): 416–40. doi:10.2307/2111130.

Fishbach, Ayelet, Ronald S. Friedman, and Arie W. Kruglanski. "Leading us not into temptation: Momentary allurements elicit overriding goal activation." *Journal of Personality and Social Psychology* 84, no. 2 (2003): 296–309. doi:10.1037/0022-3514.84.2.296.

Flett, Gordon L., and Paul L. Hewitt, eds. *Perfectionism: Theory, Research, and Treatment*. Washington, DC: American Psychological Association, 2002.

Frankl, Viktor E. *Man's Search for Meaning*. Boston: Beacon Press, 2006.

Gabbett, Tim J. "The training–injury prevention paradox: Should athletes be training harder and smarter?" *British Journal of Sports Medicine* 50, no. 5 (March 2016): 273–80. doi:10.1136/bjsports-2015-095788.

Galvin, Benjamin M., Amy E. Randel, Brian J. Collins, and Russell E. Johnson. "Changing the focus of locus (of control): A targeted review of the locus of control literature and agenda for future research." *Journal of Organizational Behavior* 39, no. 7 (March 2018): 820–33. doi:10.1002/job.2275.

Gankas, George. "GG's simple putting tips—How to putt on target." GG SwingTips Golf, August 14, 2019. YouTube video, 11:16. https://youtu.be/RA10k4rIkEs.

Gervais, Michael. "AASP 2019 keynote: Michael Gervais." Association for Applied Sport Psychology, December 18, 2019. YouTube video, 55:07. https://youtu.be/NegGVWN72EM.

Good, Darren J., Christopher J. Lyddy, Theresa M. Glomb, Joyce E. Bono, Kirk Warren Brown, Michelle K. Duffy, Ruth A. Baer, Judson Brewer, and Sara W. Lazar. "Contemplating mindfulness at work: An integrative review." *Journal of Management* 41, no. 1 (January 2016): 114–42. doi:10.1177/0149206315617003.

Gotwals, John K., and Katherine A. Tamminen. "Intercollegiate perfectionistic athletes' perspectives on success and failure in sport." *Journal of Applied Sports Psychology* 34, no. 1 (2022): 25–46. doi:10.1080/10413200.2020.1740826.

Hallinan, Joseph T. *Why We Make Mistakes: How We Look Without Seeing, Forget Things in Seconds, and Are All Pretty Sure We Are Way Above Average*. New York: Broadway Books, 2010.

Hannah, Sean T., Patrick J. Sweeney, and Paul B. Lester. "Toward a courageous mindset: The subjective act and experience of courage." *The Journal of Positive Psychology* 2, no. 2 (2007): 129–35. doi:10.1080/17439760701228854.

Harrison, Guy P. *Think: Why You Should Question Everything*. New York: Prometheus Books, 2013.

Hayes, Steven C., Kirk D. Strosahl, and Kelly G. Wilson. *Acceptance and Commitment Therapy: The Process and Practice of Mindful Change*. New York: Guilford Press, 2012.

Hogan, Ben, and Herbert Warren Wind. *Ben Hogan's Five Lessons: The Modern Fundamentals of Golf*. New York: Touchstone, 1957.

Holt, John. *How Children Fail*. Reading, MA: Addison-Wesley Publishing, 1995.

Hyatt, Carole, and Linda Gottlieb. *When Smart People Fail: Rebuilding Yourself for Success*. New York: Penguin Books, 1988.

Jackson, Susan A. "Factors influencing the occurrence of flow state in elite athletes." *Journal of Applied Sport Psychology* 7, no. 2 (1995): 138–66. doi:10.1080/10413209508406962.

Justice, Izzy. *GYRA Golf: Golf's 1st Mental Scorecard*. Bloomington, IN: iUniverse, 2020.

Lefcourt, Herbert M. "Locus of control." In *Measures of Personality and Social Psychological Attitudes: Volume 1 in Measures of Social Psychological Attitudes Series*, edited by John Paul Robinson, Phillip R. Shaver, and Lawrence S. Wrightsman, 413–99. San Diego: Academic Press, 1991.

Lopes da Silva, Fernando. "Neural mechanisms underlying brain waves: From neural membranes to networks." *Electroencephalography and Clinical Neurophysiology* 79, no. 2 (August 1991): 81–93. doi:10.1016/0013-4694(91)90044-5.

Lythcott-Haims, Julie. *How to Raise an Adult: Break Free of the Overparenting Trap and Prepare Your Kid for Success*. New York: St. Martin's Press, 2015.

Kay, Katty, and Claire Shipman. *The Confidence Code: The Science and Art of Self-Assurance—What Women Should Know*. New York: HarperCollins, 2014.

Katahira, Kenji, Yoichi Yamazaki, Chiaki Yamaoka, Hiroaki Ozaki, Sayaka Nakagawa, and Noriko Nagata. "EEG correlates of the flow state: A combination of increased frontal theta and moderate frontocentral alpha rhythm in the mental arithmetic task." *Frontiers in Psychology* 9 (March 2018). doi:10.3389/fpsyg.2018.00300.

Manson, Mark. *The Subtle Art of Not Giving a F*ck: A Counterintuitive Approach to Living a Good Life*. New York: HarperOne, 2016.

Marinho, Anna Carolina Ferreira, Adriane Mesquita de Medeiros, Ana Cristina Côrtes Gama, and Letícia Caldas Teixeira. "Fear of public speaking: Perception of college students and correlates." *Journal of Voice* 31, no. 1 (January 2017): 127. doi:10.1016/j.jvoice.2015.12.012.

Mesagno, Christopher, Stepphanie J. Tibbert, Edward Buchanan, Jack T. Harvey, and Martin J. Turner. "Irrational beliefs and choking under pressure: A preliminary investigation." *Journal of Applied Sport Psychology* 33, no. 6 (2021): 569–89. doi:10.1080/10413200.2020.1737273.

Michigan State University. "'Power poses' don't work, eleven new studies suggest." *ScienceDaily*, September 11, 2017. https://www.sciencedaily.com/releases/2017/09/170911095932.htm.

Milyavskaya, Marina, Michael Inzlicht, Nora Hope, and Richard Koestner. "Saying 'no' to temptation: *Want-to* motivation improves self-regulation by reducing temptation rather than by increasing self-control." *Journal of Personality and Social Psychology* 109, no. 4 (2015): 677–93. doi:10.1037/pspp0000045.

Mlodinow, Leonard. *Subliminal: How Your Unconscious Mind Rules Your Behavior*. New York: Vintage Books, 2012.

Morin, Amy. *13 Things Mentally Strong People Don't Do: Take Back Your Power, Embrace Change, Face Your Fears, and Train Your Brain for Happiness and Success*. New York: HarperCollins, 2014.

Ng, Betsy. "The neuroscience of growth mindset and intrinsic motivation." *Brain Sciences* 8, no. 2 (February 2018): 20. doi:10.3390/brainsci8020020.

Nickerson, Raymond S. "Confirmation bias: A ubiquitous phenomenon in many guises." *Review of General Psychology* 2, no. 2 (June 1998): 175–220. doi:10.1037/1089-2680.2.2.175.

Norem, Julie K. "Defensive pessimism, optimism, and pessimism." In *Optimism & Pessimism: Implications for Theory, Research, and Practice*, edited by Edward C. Chang, 77–100. Washington, DC: American Psychological Association, 2001.

Obler, Loraine K., and Deborah Fein. *The Exceptional Brain: Neuropsychology of Talent and Special Abilities*. New York: Guilford Press, 1988.

Ordóñez, Lisa D., Maurice E. Schweitzer, Adam D. Galinsky, and Max H. Bazerman. "Goals gone wild: The systematic side effects of overprescribing goal setting." *Academy of Management Perspectives* 23, no. 1 (2009): 6–16. doi:10.5465/AMP.2009.37007999.

Padesky, Christina A., and Aaron T. Beck. "Science and philosophy: Comparison of cognitive therapy and rational emotive behavior therapy." *Journal of Cognitive Psychotherapy* 17, no. 3 (2003): 211–24. doi:10.1891/jcop.17.3.211.52536.

Paek, Hye-Jin, and Thomas Hove. "Risk perceptions and risk characteristics." *Oxford Research Encyclopedias, Communication* (2017). doi:10.1093/acrefore/9780190228613.013.283.

Paunesku, David, Gregory M. Walton, Carissa Romero, Eric N. Smith, David S. Yeager, and Carol S. Dweck. "Mind-set interventions are a scalable treatment for academic underachievement." *Psychological Science* 26, no. 6 (June 2015): 784–93. doi:10.1177/0956797615571017.

Polk, Kevin L., and Benjamin Schoendorff, eds. *The ACT Matrix: A New Approach to Building Psychological Flexibility Across Settings and Populations.* Oakland, CA: Context Press, 2014.

Pury, Cynthia L. S., and Robin M. Kowalski. "Human strengths, courageous actions, and general and personal courage." *The Journal of Positive Psychology* 2, no. 2 (2007): 120–28. doi:10.1080/17439760701228813.

Pury, Cynthia L. S., Robin M. Kowalski, and Jana Spearman. "Distinctions between general and personal courage." *The Journal of Positive Psychology* 2, no. 2 (2007): 99–114. doi:10.1080/17439760701237962.

Pury, Cynthia L. S., and Shawn Saylors. "Courage, courageous acts, and positive psychology." In *Positive Psychology: Established and Emerging Issues*, edited by Dana S. Dunn, 153–68. New York: Routledge, 2018.

Rachman, Stanley. "The overprediction of fear: A review." *Behaviour Research and Therapy* 32, no. 7 (September 1994): 683–90. doi:10.1016/0005-7967(94)90025-6.

Reivich, Karen, and Jane Gillham. "Learned optimism: The measurement of explanatory style." In *Positive Psychological Assessment: A Handbook of Models and Measures*, edited by Shane J. Lopez and Charles R. Snyder, 57–74. Washington, DC: American Psychological Association, 2003.

Rigoni, Davide, Simone Kühn, Giuseppe Sartori, and Marcel Brass. "Inducing disbelief in free will alters brain correlates of preconscious motor preparation: The brain minds whether we believe in free will or not." *Psychological Science* 22, no. 5 (2011): 613–18. doi:10.1177/0956797611405680.

Roccas, Sonia, Lilach Sagiv, Shalom H. Schwartz, and Ariel Knafo. "The Big Five personality factors and personal values." *Personality and Social Psychology Bulletin* 28, no. 6 (2002): 789–801. doi:10.1177/0146167202289008.

Russell, William D. "An examination of flow state occurrence in college athletes." *Journal of Sport Behavior* 24, no. 1 (March 2001): 83–107.

Sagiv, Lilach, Sonia Roccas, Jan Cieciuch, and Shalom H. Schwartz. "Personal values in human life." *Nature Human Behaviour* 1, no. 9 (September 2017): 630–39. doi:10.1038/s41562-017-0185-3.

Seligman, Martin E. P. *Learned Optimism: How to Change Your Mind and Your Life.* New York: Vintage Books, 2006.

Seligman, Martin E. P., and Scott Barry Kaufman. "From Learned Helplessness to Learned Hopefulness with Martin Seligman." *The Psychology Podcast* with Scott Barry Kaufman, June 4, 2020. 57:59. https://scottbarrykaufman.com/podcast/from-learned-helplessness-to-learned-hopefulness-with-martin-seligman/.

Smith, Kristopher M., and Coren L. Apicella. "Winners, losers, and posers: The effect of power poses on testosterone and risk-taking following competition." *Hormones and Behavior* 92 (2017): 172–81. doi:10.1016/j.yhbeh.2016.11.003.

Steptoe, Andrew. *Genius and the Mind: Studies of Creativity and Temperament.* Oxford University Press, 2005.

Strecher, Victor J., Brenda McEvoy DeVellis, Marshall H. Becker, and Irwin M. Rosenstock. "The role of self-efficacy in achieving health behavior change." *Health Education Quarterly* 13, no. 1 (March 1986): 73–92. doi:10.1177/109019818601300108.

Stillman, Tyler F., Roy F. Baumeister, Kathleen D. Vohs, Nathaniel M. Lambert, Frank D. Fincham, and Lauren E. Brewer. "Personal philosophy and personnel achievement: Belief in free will predicts better job performance." *Social Psychological and Personality Science* 1, no. 1 (January 2010): 43–50. doi:10.1177/1948550609351600.

Stulberg, Brad. *The Practice of Groundedness: A Transformative Path to Success That Feeds—Not Crushes—Your Soul.* New York: Penguin Random House, 2021.

Stults-Kolehmainen, Matthew A., Miguel Blacutt, John B. Bartholomew, Todd A. Gilson, Garrett I. Ash, Paul C. McKee, and Rajita Sinha. "Motivation states for physical activity and sedentary behavior: Desire, urge, wanting, and craving." *Frontiers in Psychology* 11 (November 2020). doi:10.3389/fpsyg.2020.568390.

Talluri, Bharath Chandra, Anne E. Urai, Konstantinos Tsetsos, Marius Usher, and Tobias H. Donner. "Confirmation bias through selective overweighting of choice-consistent evidence." *Current Biology* 28, no. 19 (October 2018): 3128–35. doi:10.1016/j.cub.2018.07.052.

Thanarajah, Sharmili Edwin, Heiko Backes, Alexandra G. Difeliceantonio, Kerstin Albus, Anna Lena Cremer, Ruth Hanssen, Rachel N. Lippert, et al. "Food intake recruits orosensory and post-ingestive dopaminergic circuits to affect eating desire in humans." *Cell Metabolism* 29, no. 3 (March 2019): 695–706. doi:10.1016/j.cmet.2018.12.006.

Thomas, Owen, Andy Lane, and Kieran Kingston. "Defining and contextualizing robust sport-confidence." *Journal of Applied Sport Psychology* 23, no. 2 (2011): 189–208. doi:10.1080/10413200.2011.559519.

Tops, Mattie, and Maarten A. S. Boksem. "'What's that?' 'What went wrong?' Positive and negative surprise and the rostral–ventral to caudal–dorsal functional gradient in the brain." *Frontiers in Psychology* 3 (2012). doi:10.3389/fpsyg.2012.00021.

Vanhamme, Joëlle, and Dirk Snelders. "The role of surprise in satisfaction judgements." *Journal of Consumer Satisfaction, Dissatisfaction and Complaining Behavior* 14 (2001): 27–45.

Vîslă, Andrea, Ioana A. Cristea, Aurora Szentágotai Tătar, and Daniel David. "Core beliefs, automatic thoughts and response expectancies in predicting public speaking anxiety." *Personality and Individual Differences* 55, no. 7 (2013): 856–59. doi:10.1016/j.paid.2013.06.003.

Vrticka, Pascal, Lara Lordier, Benoît Bediou, and David Sander. "Human amygdala response to dynamic facial expressions of positive and negative surprise." *Emotion* 14, no. 1 (February 2014): 161–69. doi:10.1037/a0034619.

Wenglert, Leif, and Anne-Sofie Rosén. "Measuring optimism–pessimism from beliefs about future events." *Personality and Individual Differences* 28, no. 4 (2000): 717–28. doi:10.1016/S0191-8869(99)00133-6.

Wenzel, Amy. "Modification of core beliefs in cognitive therapy." In *Standard and Innovative Strategies in Cognitive Behavior Therapy*, edited by Irismar Reis de Oliveira, 17–34. Rijeka, Croatia: InTech, 2012.

Wilson, Robert C., Amitai Shenhav, Mark Straccia, and Jonathan D. Cohen. "The Eighty Five Percent Rule for optimal learning." *Nature Communications* 10 (November 2019). doi:10.1038/s41467-019-12552-4.

Yeager, David Scott, and Carol S. Dweck. "Mindsets that promote resilience: When students believe that personal characteristics can be developed." *Educational Psychologist* 47, no. 4 (2012): 302–14. doi:10.1080/00461520.2012.722805.

Yoshida, Kazuki, Daisuke Sawamura, Yuji Inagaki, Keita Ogawa, Katsunori Ikoma, and Shinya Sakai. "Brain activity during the flow experience: A functional near-infrared spectroscopy study." *Neuroscience Letters* 573 (June 2014): 30–34. doi:10.1016/j.neulet.2014.05.011.

Index

About the Author

Photo by Ashley Hamm

Known for building personable, knowledgeable, and confidential relationships with his clients, Raymond Prior, PhD, is one of the most sought-after names in performance psychology. His clients include major champions, world champions, Olympic gold medalists, individual and team national champions, National Coach of the Year Award winners, individual and team conference champions, and countless NCAA All-Americans in a variety of sports. Raymond also works with non-sport performers, including Grammy winners, Oscar winners, and Emmy winners performing onstage and onscreen. As an author and researcher, Raymond has contributed chapters to a variety of performance psychology texts, and his research has been published in the *Journal of Applied Sport Psychology*.